Stan Grant is a Wiradjuri and Kamilaroi man. A journalist since 1987, he has worked for the ABC, SBS, the Seven Network and Sky News Australia. From 2001 to 2012 he worked for CNN as an anchor and senior correspondent in Asia and the Middle East. As a journalist, he has received a string of prestigious international and Australian awards. In 2015, he published his bestselling book *Talking to My Country*, which won the Walkley Book Award, and he also won a Walkley Award for his coverage of Indigenous affairs. In 2016 he was appointed to the Referendum Council on Indigenous recognition. Stan is now Chair of Indigenous/ Australian Belonging at Charles Sturt University and International Affairs Analyst at the ABC.

Also by Stan Grant

The Tears of Strangers
Talking to My Country
Australia Day

WITH THE FALLING OF THE DUSK

STAN GRANT

HarperCollins*Publishers*

HarperCollins*Publishers*

Australia • Brazil • Canada • France • Germany • Holland • Hungary
India • Italy • Japan • Mexico • New Zealand • Poland • Spain • Sweden
Switzerland • United Kingdom • United States of America

First published in Australia in 2021
by HarperCollins*Publishers* Australia Pty Limited
Level 13, 201 Elizabeth Street, Sydney NSW 2000
ABN 36 009 913 517
harpercollins.com.au

A catalogue record for this book is available from the National Library of Australia.

ISBN 978 1 4607 5803 8 (paperback)
ISBN 978 1 4607 1179 8 (ebook)
ISBN 978 1 4607 8745 8 (audiobook)

Cover design by Darren Holt, HarperCollins Design Studio
Cover image by Marcus Lenk on Unsplash
Author photograph by Kathy Luu
Typeset in Minion Pro by Kirby Jones
Printed and bound in Australia by McPherson's Printing Group
The papers used by HarperCollins in the manufacture of this book are a natural, recyclable
product made from wood grown in sustainable plantation forests. The fibre source and
manufacturing processes meet recognised international environmental standards, and carry
certification.

To Brad and Sarmad, my brothers of the road – RIP.

Storm and stress today rocks our little boat on the mad
waters of the world-sea; there is within and without the
sound of conflict, the burning of body and rending of soul;
inspiration strives with doubt, and faith
with vain questionings.

– W.E.B Du Bois

CONTENTS

A TRAIN TO CHINA

I took my first good look at China from the window of a train on a frozen Christmas morning. I had lived in Hong Kong and made several trips to the China mainland, but this was different: I was here to stay. My first morning in my new home.

I woke early in my sleeper cabin as the sun was rising, and with the smooth of my hand smeared the condensation from the window. It's a curious thing, but my body clock, no matter where I am in the world, no matter what time I have gone to sleep, remains aligned to the sun. As the earth stirs for a new day, so I am gently nudged awake. It is good for a soul such as mine to stir early, to snuggle into silence and allow my mind to follow where my thoughts lead. I had a lot on my mind that day.

My family was still rugged up and asleep. They had, without reservation, excitedly embraced this adventure. So here we all were on a slow train. I wanted my children especially, even if asleep, to feel the movement, the rhythms of the train and the pull of the earth that would work this new place into them. The journey is part of the story that comes from my ancestors, Aboriginal people of Australia whose tracks form a songline across country as vast and foreboding as the one I was now in. It is in the journey that I seek permission, that I ask if this place will let me in.

I have done this everywhere I have been, on long road trips or just walks around unknown streets in new cities. These are my quiet rituals of belonging. I want to allow the place to make space for me; to welcome me; to show me what matters. It may be somewhere to eat, a park bench or a bookstore, but these places invite me in, and in this way I join my stories with all the stories that have come before. What was it the psychologist Carl Jung said? Land assimilates its conqueror. We may think we are masters of all we survey, that we rule the land, that we leave our footprint, yet with every step the land is changing us.

It was cold inside the train, and I shivered a little. Steam rose from my breath, and through the streaky window I looked out on this place. What roads led me here? What twists of fate and providence? I have always lived a restless life, always wandering – and wandering is the happiness of the anxious soul. I had forever been moving. My childhood memories are a blur of places and people, dark nights and long roads. I was never more content than when squeezed in with my siblings in the back seat of a car, watching the headlights scatter the darkness. I would count off one by one the white illuminated posts by the side of the road. Sometimes I would catch a glimpse of a kangaroo. I was forever lost in thought, until the movement of the car and the hum of the tyres on the road would lull me to sleep. One small town bled into another, and I grew older, but I never lost the lure of the journey.

Journalism was the perfect calling for someone so anxious and restless. From the moment I walked into a newsroom I felt I belonged. It was freedom. I was in a world of ideas and argument and words. I wanted to chase the story; I wanted to go where the story led. Journalism is not for the timid or those who live by a clock. It is for the reckless and the irascible and the tireless, even the foolish. I can understand the desire for certainty and security, but that wasn't what I wanted. I have never met a good journalist who knows when to switch off. My first instinct was always to say yes – to a new story, a new job, a new home, yes, yes, yes. Journalists run into the fire; they run towards the gunshot. Journalists don't like no and they don't say no. My restlessness, my instincts, had taken me around the world, from the islands of the Pacific to Africa, to the great cities of Europe, to the deep history and blood feuds of the Middle East, and now I was on a train to China.

China had always lived in my imagination. That big mysterious place on a map that I recalled from childhood, pinned to the wall of my classroom. I remembered sitting on the floor, hands tucked under my legs, and watching black-and-white film of a land crowded with people, grey suits and bicycles. Everyone appeared to move quickly. I started school at the height of China's Cultural Revolution, and I imagine every primary-school-aged child in Australia at the time would have heard the name Mao Zedong, the revolutionary leader of communist China. I recall the time I first saw his image: a portly, serenely smiling figure standing amid a crush of young, feverish faces, all waving Mao's *Little Red Book*, the sayings of this man they called the Great Helmsman.

This was at the height of the Cold War, when the world lived in the shadow of nuclear catastrophe. I can recall watching a film of American kids doing 'duck and cover' drills, sheltering under the desks to avoid radioactive fallout in the event of an attack. The communists were the enemy: the Soviet Union and China.

The ABC TV program *Behind the News* started the year I started school, and this was how I came to know the world, to think of places beyond my own. My class would gather around a television and watch images of the Vietnam War, man on the moon, protest, conflict and chaos everywhere. It left its mark on me, even without me realising it – which are the best lessons. It ignited something inside that one day would set me on a journey to tell the stories of foreign places and a world in change.

Back when I was a boy, China was always a hungry land. Who of my age doesn't recall being told to eat all your food because there were children starving in China? This man Mao and his Great Leap Forward had led his country to famine, and tens of millions died. I must have heard somewhere that phrase 'the sick man of Asia' – that's what China was called then. It was a big country that could not feed itself.

China was the stand-in for all things foreign or forbidden. There was a schoolyard myth – you know the one – dig a hole deep enough and it would lead to China. So I did, and it didn't. I learnt about the Chinese in the Australian gold rush of the nineteenth century. I stared at those sepia-toned photos of sinewy, dark-skinned men wearing what looked like a cross between an apron and a dress, with pigtails and usually pushing wheelbarrows. The Chinese were some of the earliest foreigners to come to Australia, yet it says something about how we see our country that they have always been outsiders. That's because Australia, for all its later embrace of what we like to call multiculturalism, is still, at its core, white. A white person in Australia will never be asked, 'Where do you really come from?' A third- or fourth-generation Chinese Australian will never cease having to explain themselves.

In the days of the White Australia policy, when we wanted to keep the 'coloured' races out, I – like all children – was raised to fear the 'yellow peril': those imagined hordes from the north who, we were told, would overrun us. Then in the early 1970s I was swept up in the kung fu craze: I had a poster of the Hong Kong actor Bruce Lee with scars across his ripped abdomen and sang along with Carl Douglas's only hit song, 'Kung Fu Fighting'. When the white American actor David Carradine squinted as though staring into a blazing sun and pretended to be a monk from the Shaolin temple, his program, *Kung Fu*, became a worldwide hit. We all copied his moves, his kicks and bends and rolls. My brother and I acted out fighting scenes in slow motion.

China was distant and exotic and mysterious and exciting and frightening. Its people had their own culture and language, their own philosophy, faith and story. These people looked so different. Let me correct that: they are not just *a people* but many diverse *peoples*, for China is not one thing; it never has been. What we now call China is the product of thousands of years of war and revolution and empire. Turmoil is a constant state of being. The famous fourteenth-century Chinese novel *Romance of the Three Kingdoms* opens with the line 'The Empire long divided must unite; long united must divide'. Empires would rise and fall, each Emperor casting a long shadow even though all around them there was treachery. To the Chinese, China was the world. They called it the Middle Kingdom – the centre of all civilisation – and the emperor was the Son of Heaven.

But that was long ago. This China that would be my home had been humiliated; it had been conquered, exploited, dominated by foreign powers. It had been weak. And this disgrace ran deep; every Chinese child was schooled in vengeance. For them, the West was decadent and poisonous. They would take what the West had to offer – these sons and daughters of China would grow rich – but they would always be Chinese. They would complete the great rejuvenation and return their motherland to its rightful place at the apex of global power.

From my train window, it would have been easy to see this land as strange, somehow. It is common for people – and here I mean European people, people of the West – to use that word *strange* when confronted with something different. Strange because Europeans assume they are normal. That's what happens when a people fashion the world after their own image – just as the Chinese themselves once did.

Over the past three centuries, the West had supplanted China at the centre of the world; it had defeated China's armies, occupied Chinese land and plied its people with opium. China was the past and the West was the future. Europeans could lay claim to the invention of modernity: a seventeenth-century explosion of science, technology and philosophy that changed how we think, work and make war. Liberty, freedom and democracy were the shibboleths of this new age. It was a time of reason, of discovery, of empire and colonisation. As the great nations of Europe claimed the world, they also turned on each other. The twentieth century had witnessed war unparalleled in its savagery. Yet these wars of modernity did not challenge the fact of modernity itself. Capitalism, communism and fascism arose, all mortal enemies but all sprung from the same well: they were competing utopian visions of what it was to be modern, to be European. To be modern was to be beyond history, in a perpetual state of new beginnings, informed by the past but not beholden to it. History to Europeans was an arc of freedom, a sundial of progress moving assuredly from East to West.

The great eighteenth-century German philosopher Georg Hegel believed that China was a place without history. To him, world history began only with the ancient Greeks. The West measures history in a straight line, and even catastrophe is something to be left behind. In the West, even as we commemorate old battles and remind ourselves, 'never again', forgetting is prized more than remembering. Liberalism and democracy demand endless progress; they don't cope well with too much history. That helps explain why China is still seen through Western eyes as 'strange'. History, for the Chinese, is never over. That's the difference between a civilisation and a nation: civilisations have long memories, while nations are always about tomorrow.

That's what I saw from my train window – the space between the future and the past, between becoming and being, between progress and eternity. This China was not strange to me; it was all too familiar. To stare onto a hard, cracked land was comforting in its way, because I could see myself here. Because I too came from a hard place and a hard history. Like the Chinese, I was born into a family and a people swept away on history's tide. The modern world had washed over us and we were left like survivors of a shipwreck, clinging to the debris of our lives. My ancestors had been invaded, colonised, massacred and then cast aside in a new country – a new European country – that had been built on our loss. What was left is an existential sadness. I could say that I shared the sadness of this land. I know what the Chinese mean when they say they will eat a thousand years of bitterness. It means they will endure; they will survive whatever the world throws at them, and it will make them stronger.

I also saw a country haunted by history. This land seemed to pulse with memory. In the cold morning light, with just the rattle of the train to break the silence, I could hear the whisper of all the people who had lived here. These are the lands that speak to me: forever lands, places where borders and dates and flags and armies, all those markers of what we might call a nation, matter less than the earth itself. Lives, countless lives, born into a place, those who loved and laughed and cried and laboured and died and then returned to the earth, they never disappear. They become part of the place itself, and all those memories hang in the air. In the distance I saw an old Buddhist pagoda surrounded by hills with barely any trees, and there, on a flat piece of ground, was a lone man working his field with a horse-drawn plough.

It was Christmas Day – I had to remind myself of that. Christmas Day in a place where there was no Christmas, where there was no God. Think about that – the man in the field would likely have never heard of Jesus. His life had been lived under the Chinese Communist Party, which had banished religion. Back home in Australia, my family – my parents, brothers and sister and their children – would be awake soon, and the kids would start tearing at their wrapped presents under the tree. My mother would start cooking, and other family members would drop by, and the food and company would last all day. I missed my family most at Christmas. I missed Australia most at Christmas: hot, sticky, flyblown Christmas. But as much as I loved my country, I could never stay. There was something in our history that I just had to get away from.

My wife and our boys were still fast asleep. The day before, we had closed the door on our life in Hong Kong and boarded this train for Beijing. We had told the kids that it was the Polar

Express: a train bound for the North Pole and Santa Claus. They had played along and strung up stockings outside their sleeper carriage. We had filled them with presents while they slept. My wife had made an advance trip to Beijing to find us a house, and had bought bicycles for each of the boys and set them up inside our new home for a surprise when the kids opened the door. This was the move I had been hoping for: now free of the news presenter's desk in Hong Kong, I was on my way to a life of adventure as China correspondent for CNN, one of the biggest news networks on the planet.

The return of China as a great power was already shaping the fate of the world. In the years ahead, it would exercise a great hold on me: it would become the defining story of my career. This country was in the midst of an economic revolution that had lifted more than half a billion people out of poverty. China was now the engine of global economic growth and the world's factory, producing our phones, shoes, shirts, televisions, refrigerators. There was barely anything the Chinese did not make, and more cheaply than any other country. Gone were the bicycles and old grey suits; in their place were fashion brands, Audis and McDonald's fast food. The Communist Party was defying the Western liberal belief that said a country cannot become rich without becoming free. The Party was instead doubling down on its power: it would stop at nothing, not even the slaughter of its own people, to keep its iron grip on the nation. All predictions pointed to China becoming the most economically dominant nation on the planet, an authoritarian superpower.

As the train pulled past, I stared at the man in his field. What things he had seen. Even from my window, just a snatched glimpse, I could see this man looked old. He had been born into a country hidden from view. The twentieth century was a time of upheaval and breathtaking violence for China, the end of empire and the tumultuous birth of a new People's Republic. This man had likely seen famine and mass starvation. Like nearly all Chinese, he would have been raised to revere Chairman Mao, whose portrait would have held pride of place on the wall of his small village home. I wondered if this man had been a soldier in the People's Liberation Army. Had he denounced the bourgeois enemies of the state during the Cultural Revolution? I wondered if his son or daughter now lived far from the ancestral home, in a city, working in a factory and sending money back home, dreaming of riches in a China that was reclaiming its place in the world.

Although from different worlds, this man and I shared a lot – our lives stood at the crossroads of history. We were twinned with fate. We belonged to old cultures whose worlds had been upended by the march of modernity. History lived in us: every one of our ancestors had a hold on us. This man had likely never strayed far from his village, yet the world had come to him as China shook itself from its slumber and began to throw off the yoke of a hundred years of humiliation. And me? I had left my country to find a place in the world, and my wandering had brought me here. I believe there are no mere coincidences; nothing is simply happenstance. Every step we take, every choice we make, every stranger's face we see can change who we are. I swear that, as my train moved past this man, as I looked back at him for one last glimpse, he stared right at me.

My wife soon woke, and she turned to me still half-asleep. 'Merry Christmas,' she said. I looked at her and smiled, then looked back out at this place called China. I heard my wife behind me: 'Home,' she said.

THE VIRUS

I first saw something stirring on the ground; a mound of bird feathers suddenly rustled and the vague outline of a creature began to form. At first I wasn't sure what I was seeing, but slowly it shook itself down and became more visible. What appeared was a medium-sized dog. Something, though, was not right – the animal was unsteady on its feet, and what was left of its fur was matted and dirty. I could see red raw skin and weeping sores. It seemed to fix me in its sight and began to move closer; my cameraman started filming.

As the dog drew nearer, I could see its eyes were bright red and swollen, pus oozing from an infection. It was the sickest and sorriest animal I had ever seen alive; in fact, it was barely clinging to life. The most humane thing to do would be to put it down. The dog didn't make it all the way to me – it didn't have the energy. After a few weak steps it slumped again to the ground.

This was my introduction to a Chinese animal market in Guangdong Province, in southern China. A virus had broken out from a market just like this one – a lethal virus unseen before that was striking down anyone who came in contact with it. The first symptoms were intense muscle pain, lethargy, fever, a cough and a sore throat. For every ten people who came down with the virus, one would die. It spread rapidly throughout the population, shutting down some businesses and keeping people indoors. Those who ventured out usually wore masks to reduce the risk of infection. Public health warnings told people to avoid crowded spaces and reduce contact with others. Riding on an escalator or entering a lift might be enough to put your health or even life at risk.

At the time, I was living in Hong Kong with my family and working for CNN. We were on the frontline of the outbreak of what became known as Severe Acute Respiratory Syndrome, or SARS. The first case was reported in November 2002, when a farmer in Guangdong fell sick and died. It took several months for the world to become aware of the seriousness of SARS. The Chinese government had been secretive and slow to act. By the time the World Health Organization raised the alarm, several thousand people were infected worldwide, and hundreds had died.

In the search to pinpoint the spread of the disease, all eyes had fallen on China's notorious 'wet markets'. The virus was linked to the sale and consumption of civet cats that had been infected by cave-dwelling bats. Now CNN had sent me to a wet market to get close to the source of the outbreak. Here, I came face to face with the diseased dog. But there was worse to be seen, much worse: stomach-churning scenes of dogs and cats crammed into cages, urinating and defecating on each other, barely able to breathe. Indeed, some were already dead.

Anything from insects to rodents to snakes and frogs to cats and dogs were available to buy. People would wander through and choose which animal they wanted, and it would be killed, skinned, gutted and chopped up right there. I suppose it wasn't so different to our butchers' shops, except there was no pretence of hygiene and the manner of death was cruel: some animals were simply clubbed over the head. There was a myth that the adrenaline from fear added flavour to the meat, so some animals – dogs especially – would be killed more slowly.

My crew and I wanted to film a story showing the food journey from market to plate, and we decided to follow a truckload of cats. The animals were in tiny cages, squealing and howling, some scratching and fighting each other, and we followed the truck to a local restaurant. The restaurant was called the King of Cats; we planned to smuggle ourselves in and pretend to be customers.

We fixed our small camera to film surreptitiously, then took a seat and perused the menu while the cages of cats were offloaded outside. The restaurant's speciality was a stew of cat meat, snake and chicken. There was no way I could eat here, but we filmed as a customer pointed out a cat in one of the cages, and the waiter opened the latch and lifted the animal out by the skin at the back of its neck. The cat was squealing and kicking as it was carried through the restaurant. Soon the waiter returned and delivered a bubbling pot and bowls of rice to a table of hungry men.

The outbreak of SARS brought China front and centre into the lives of people everywhere. What happened in an animal market in a far-flung province could kill people thousands of kilometres away. It wasn't that the Chinese enjoyed exotic food – I can't judge that too harshly, as I've eaten many animals in my time: camel, horse, impala, warthog, giraffe, marmot, crocodile, kangaroo and goanna – but the lack of regulation and cleanliness, not to mention the cruelty. I had heard stories of restaurants where patrons could select body parts from bears or monkeys – a leg of a monkey, for instance – and it would be severed in front of them. I have never been able to verify this, but I mention it because it's entirely believable. In remote parts of China I have seen the carcasses of dogs strung up outside roadside restaurants. I have eaten some admittedly very tasty meals right next to open sewers. When you're hungry, you'll overlook anything.

It wasn't just the threat of SARS that put the world at risk, but the secrecy of the Chinese Communist Party. It has no problem lying to its own people, so it would not stop at lying to the rest of us. China is a nation built on fear and top-down control: provincial leaders would rather hide the truth than confess any failing to the centralised party powerbrokers.

The SARS crisis came and went. The spread of the virus was limited, and a wider disaster was averted. But the world now confronted just how vulnerable it was to this enormous, increasingly powerful but still, in so many ways, impenetrable and inscrutable country. China had opened up to the world, and become the world's factory. At the time of the SARS outbreak, it was in the midst of an economic revolution transforming the lives of hundreds of millions of ordinary Chinese. Now they could buy homes and send their children to school. Chinese tourists were travelling the globe, while at home they watched Hollywood movies and danced in nightclubs to Western music. You could be fooled into thinking China was becoming like us.

Fools we were. The Chinese Communist Party had its eyes set far ahead: it would return China to global dominance. It would beat the West at its own game. The Party would embrace capitalism but never relinquish its power. SARS gave us a taste of what was to come, how another illness would emerge from a Chinese wet market and upend the world, killing millions and infecting millions more, and driving our economies to the wall. In the years after SARS, Western countries would be mired in war, crippled by financial crises and beset by political turmoil. In the battle between democracy and authoritarianism, the Chinese Communist Party would claim the upper hand.

*

We are living at a time of death. It is at our door. Death is a touch or a breath away. Death is joined with fear; that is its power. We know that death is inevitable, but it is imminent now and that terrifies us. It is the fear of death that steals our life. That's what the French writer Albert Camus told us in his book *A Happy Death*, the story of a man's search for happiness while confronting the meaninglessness of existence.

Camus wrote of his protagonist, Patrice Mersault: 'He realised now that to be afraid of this death he was staring at with animal terror meant to be afraid of life.' Camus told us that to conquer the fear of death is to truly live. Yet so many of us, perhaps most of us, surrender to fear. In 2020, all of us, no matter where in the world, have faced death and fear. The novel coronavirus named COVID-19 – and our response to it – have stolen our lives. The mere threat or risk of contracting this illness has shut us down.

We have sheltered behind locked doors, separated from those we love. The state rules our lives. Government-enforced lockdowns have crippled our businesses, closed our schools, emptied our cinemas, music halls and sporting arenas. At times, even venturing outside risked punishment: we could be fined or even jailed. This is not who we are. This is not who we are, or at least not who we tell ourselves we are. Our societies are meant to be founded on freedom and liberty. But that has as often been a myth. In the year of COVID-19, we have sacrificed freedom.

This past year has left me deeply troubled. I bristle against control. I have seen where the loss of freedom can take us. As a journalist, I have spent much of my career reporting the most repressive and violent regimes on earth, and I know how easily and quickly people can descend into terror and tyranny. Even as I understand and accept that obedience right now is a virtue, that it may keep us and others alive and give us a chance of beating this virus, there is something we should fear more than the coronavirus. There is another virus, and it feeds on fear too: it is the virus of tyranny, and it is already loose in our world.

Throughout human history, the virus of tyranny has laid waste to entire civilisations; it has shattered our treasures and obliterated cultures. It has come on horseback, set upon us by marauding armies; it has been carried in the air and on the seas. No one is immune to this disease. It sends us to war, or condemns us to the gallows. Countless millions of lives have been sacrificed to this virus, and it will go on taking lives. We call it by many names – despotism, authoritarianism, autocracy – but its ends are the same: to create states of terror; to break our will and harvest what has been called a 'harmony of souls'.

In the words of Joseph Stalin: 'The production of souls is more important than the production of tanks.' Human beings are weaponised in the cause of tyranny. Historian Timothy Snyder who has devoted his career to the study of tyranny, says that Nazi and Soviet regimes turned people into numbers. I have chosen very carefully and very deliberately to link the spread of tyranny to the spread of a virus, because tyrants understand this deep, primal fear we have of disease, and they use it to manipulate us and persecute others.

They define their enemies as diseases or infections, and they seek to inoculate their own societies. Stalin's henchman Vyacheslav Molotov spoke of purging or assassinating people who 'had to be isolated', he said, or they 'would spread all kinds of complaints, and society would have been infected'. The architect of Hitler's holocaust, Heinrich Himmler, in sending millions to the gas chambers said he was exterminating 'a bacterium because we do not want in the end to be infected by a bacterium and die of it'. He said, 'I will not see so much as a small area of sepsis appear here or gain a hold. Wherever it may form, we will cauterize it.'

And then there is Adolf Hitler, who compared himself to the famed German microbiologist Robert Koch. As Koch found the bacillus of tuberculosis, Hitler said, 'I discovered the Jews as the bacillus and ferment of all social decomposition. And I have proved one thing, that a state can live without Jews.' To Hitler, Jewish people were 'no longer human beings'. He described the holocaust as a 'surgical task ... otherwise Europe will perish through the Jewish disease'. Authoritarian regimes seek to sterilise and purify society. In Hitler's case this focused on the purity of the German race. It is no mistake that tyrants use the language of virus, disease and contamination. Just as a virus is to be eradicated, so people are to be removed, eliminated or exterminated.

These attitudes do not belong to a time past: there are leaders today who exploit the same fears, who focus on difference and create division using the same language of disease. Recall what US president Donald Trump said of Mexican immigrants – that they are responsible for 'tremendous infectious diseases pouring across the border'. In China, the Communist Party has locked up a million Uighur Muslims in 're-education camps', where human rights groups say they are brainwashed with communist ideology. In an official party audio recording translated by Radio Free Asia, the Uighur ethnic minority is described as being 'infected by an ideological illness ... they must seek treatment from a hospital'. According to the recording, 'if we do not eradicate religious extremism at its roots, the violent terrorist incidents will grow and spread like an incurable malignant tumour'.

Albert Camus warned of the virus of tyranny in his novel *The Plague*, the story of a rat-borne disease that overruns an entire city. His was a bleak vision of death and fear – of a city sealed off and a people locked down, and shot when they try to escape. Published in 1947, just two years after World War Two, and as the West was still celebrating the victory of freedom, Camus' plague is an allegory of authoritarianism. Camus wanted to tell us of the courage that swells within us, that when the plague is at its worst, brave people fight against it. But he cautioned us too that the plague can return: it is 'a bacillus that never dies or disappears for good', and it bides its time 'slumbering in furniture and linen. It waits patiently in bedrooms, cellars, trunks, handkerchiefs, old papers, until one day it will rouse up its rats again ...'.

In coronavirus, tyranny may have found the perfect host: a disease that brings the threat of death, a fearful population and all-powerful government that can set aside all liberty to fight this unseen enemy. French philosopher Michel Foucault long ago made the link between the plagues of the seventeenth century and authoritarian control. Behind state-imposed discipline, he wrote, 'can be read the haunting memory of "contagions"'. The memory not just of a virus, but of rebellion, crime, all forms of social disorder, where people 'appear and disappear, live and die'. It is the state that brings order to the fear: 'everyone locked up in his cage, everyone at his window, answering to his name and showing himself when asked'.

In the response to the plague, Foucault saw the forerunner of the modern prison: the panopticon, the all-seeing eye. The plague-stricken village, wrote Foucault, is 'traversed throughout with hierarchy, surveillance, observation, writing; the town immobilized by the functioning of an extensive power that bears in a distinct way over all individual bodies – this is the utopia of the perfectly governed city'.

The coronavirus shutdown reminds us that freedom is the province of the state: it can grant freedom, define its limits or take it away. The crisis has centralised government control. Around the world, governments are using physical and biological surveillance to control the pandemic. Russia is using facial recognition to catch those violating quarantine. Drones and artificial intelligence are being used to spy on people. Social-media shaming is used to out those breaking the rules. Tech giants Apple and Google provide governments with access to the data of billions of people.

Our freedom was unravelling before coronavirus. As part of the war against terrorism, Western democracies had eroded civil liberties: to fight one enemy – terrorists – we invited another – tyranny. Over the past two decades, in a growing number of countries, would-be autocratic strongmen have seized power. The rule of law and freedom of the media has been wound back; it is harder to tell where real news ends and fake news begins. Technology has invaded our privacy. The virus of tyranny has already found its way into the bloodstream of liberal democracy. We have edged closer to what the Romanian political scientist Vladimir Tismăneanu – who experienced the brutal regime of Nicolae Ceauşescu – has called 'the age of total administration and inescapable alienation'. When we shut ourselves down, when we surrender our liberty, we risk weakening our immunity to the virus of tyranny. To fight coronavirus, we have become, to some degree. authoritarians.

*

Slowly we have emerged from hibernation. The lockdown has eased. We can visit friends and family again, albeit in small numbers. We have returned to our favourite coffee shops, even gyms and swimming pools. Schools are open. We no longer speak of normal; now we have Covid normal. Now there are vaccines. But will we ever recover the lives we had? The virus has exposed our fragility. Businesses that have shut may never reopen. Those who have lost their jobs may never work again. Our democracy itself has been interrupted and may never look quite the same.

The state-ordered lockdown and isolation to fight coronavirus reminds us of what Tismăneanu has called 'the frailty of liberal values'. A swim at the beach or a coffee with friends are democracy's simple rewards. To lose these gentle pleasures loosens our grip on democracy itself. For it is in those quiet rituals of the everyday that we give our lives and our polity meaning. Democracy is delicate, and it draws its strength from us. In the shared joys and common courtesies of daily life, we affirm to each other our allegiance. Coronavirus has not just threatened our health, it has threatened our way of life. Like those who have endured war and catastrophe, we will never be the same.

It has been said that a pandemic is a social phenomenon with a medical aspect. The coronavirus, like previous pandemics, both reveals and accelerates. In this case it has revealed the fragility of democracy and the looming threat of authoritarianism. In his post–Cold War landmark study of democracy, *The End of History and the Last Man*, American political scientist Francis Fukuyama wrote something that should make us all nervous: 'The totalitarian state, it was believed, could not only perpetuate itself indefinitely, it could replicate itself throughout the world like a virus.'

That word again: virus. Authoritarianism infects us where we are weakest – where we are most fearful – and it mutates and it spreads. This is a long way from Fukuyama's vision when the Berlin Wall came down in 1989. As a young academic, he used the phrase 'the end of history' to describe what he saw as the triumph of liberal democracy. When the Soviet Union disintegrated just two years later, Western liberal democracy indeed appeared triumphant. To Fukuyama, the great ideological battles of humanity had been fought and won. Drawing on the philosopher Hegel, Fukuyama believed that history was the march towards freedom, and now history itself was at an end. As he wrote back then, authoritarianism was in crisis and only 'liberal democracy, the doctrine of individual freedom and popular sovereignty', remained as an 'ideology of potential universal validity'. We had found, in Fukuyama's words, 'the endpoint of mankind's ideological evolution – the final form of government'.

Albert Camus, though, years before, had warned: 'The individual cannot accept history as it is. He must destroy reality, not collaborate with it, in order to affirm its own existence.'

If history had reached an end in 1989, then the Chinese Communist Party had not read about it. In the same year the wall came down in Germany and the Soviet Union lurched towards collapse, China's Supreme Leader, Deng Xiaoping, ordered his troops to shoot down pro-democracy protesters in Tiananmen Square. History had no sooner ended than it began again.

*

We find ourselves now at a hinge point of history. To understand the gravity of this moment, we need to take a snapshot of our world. Thirty years after the end of the Cold War, there is talk of Cold War 2.0. The United States is staring down a new rival: China. We are witnessing a return of 'great power rivalry', yet China is economically more powerful today than the Soviet Union was then, and the United States is unquestionably diminished. America is politically fractured, and deeply divided along racial and class lines. It is in the grip of an opioid epidemic and a frenzy of gun violence, and of course it has been devastated by the coronavirus. Alarmingly, life expectancy in the country is decreasing.

So damaged and polarised is the United States that *The Atlantic* magazine in December 2019 entitled its edition 'How to Stop a Civil War'. The headline becomes more chilling when we consider that *The Atlantic* magazine was founded in 1857 to campaign for the abolition of slavery, just a matter of years before the civil war of the 1860s. In 2019 talk of civil war may have seemed exaggerated until 2021 when Donald Trump incited his followers to storm the Capitol building. Trump refused to accept that he had lost the election; America would not have a peaceful handover of power. What the world witnessed was an insurrection in the so-called heart of democracy. What it revealed was that democracy itself is rotten.

America is an exhausted nation. It has been beset by crises for decades: the al-Qaeda-orchestrated terrorist attacks of September 2001, the wars in Afghanistan and Iraq, the banking collapse and global financial crisis of 2007–2008. It is today a nation worn down and poorer; it is less sure of itself, and the world is less sure of American leadership.

A decade ago, the journalist and political commentator Fareed Zakaria coined the phrase 'the post-American world': he saw a world in which the United States was still powerful but no longer dominant. Others had caught up. Is this now the post-American world? China is on track to become the biggest economy in the world, and it is building a military that it says will fight and win any war. The two nations have been on a collision course. In 2017 the United States declared China a strategic competitor, and in 2019 the two powers waged a trade war that damaged both nations.

There are serious concerns that China and the United States could be on course to an even greater conflict. Any clash between the nations would likely be catastrophic, but as much as we may try to wish it away, military strategists in Beijing and Washington are right now preparing for such an eventuality. Global think tank the RAND Corporation prepared a report in 2016 for the American military, and its title could not have been more direct: *War with China: Thinking Through the Unthinkable*. It concluded that China would suffer greater casualties than the United States if war was to break out now. However, it cautioned that as China's military muscle increased, so would the prospect of a prolonged destructive war.

We know where the conflict would possibly start: the South China Sea. Beijing has claimed disputed territory and already expanded it and militarised it. Air force runways have been built on land dredged up from the ocean floor. Loudspeakers warn foreign ships to stay out of what China claims as its waters. American and Chinese warships sometimes come within metres of each other. This is our worst nightmare: an accident, a miscalculation that escalates beyond control. Or perhaps Taiwan will be the trigger. Xi Jinping has declared he will reunify the island with the mainland, by force if necessary. Some historians see an overlay with the drift to world war in 1914 or 1939. Writing about the lead-up to World War One, Christopher Clark, in his book *The Sleepwalkers*, says that political leaders had become hostage to events: 'Causes trawled from the length and breadth of Europe's pre-war decades are piled like weights on the scale until it tilts from probability to inevitability.'

Are the weights tipping the scales again? The Indo-Pacific is a tinderbox of old enmities, expanding militaries, disputed territories, unfinished conflicts and nuclear-armed states. The founding dean of the Harvard University Kennedy School, noted historian Graham Allison, has looked back to 400 BC and the lessons of Thucydides, the historian of the Peloponnesian war between Athens and Sparta. The 'Thucydides trap' holds that when a rising power meets a waning power, war becomes inevitable. Allison fears the world is lurching towards conflict unseen since World War Two. In his book *Destined for War: Can*

America and China Escape Thucydides' Trap?, Allison writes: 'It was the rise of Athens and the fear this instilled in Sparta that made war inevitable.'

Then it was Athens–Sparta. In 1914 it was Germany–Great Britain, and now it is China–United States.

'As far ahead as the eye can see, the defining question about global order is whether China and the US can escape Thucydides' trap. Most contests that fit this pattern have ended badly,' Allison writes. On the current trajectory, war is 'not just possible, but much more likely than currently recognised'.

Now a virus that came out of China has only added to our global instability. As Australia's Prime Minister Scott Morrison said, our world is 'poorer, more disorderly and more dangerous'. Reflecting this threat, Australia has updated its defence strategy significantly, increasing spending and investing in new weaponry. War, it must be said, is still unlikely, but we are not alone in preparing for what was not long ago unthinkable.

Certainly the world is very different to the time of Thucydides. Even compared to 1914, we are a more interconnected, economically entwined global community. It is the fact of our interconnectedness and our urbanisation that has assisted the rapid spread of coronavirus: the world is just a quick flight away. The great peace that has stretched from the end of World War Two has made us smarter, richer and healthier. Since the 1960s, peace in Asia has allowed unprecedented growth and transformed the region. Chinese scholar Wu Zurong, in a 2015 article for *Foreign Policy* magazine titled 'No Thucydides Trap', wrote of how globalisation and the links between China and the US militate against war. China, he wrote, seeks 'a modern relationship ... [a] win-win scenario'.

In a speech in the United States in 2015, China's President Xi Jinping spoke of an opportunity for the two powers to boost global security, but he also issued a warning: 'Should they enter into conflict or confrontation, it would lead to disaster for both countries and the world at large.'

How does Graham Allison answer his question: can America and China escape Thucydides' trap? He believes our fate depends on realism on all sides. Vital interests must be clearly defined; America must strengthen its democracy, and China address its failures of governance: both face threats from within. There is a need, he writes, for great thinkers to devise a grand strategy. Allison concludes with a quote not from Thucydides but from Shakespeare: our destiny lies 'not in our stars, but in ourselves'.

I can think of something else Shakespeare wrote in *Macbeth*:

> And all our yesterdays have lighted fools
> The way to dusty death.

*

John Adams, one of the founding fathers of the United States and its second president, once said: 'Remember, democracy never lasts long. It soon wastes, exhausts, murders itself. There never was a democracy that did not commit suicide.' Is that what we are seeing in our time? Is this the inevitable death of democracy, before it has even had time to grow old? The turmoil of the world is set against a weakening democracy and a seemingly ascendant authoritarianism. Freedom House, an organisation that measures the health of democracy, now counts thirteen straight years of declining freedom in the world. It says we are witnessing the return of the iron fist, the resurgence of political strongmen who seek to exploit fear and anxiety and govern over division.

It is only thirty years since Fukuyama's 'end of history' – is this where it has taken us? It wasn't supposed to be this way. The second half of the twentieth century was a boom time for democracy. Germany emerged from the trauma of Nazism; South Africa threw off the yoke of apartheid; decolonisation across Africa and Asia created free, democratic nations; and in other parts of the world – in Latin America and in Europe – autocratic regimes were swept aside. Between 1970 and 2010 the number of democracies in the world increased from 35 to 120: according to Freedom House, 63 per cent of the world's people lived in democracies.

To its defenders, democracy's appeal is obvious. As an essay in *The Economist* magazine in 2018 pointed out, 'Democracies are on average richer than non-democracies, are less likely to go to war and have a better record of fighting corruption. More fundamentally, democracy lets people speak their minds and shape their own and their children's futures.'

To paraphrase Winston Churchill: democracy is the worst form of government, except for all the others. Easy to say when democracy is designed for you. Democracy grew out of ideas of Western universalism, too often imported at the barrel of a gun. To much of the world, Western triumphalism sounds like humiliation. There is a blowback now that is shaking the West's faith in itself. Today what we have called the global liberal order is unravelling. Global politics was in a state of flux before COVID-19 escaped the Chinese city of Wuhan and put our lives into a tailspin. War, economic collapse, a refugee crisis, political populism – all have tested us. None of us has escaped unscathed.

Terrorism has struck in cities from Paris to London to Jakarta to Sydney to Christchurch. People who lost their savings, their jobs or their homes in the financial meltdown a decade ago are still struggling to recover. Some never will. These shifting fault lines have exposed deep socio-economic inequalities, extant racial divisions and simmering political antagonism.

The Indian writer Pankaj Mishra has called this 'the age of anger'. The West has poisoned itself with the very seeds it has sown. The Chinese-American lawyer and academic Amy Chua says we are witnessing the resurgence of tribalism. The old political left–right binary fails to explain what we are living through. This is the politics of identity. Religion, race, ethnicity, nationalism: these are the drivers of our age. Immanuel Kant's idea of a perpetual peace of shared humanity and universal rights shatters against age-old enmity, historical grievance and resentment.

I am reminded of the words of the great Irish poet William Butler Yeats:

> Things fall apart; the centre cannot hold;
> Mere anarchy is loosed upon the world;
> The blood dimmed tide is loosed, and everywhere
> The ceremony of innocence is drowned;
> The best lack all conviction, while the worst
> Are full of passionate intensity.

As a reporter I have traversed this world of intensity and hate. From bombed-out marketplaces in Afghanistan, Pakistan and Iraq to the closed world of North Korea and the authoritarian behemoth of China, I have indeed followed the trail of blood where the ceremony of innocence is drowned. I have seen how identity excludes and shrinks our world, how it is weaponised. Hutu versus Tutsi in Rwanda, Catholic against Protestant in Northern Ireland, the Muslim blood feud of Shia and Sunni, Hindu against Muslim ... on and on it goes.

I have touched the outer limits of our humanity, and it has proved to me one thing: the Indian philosopher and economist Amartya Sen is right when he warns that identity can kill, and kill with abandon. Let me turn again to Yeats. In his poem 'The Rose Tree', he imagines a conversation between two Irish rebels, Pearse and Connolly:

'But where can we draw water,'
Said Pearse to Connolly,
'When all the wells are parched away?
O plain as plain can be
There's nothing but our own red blood
Can make a right Rose Tree.'

Nothing but our own red blood. This is the blood of vengeance and anger and grievance. It is the blood of identity, poured through the strainer of history. Everywhere there is resurgent populism, nationalism, sectarianism, tribalism. All of it feeds on history. Think of what Xi Jinping tells the Chinese people: remember the hundred years of humiliation by foreign powers. Or Vladimir Putin, who laments the end of the Soviet empire as the 'greatest catastrophe of the twentieth century'. In Turkey, Recep Tayyip Erdoğan reminds his people of the greatness of the Ottoman Empire. In Hungary, Viktor Orbán – a populist leader who has boasted of his 'illiberal democracy' – tells his people they were cheated after the end of World War One, when the country lost two-thirds of its territory, and vows never again. The Islamic State is still fighting the Crusades, and dreams of rebuilding the caliphate ahead of the final battle of humanity.

The German philosopher Friedrich Nietzsche told us we all 'suffer from a consuming historical fever'. History – the vengeance of history – is the poison in the blood of our identities. Nietzsche warned of the 'man of ressentiment': his is the unquenchable thirst for revenge; the refusal to let go; suffering forms the core of his identity. To Nietzsche, the 'man of ressentiment' is a prisoner of his past, caught in a time warp. He always returns to the source of injustice that he cannot fix and does not want to fix.

*

This toxic identity that has made our world so perilous has taken root too in democracies, as American political scientist Mark Lilla says, spreading like a cancer. He argues that the politics of identity is shattering the idea of shared citizenship. The word 'we', he says, has been banished 'to the outer reaches of respectable political discourse'. Lilla says this is a 'disastrous foundation for democratic politics'. America, he writes, is in a 'moral panic about racial, gender and sexual identity that has distorted liberalism's message'.

At worst, this is pitting groups from the left and right into open and often violent conflict. In the United States, white supremacists have clashed with anti-fascist activists. In South Carolina, a young man named Dylann Roof walked into a black church and gunned down people in prayer; he was in the grip of that malignant historical fever, a man out of time still fighting a long dead war, a civil war in which America had to fight for its soul. In Christchurch, New Zealand, Muslim men and women were gunned down in a mosque. In Paris, concert goers at the Bataclan theatre were slaughtered by people with a distorted, hateful view of faith. Islamic fundamentalists, white supremacists, right-wing or left-wing extremists: they all drink from the same poisoned well.

Those are the extreme examples of identity hate. Yet they come from somewhere – they are born of a world where we no longer see ourselves in each other. In democracies today there are those who seek power through division, who revel in carnage and exploit fear and anxiety. They vow to return their people to some imagined golden age, while at the same time defining who the true people are: who belongs and who does not, who are the viruses to be cleansed. And these populists are often popular. They are seizing power with a simple, seductive message for people who are tired or angry or left out, left behind and fearful.

This is the state of democracies today, a competition for recognition and power that is rendering our polity fractured and unworkable. Talk of unity or hope cannot but sound trite or naive when politicians and political parties can so persuasively appeal to a constellation of difference. We define ourselves not by what we are but what we are not.

*

Into this mix of great power rivalry, fear of war, rising authoritarianism, retreating democracy, political populism, nationalism, tribalism and toxic weaponised identity we now add the coronavirus. The year 2020 was unlike any other in our recent memories. A horrible year. We have experienced fear and vulnerability; some have lost loved ones, others have fallen ill; too many have lost their livelihoods, and we have all lost a little of our freedom. The great strength of liberal democracy – freedom – has not been enough to defeat COVID-19.

For a decade I lived in, worked in or visited China, covering the story of this emerging authoritarian superpower. I felt what it was like to live in a country where the state controls information and movement – where the Communist Party reaches into every aspect of life. In 2020–21, all of us have felt a little of what life is like in China: monitored, suspicious of each other, with our liberty curtailed. To defeat the virus, we have had to surrender what is most precious to us. China's President Xi Jinping boasts that his style of government is superior to that of the West; I can imagine him asking: where is your freedom now?

Of course, we can argue that state-enforced restrictions have been necessary, and our willingness to comply has helped limit the spread of the virus. But is this revealing the limits of liberal democracy built on freedom and individual liberty? The German political theorist and Nazi Party member Carl Schmitt, writing in the 1920s and '30s, argued that liberal governments are weak when faced with emergency. He believed that the technical nature of liberal constitutionalism – our checks and balances – left it unable to deal effectively with exceptional situations. In his book *Political Theology*, Schmitt argued that the sovereign 'decides whether there is an extreme emergency'.

A communist dictatorship, he warned, was better positioned to deal with that exception. Why? Because that dictatorship itself was born out of emergency: revolution. Top-down state control is in the DNA of communism, he wrote: 'everything is justified that appears to be necessary for a concretely gained success'. Schmitt was writing against what he saw as the threat of communist Russia, and he believed only the Nazis could counter that threat. In the 1930s, Germany showed us how a cultured, intelligent, democratic nation can fall to tyranny. Australia's Prime Minister Morrison is just one of many who have likened our era to the 1930s, when a world gripped by depression saw the rise of fascism and descended into catastrophic war.

This is a bleak outlook. And these are bleak and testing times. Will democracy meet this challenge? While democracy can be the best vaccine against tyranny, it carries within its own tyranny. To many people – the poor and oppressed – democracy is a sham: a game played by and for the elites. When the threat of coronavirus passes, will we reclaim our liberty? Will democracy meet the challenges of this age? What we have set aside in an emergency we must not allow to be normalised. We must push back against attempts at greater surveillance or control of our lives. Democracies united around common purpose made the world a better place after World War Two. The world will need that collaboration, that commitment to a common future, to ensure we defeat the tyrannies of our time.

Thirty years ago we declared the end of history, but history does not so easily end. The West was guilty of hubris and triumphalism: of thinking that countries like China would bend to our will. Now we are at a deep inflection point of history and the world we have known is no longer assured. We have felt the loss of freedom – surely now we know precious it is.

I recall how Aleksandr Solzhenitsyn, banished to the gulag, felt the brutality of the Soviet Union. Yet it could not take his soul. Even there he found freedom and he found love. 'Of all the cells you've been in, your first cell is a very special one,' he wrote in his book *The Gulag Archipelago*. He would remember it all his life, he said, just like a first love. His cellmates were his family: 'It was not the dirty floor, nor the murky walls, nor the odour of the latrine bucket that you loved – but those fellow prisoners ... and that something that beat between your hearts and theirs.' In that cell, Solzhenitsyn said, his soul would heal. That cell became not an abyss but the most important turning point in his life.

His words are majestic. They eschew all hate or revenge; they surely inspire courage in the most timid soul. In the time of his greatest trial, he pulled humanity closer rather than pushing it away.

> Now for the first time you were about to see people who
> were not your enemies. Now for the first time you were
> about to see others who were alive, who were travelling your
> road, and whom you could join to yourself with the glorious
> word 'we'.

In a world where we are putting up more borders and razor wire to keep people out, and identity has become a poisonous new faith, we need these words of Solzhenitsyn more than ever. Solzhenitsyn remembers the sound of the cell door opening for the first time and 'three unshaven, crumpled pale faces' turning to him and smiling. He had forgotten what a smile was. 'Are you from freedom?' they asked.

*

Solzhenitsyn is one of the many writers I have turned to on my journey. Those writers who never stop believing in freedom. Those who look to join the crimson thread of humanity, to find what is common to us all. Those who will not bow to tyranny or surrender to hate.

I have found the same in the people I have met on this journey: those small lives that together add up to the glory of what it is to be alive. I have drawn strength from the quiet courage and dignity of those people who endure uncertainty and upheaval and somehow never relinquish hope. I have seen it in the face of a father who lost one of his children in the devastating Pakistan earthquake of 2005 and then carried his surviving injured child forty kilometres down a mountainside to find medical relief; there, he pitched a tent, looked for work and started again. I saw love in the tears of a father who held his daughter's hand after she was badly injured: she was suffering broken bones and internal bleeding, and in the middle of a war-torn country with scant medical supplies, she would surely die. Her father sat alongside her, stroking her hair and waiting for his little girl to pass. I saw determination in a peasant worker in a remote hillside village in China looking after two of his children, both blind from preventable eye disease, as they waited for doctors to arrive to save his children's sight.

I have seen resilience, I have seen courage, I have seen despair and, yes, even hopelessness on my journey through a world unravelling and putting itself together again. It is a journey I want to take you on now – a journey to history's end. It is a journey from day to dusk and into a dark night … and from there to where history begins again.

1

THE END OF HISTORY

One of the most famous portraits of Napoleon has him standing before the tomb of Frederick the Great of Prussia. His arms are folded, and he bows his head just slightly. It is staged so that he appears humble and respectful. One of Napoleon's biographers, Philip Dwyer, says the portrait was a powerful tool of propaganda: 'both a mark of respect for Frederick as general and sovereign and a means of enhancing Napoleon's own reputation by obliging people to compare him to Frederick, one of the greatest generals of the eighteenth century'. Napoleon had crushed the Prussian army under Frederick William III in the battles of Auerstedt and Jena on 14 October 1806. The Kingdom of Prussia now came under the empire of France.

At the time, the philosopher Georg Hegel was living and teaching in Jena. He glimpsed Napoleon riding through the town. Hegel was moved to describe the great general as 'the soul of the world'. In that moment Hegel had an epiphany: Napoleon was more than emperor, more than general: he was the fulfilment of human destiny. All of human endeavour, all thought, war, sacrifice, life and death, thought Hegel, had led to this moment. To Hegel, Napoleon was a force from which history was set in motion. This was what humanity was destined for. Napoleon was the absolute spirit. Hegel saw the Battle of Jena as more than just a military victory: it was a moment of transcendence, a break from all that had come before. As he described Napoleon 'dominating the entire world from horseback', Hegel gave flight to a radical idea: the end of history itself.

To some, this is an evil notion: a belief that our fate is sealed, that people are at the mercy of an historical puppet master. To his critics, Hegel promotes the narrative of the 'great man of history' – the tyrant who seeks to bend time to his will. Terror and murder are forgiven in the quest for Hegel's absolute freedom. Hegel becomes some philosophical spectre haunting our age. He is the voice who whispered into the ears of Hitler and Stalin. His legacy is the gas chamber and the gulag. Hegel cursed the twentieth century, bequeathing us a legacy of virulent nationalism that led to world wars. The philosopher Karl Popper listed Hegel among the enemies of the Open Society: Hegel is 'the perversion of everything that is decent'. The Marxist extreme left and the fascist extreme right, Popper says, 'all base their political philosophies on Hegel'. Yet Hegel looms over us: there is no way to understand our age without seeking to understand Hegel.

Hegel's 'end of history' casts a long shadow. Even those who have never heard of him, let alone read him, live in a world Hegel made. It is not possible to imagine the modern political state without Hegel. One Hegelian philosopher, Stephen Houlgate, has called this eighteenth-century thinker 'the most important political philosopher of the post-French Revolutionary modern era'. Although his idea would become so incendiary, Hegel himself alluded to the end of history just once, when he said: 'world history moves from east to west; for Europe is the end of world history plain and simple'. Europe, to Hegel, represented the apex of freedom. His arc of history begins in imperial China, where only the emperor is free; in ancient Greece the seeds of democracy are planted but only some people are free; the French Revolution of 1789 promises freedom for all. Freedom, says Hegel, is the engine of history. Rather than being dragged along in its wake, it is our restless, brave pursuit of freedom that makes history move. For Hegel, people are their own idea: our struggle to be free gives shape to our world. And it is a divine quest: freedom is a gift from God.

Freedom or tyranny: how can one man be responsible for both? Because history is hard, brutal. The grievance of history is passed on from generation to generation: a blood debt that demands payment over and over. Hegel called history 'the slaughter-bench on which the happiness of peoples, the wisdom of states, and the virtue of individuals have been sacrificed'. The French Revolution – Hegel's historical high point – itself descended into terror. Maximilien Robespierre's Committee of Public Safety – the de facto government – launched a campaign of violence in which thousands were killed and hundreds of thousands imprisoned. It was the age of the guillotine. To Robespierre, tyranny was the price of freedom. Without terror, he said, 'virtue was powerless'. Hegel agreed: tyranny was 'pure, horrible power', but 'necessary and just' if it preserved the state, because only the state can deliver us to a place beyond tyranny. For Hegel, the state is 'the justification of god'. It is only when we surrender our freedom to a collective will to live together, bound by a system of laws, that we can know true freedom. The state, he says, 'not only writes history's prose, it provides its content'. No wonder Karl Popper was so horrified. To Popper, Hegel's state sacrifices 'conscience' for 'blind obedience'. Hegel puts humanity on the road to 'totalitarian nationalism'. It is an 'an appeal to tribal instincts, to passion and to prejudice'.

The mere mention of names like Hegel, let alone talk of philosophical ideas, can understandably be eye-glazing for many people. The language is dense and opaque: scholars spend lifetimes analysing each word, each sentence, trying to deconstruct the ideas, and they go to their graves befuddled, confused and frustrated. The great philosophers conduct their own conversation across time. They are gravediggers, exhuming the bodies of thinkers past and picking over their bones for traces of something they can call truth. Hegel reached back to the Greeks, to Socrates and Plato, for his ideas about democracy and the state. He also devoured the works of the philosophers of the Enlightenment, that explosion of new thinking from the seventeenth to the nineteenth centuries. As one of its foundation thinkers, Immanuel Kant, put it, this period was 'man's emergence from his self-incurred immaturity'. The Enlightenment was the Age of Reason, the time when humanity cast aside superstition in favour of reason, when old regimes fell to new beliefs about liberty, and rights. Hegel confronted Kant as Kant had locked horns with David Hume, the great Scottish Enlightenment figure who famously told the world that 'reason is the slave of passions'. Kant said Hume 'woke me from my slumber'; Kant surely did the same for Hegel.

These thinkers shook me to life as well. For me philosophy isn't so much about answering the great questions of life as asking better questions. As I reported from around the world, as I looked into the faces of terrorists, as I walked through bloodied market places, as I sat with people huddled in fear, as I watched governments fall, or despots prosper, I needed to know more than simply what happened. I needed to know if morality mattered, if justice was just a mirage, if there was any such thing as truth. Journalism alone could not give me that. It put me at the front row of history, but I needed more – I needed to understand what drove history. For that I had to rob graves myself.

Hegel said: 'Philosophy is something lonely, it does not belong on the streets, and in the market place.' There are 'bayonets, cannon, bodies', he wrote, but of philosophy the 'soul of its commander is spirit'. In 1989, 200 years after the French Revolution, interest in Hegel was rejuvenated by the fall of the Berlin Wall and later the crumbling of the Soviet Union. As Francis Fukuyama said, this moment was the true 'end of history'.

*

It is received wisdom now that 1989 was a turning point: a moment when the world changed forever. Certainly the fall of the Wall and all it symbolised is fixed in our memory. It exists as a moment in time, something that could be captured in a photograph. But the plates were shifting well before then. We need to go ten years further back, to 1979, and we can see that the dominoes were in place. Everything that would happen in the decades to come had its beginning in a year when I was becoming conscious of a world beyond my own.

In 1979, the British punk rock band The Clash let fury have the hour. Anger can be power, they told us. The Clash was always the most articulate and political of the groups that thundered out of England in the mid-1970s and tore up the rock 'n' roll rule book. No more Elvis, Beatles or Rolling Stones – that was the catch-cry of a frustrated, impatient, alienated youth. They rejected the optimism of the 1960s. They wore safety pins in their clothes, not flowers in their hair. They were the children of Britain's 1973–75 recession. They were unemployed and without hope. In the words of seminal punk band the Sex Pistols, they were the flowers in the dustbin of history. How Hegel would have recognised them.

In the dying weeks of 1979, The Clash released *London Calling*, today considered one of the greatest albums in the history of rock. It was a startling array of musical genres, from jazz to blues to rockabilly to funk and disco, all sweetening the sound of a cry of anguish from a generation shaped by the Cold War and living in fear of nuclear war. The ice age is coming, they told us; we need to brace for meltdown.

That same year Margaret Thatcher had led a Conservative government to power as Britain's first female prime minister. In a couple of years Ronald Reagan, a former Hollywood actor turned California governor, would become president of the United States. A few years later, Mikhail Gorbachev became the leader of the Soviet Union; he would be the last.

In 1979 the Red Army invaded Afghanistan, triggering the rise of the Taliban and solidifying the place of al-Qaeda. The fuse was lit for the 2001 terrorist attacks on America. In Iran, Ayatollah Khomeini launched an Islamic revolution that toppled the Western-backed Shah of Iran. As Christian Caryl wrote in his book *Strange Rebels: 1979 and the Birth of the 21st Century*, 'The forces unleashed in 1979 marked the beginning of the end of great Socialist utopias that had dominated so much of the 20th century.' Ronald Reagan would soon forecast the end of the 'evil empire'. The march of freedom and democracy, he said, 'would leave Marxism-Leninism on the ash heap of history'. The Chinese Communist Party had other ideas. Deng Xiaoping – recently installed as Supreme Leader – began a series of economic reforms that would put his country on a collision course with the West. Deng would offer a new model: socialism with Chinese characteristics. The political planets were aligning; we were on the cusp of enormous change.

In 1979 I was sixteen and experiencing my coming of age. The punk bands spoke to me, far away as I was from London's Oxford Street. It was the sound of the music that first seized me: loud, fast and urgent. It was simple to play – and that was the point, anyone could do it. I played guitar; I couldn't emulate Jimi Hendrix but I could play the Pistols' 'Anarchy in the UK'. These were my bands, people mostly just a couple of years older than me. I shared their fears. I was a Cold War kid who had grown up with the looming threat of war and catastrophe. These were truly anxious times. This was my political awakening, and punk music was its soundtrack.

The punk bands wrote about fascism, so I sought out books on fascism. When The Clash sang about the Spanish Civil War, I read up on Franco. Punks latched on to any idea – restless youth searching for something to believe in. Some flirted with Nazi regalia – a dumb fashion statement, really – while others wanted to tear down capitalism. Like many impressionable youths, I was emotionally drawn to Marxism. I read *The Communist Manifesto* before attempting – but not understanding – *Capital*. To an idealistic but naive young man, the idea of a socialist utopia of freedom, and equality for all, made sense to me. But in the years ahead I would come to see utopian dreams for the nightmares they are. Humanity's quest for the ideal society offers only the illusion of freedom or equality; what we get instead is despotism, top-down control, social engineering and the destruction of the human soul. In 1979, while I was high on The Clash, with a head full of politics, life behind the Iron Curtain was far from a workers' paradise. People were hungry; their lives were controlled; the entire system was rotting from the inside.

Thatcher and Reagan formed a formidable partnership. Thatcher smashed the unions to re-engineer the British economy. She fought and won a war against Argentina in the Falkland Islands. Reagan promised to return his country to again be that shining city on a hill. It was sunshine in America, he said. And for a time that was true: neoliberalism, as it became known, dramatically recast our economies and reshaped our lives; we grew richer and people were lifted out of poverty. But in time this neoliberal experiment, which elevated the market above all else, exhausted itself. We lost sight of human beings: as Thatcher famously said, there is no such thing as society, only economies. She was channelling the high priest of neoliberalism, the Nobel Prize–winning economist Friedrich Hayek, who saw the market as the highest form of justice. From our vantage point today, we can see how neoliberalism consolidated power in the hands of elites, and spawned a populist backlash among those left behind that has shaken world politics, and the consequences of which we are still to see.

But in the 1980s there was hope. The great Cold War enemies, Russia and America, were talking. From their first summit, in Geneva in 1985, Reagan and Gorbachev slowly built trust and, remarkably, agreed to reduce their nuclear arsenal. The world was stepping back from the brink.

By the early 1980s The Clash had burnt themselves out, and their songs didn't sound so ominous anymore. The anger of punk had given way to a new, softer sound. Neoliberalism was redefining music too, as British kids swapped their mohawks for blow-waves. They dressed in Edwardian clothes and styled themselves as 'New Romantics'. Duran Duran shot film clips on yachts with pretty young women. Guitars were replaced by tinny synthesisers, and I had gone from being a faux rebellious youth to a budding young journalist. The Cold War was about to end, and I was set to start my journey into this new world: a world beyond history.

*

I stumbled into journalism. I had a vague idea that I wanted to do something with my life that involved writing, but I had no clue how I might go about that. When I left school I found a job as a mail boy at the Australian Institute of Aboriginal Studies. It was easy, hassle free and fun. My uncle was the janitor there and I would spend my morning delivering internal mail to the assorted academics who worked at the institute, and then my lunch hour sitting with Uncle Mick and listening to his stories about his childhood.

I was always fascinated by stories; my family members are storytellers. As a child I would sit at my mother's feet as she spun me the most incredible ghost stories and tales of adventure. Other times she would tell me about her life growing up: the hardship – and there was a lot of that – but also the love and humour that got them all through. Aboriginal people pass our stories down through the generations in this way: we learn about our land, our culture and our complex kinship systems. None of these stories are written down; all are memorised and thus kept alive from generation to generation. My great-grandfather Bill Grant was known among his people as 'the storyteller'. Those who remember him from their childhoods say he would travel with the stump of an old carved ceremonial tree – once common ritual markers among Aboriginal people – and sit alongside it while he spun stories around a campfire deep into the night. I like to think there is something of him in me.

It was while working as a mail boy that my life took a remarkable turn. A young Aboriginal woman, Marcia Langton, was working at the institute while she completed her PhD in anthropology. Marcia was a firebrand activist, already a veteran of many protest marches for Aboriginal rights. She had a fearsome – and entirely deserved – reputation: she suffered no fools and demolished any obstacles. She zeroed in on me in the institute's library, where I would stack books and photocopy material for the resident scholars. Marcia pulled me aside to give me a lecture about how I was wasting my life, and how my parents had not sacrificed and worked hard so that I would be a mail boy all my life. Marcia told me I needed to go to university, but the whole idea was so unlikely as to be ludicrous. No one in my family had been to university; in fact, in my parents' generation Aboriginal kids were often not allowed to go to school with white children. When I entered high school laws had changed but attitudes had not.

When I was fifteen, I – along with a group of other Aboriginal boys – was told by the school headmaster that I would amount to nothing and should stop wasting my time even showing up at school. This was common in 1970s Australia; there were no great ambitions for Aboriginal people. I probably would have dropped out, but my father got a job working at a sawmill in Canberra. Suddenly I had gone from a school where many of the students were Aboriginal – and most of them related to me – to a school where my sister and I were the only children of colour.

Canberra was the whitest of cities, but in its own way that saved me. It wasn't easy – I was an oddity, and my sister and I experienced schoolyard racial taunts – but I was a good sportsman and I could stand up for myself, and in time I made friends and settled into white suburban Australian life. It was a relief in some respects to be away from the harshness of life in Aboriginal communities and the much more brutal small-town racism. In my hometown I was regularly involved in schoolyard fights as black and white squared off against each other. Now, in Canberra, I turned up, played football and did my homework. I did well enough to finish school and pass my exams to qualify for university, but I never seriously entertained the idea until that day with Marcia.

Within weeks, Marcia had helped me fill in the university application forms and I was on my way to Sydney to study politics and philosophy and history. I had always been an avid reader, and I was obsessed with the news; now I had a chance to study and think about the world.

I had come of age at a tumultuous time in Australian history. As a child I remember being transfixed by images of the Vietnam War on the television news; with other children I gathered around a black-and-white TV to watch man walk on the moon. In Australia this was a time of protest and rapid social change: three decades of conservative government was swept aside and a new – albeit short-lived – left-wing Australian Labor Party government took power in 1972. In the same year Aboriginal political activists, inspired by the Black Panther movement in America, set up a tent embassy on the lawns of Parliament House to draw attention to the ongoing suffering of Aboriginal people mired in poverty and neglect. The idea of pitching a tent was genius: it contrasted poignantly with life in this rich, modern democracy. Political scientist Donald Horne had somewhat sardonically dubbed Australia 'the lucky country' but Australians took it as a statement of fact – indeed, a compliment. But the Tent Embassy spoke to the unlucky Australians.

I was shaped by these times. The news images are stamped in my mind. I suppose in some way all of this was preparing me for a life in journalism. Getting my break in news was another twist of unlikely fate. I had been working as a copy boy at *The Canberra Times* – a menial job that involved getting the dinner orders for the journalists on the night shift and running news copy between the editorial desks – when I was told that the Macquarie Radio Network was looking for a cadet journalist (an entry-level traineeship position, once the gateway to a journalistic career). I applied and was called for an interview. The news director and I hit it off from the start; noting my dark skin, he asked me what nationality I was, and when I told him I was Aboriginal he said his stepbrother was also Aboriginal. I have no doubt that personal connection helped me win the job.

It was 1984, and I was twenty years old. A few years before, I was delivering mail and lacking in ambition, but a chance conversation with Marcia Langton (herself now a distinguished academic, public intellectual and senior professor at the University of Melbourne) had altered the course of my life. And I had entered journalism at a fortuitous time. The world was on the cusp of enormous change, and I would be pulled along in its wake. Ahead of me was a journey into more than sixty countries, into war zones, natural disasters; I would cover rebellions and watch nations rise and fall. The geopolitical plates were already moving. In Moscow a young man named Mikhail Gorbachev had risen rapidly through the ranks of the Communist Party, and in 1984 would deliver a speech where he criticised the old Soviet system. He had introduced himself as a reformer; soon he would lead the country and help lift the Iron Curtain.

*

Philosophy. It always comes back to philosophy for me. The world as we know it is an idea. The Cold War was a clash of ideas. Communism versus capitalism; the Soviet Union versus the West; Moscow versus Washington – a tussle over competing visions of the world. But these enemies were also siblings born of the Enlightenment. Into the twentieth century, Europe and the United States dominated the globe. Eighteenth-century revolutions in France and America had given us new ideas of freedom, liberty and happiness. In 1917 the Bolshevik revolution overthrew the Russia monarchy. It is one of the key events of thirty years of unending revolution and war in Europe. From 1914 to 1945, the continent – and, by extension, the world – tore itself apart. World Wars One and Two have been called the European Civil Wars. In his book *The Cold War: A World History*, Odd Arne Westad writes: 'A whole generation of Europeans learned that killing, destroying and hating your neighbours were regular normal aspects of life.'

By 1945, the fascist nightmare of Nazi Germany was defeated, and two wartime allies, Russia and America, now faced each other down. The Cold War divided up the world; at times, in places like Korea, Vietnam and Cambodia, it turned hot with millions of deaths. The world stood on the brink of nuclear catastrophe – what was known as 'MAD', for 'mutually assured destruction'. How close we came, several times: one miscalculation, overreaction, accident or false move away from disaster. Communism and capitalism offered competing universal ideas: the market or Marxism; democracy or the Soviets' version of 'freedom'. Mikhail Gorbachev had known nothing but war or cold war; he was a student of philosophy, he had read the great thinkers, and now his time had arrived.

To understand Gorbachev the man, we must meet Gorbachev the boy. He was born into a peasant family on 2 March 1931. His father was Russian and his mother's side Ukrainian. In a country that was officially atheist, his grandmothers on both sides were religious. The young Mikhail grew up with God and Marx. He was also raised in famine and war. In the 1930s, the Russian people were starving; some of Gorbachev's own relatives died of hunger. Soviet policies of collectivisation – whereby rural farming families would yield their crops to feed those in the cities – and severe drought had triggered a famine. Mikhail's grandfather was banished to Siberia for violating the rules. Later, his maternal grandfather was imprisoned in a Stalinist purge for being a counter-revolutionary. As political scientist Archie Brown points out in his book *The Human Factor* – a study of the lives of Gorbachev, Thatcher and Reagan – the families of those arrested were 'guilty by association' and shunned by their communities. Gorbachev himself has written that his family was 'an enemy of the people', and the treatment his relatives received 'has remained in my memory'. Gorbachev's father later served in the Red Army, battling Hitler's invading forces in World War Two. At one point he was feared dead. Young Mikhail was forced out of school to work the fields. Gorbachev wrote: 'Our generation is the generation of children of war. It scorched us, it put its imprint on our character and on our perception of the world.' This explains why Mikhail Gorbachev grew up to change the world.

In 1988, Mikhail Gorbachev arrived in the capital of capitalism, New York. He visited Broadway and even took a photo under a neon Coca-Cola sign. The United Nations headquarters hung out a banner welcoming him. In her magnificent book *Post Wall, Post Square*, historian Kristina Spohr recounts a story that, from where we sit today, sounds almost too bizarre to be true. But it is. On Gorbachev's tour list was a visit to Trump Tower, where he was to meet a brash young New York real estate developer, Donald Trump. At the last minute the Soviet General Secretary had to cancel. Later that day a Gorbachev impersonator was spotted strolling down Fifth Avenue. Spohr writes: 'Trump and his bodyguards rushed down from his office thinking that the Soviet leader had changed his mind and was now keen to view his temple of consumerism. Squeezing onto the sidewalk, the tycoon enthusiastically pumped the fake Gorbachev's hand.' Trump of course later claimed he knew all along it was a stunt.

While Donald Trump was making and losing money, Gorbachev was making history. His speech to the United Nations is remarkable. It joins the philosophy of Hegel with a new world order: it marks another step on what Hegel would have seen as humanity's march of freedom. Gorbachev returned to Hegel's time – to that time of tumult and terror. He ties Hegel to the defining revolution of communist Russia.

Two great revolutions, the French Revolution of 1789 and the Russian Revolution of 1917, have exerted a powerful influence on the actual nature of the historical process and radically changed the course of world events. Both of them, each in its own way, have given a gigantic impetus to man's progress.

Progress: the journey to the absolute state. Gorbachev, following Hegel, saw human history as a story of sacrifice, a struggle of life and death. History, he said, was marked by war, but 'parallel with the process of wars, hostility, and alienation of peoples and countries, another process, just as objectively conditioned, was in motion and gaining force: The process of the emergence of a mutually connected and integral world.' A new world. Out of an old order, a new order rises. The end of history.

Freedom, Gorbachev said, is the universal right of all people. A new age demanded an end to hardened ideology, but not an end to philosophy. The Soviet Union was not yet ready to surrender but it could no longer shut itself off from the West. That, Gorbachev, said 'would lead to spiritual impoverishment'. Gorbachev vowed to put an end to wars and conflict, hunger and poverty. He announced he would cut the size of the Soviet army and begin pulling his soldiers back from occupied countries. The Soviet Union would undergo a process of reform towards democracy. It was time to reset relations with the old enemy, America. As Gorbachev said: 'The world has changed, and so have the nature, role, and place of these relations in world politics.' What Gorbachev set in train eventually cost him power and brought down the Soviet Union.

At the United Nations in 1988, Mikhail Gorbachev received a thunderous standing ovation.

*

Deng Xiaoping was ten years ahead of Gorbachev. He had seen the future and he knew that his country was at a crossroads. In 1979 Chinese pro-democracy activists were growing restless and they had the support of senior figures in the Communist Party. Mao Zedong had been dead for three years, his body lying in state in Tiananmen Square, but there were those in the Party who wanted to pick over his remains, to challenge his legacy. Deng was now paramount leader, having succeeded Hua Guofeng, who led the country immediately after the death of Mao Zedong.

Deng had seen up close the failings of the 'Great Helmsman' Mao. He had been purged from the party and rehabilitated. Deng was looking to the outside world and in 1975 had led a delegation to France. He returned a believer in overseas study tours: 'The more we see, the more we realise how backward we are,' he said. It was a sentiment he would repeat on trips around the country, admitting that the Communist Party had failed the people. On a visit to the city of Liaoning, he said: 'If we can't grow faster than the capitalist countries then we can't show the superiority of our system.' After years of Mao's iron fist, key party leaders were ready to embrace new ideas. Other delegations to Japan and Europe opened the eyes of these diehard communists; they could not deny the rapid development of capitalist economies. They had been raised on Mao-era propaganda that the West was backward and decadent; they now realised how wrong they were and what China was missing out on.

The Party had been committed to what it called the 'Two Whatevers': resolutely uphold *whatever* policy Chairman Mao made, and unswervingly follow *whatever* instructions Chairman Mao gave. Now, three years after Mao's death, the Party had more fully embraced the 'Four Modernisations': agriculture, industry, defence, and science and technology. The 'Four Modernisations' had been adopted in 1977, as part of a call for China to become a high production society. The old idea of Party support from cradle to grave gave way to more competition and workers being paid according to their productivity. In 1978, a new slogan appeared, a 'Fifth Modernisation': democracy. It was written on the walls of the capital, Beijing. Near Tiananmen Square, at a place called Xidan Wall, was an official bulletin board. Notices and newspaper clippings would be put up there. During the Cultural Revolution it was used to post messages denouncing leaders deemed traitors to the Party. In late 1978, posters started appearing criticising Chairman Mao. When no one was punished, the protest grew, with messages denouncing Marxism. Xidan Wall quickly became known as Democracy Wall.

In December 1978, Deng addressed the Party Congress and told the Chinese people it was time to 'emancipate their minds'. China, he said, must throw off the past and become a 'modern and powerful socialist state'. The Communist Party had a new slogan: 'Practice is the sole criterion of truth'. Ideology was not enough – the proof was in the outcome, and China was lagging the world. Deng Xiaoping's biographer Ezra Vogel chronicles how Deng wanted to shift the focus from class struggle to economic reform. With an eye on the momentum growing around the Democracy Wall, Deng even told the head of the Japanese Democratic Socialist Party, Sasaki Ryosaku, that people had a right to express their views. Deng was preparing for a trip to the United States, and before leaving he instructed one of his lieutenants to draft a speech supporting the democracy protesters, which he would deliver to the Communist Party leadership when he returned.

From where we sit now, with China winding back freedoms and taking yet another authoritarian turn, this looks like a remarkable moment: a 'sliding doors' moment when the country may have taken an entirely different direction. In the United States, Deng took in all the sights and sounds of Western capitalism: he wore a cowboy hat and attended a rodeo, listening to country music star Willie Nelson; he and his delegation visited Disneyland; Deng dined with Henry Kissinger. While he was away, the democracy protesters grew bolder. Ever more strident messages were posted, now calling for democracy and human rights. Demonstrations went all the way to the front gate of Zhongnanhai, the compound that housed the most powerful Communist Party figures. Essays appeared directly challenging Party rule. A former soldier, Wei Jingshen, posted his own critique of the party at Democracy Wall, demanding that people be the masters of their own destiny. It was a remarkable document, with Wei directly criticising Deng Xiaoping and even calling him a dictator. Wei wrote that the people 'do not want to serve as mere tools for dictators with personal ambitions for carrying out modernisation'. Wei became a leader of the freedom movement. When Deng returned to Beijing, he feared the situation was getting out of hand. This wasn't just criticism or students venting frustration; now it was a threat to the Communist Party itself, and Deng would have none of that.

In the coming months, under Deng's instruction, officials in Beijing banned the posting of any pro-democracy or anti-Party material. There was no more criticism of Mao Zedong. Wei Jingshen was arrested; he would spend eighteen of the next twenty years in prison, before being deported to the United States, where he lives today. Over a three-month period, Deng Xiaoping had gone from tolerating or even tentatively encouraging the Democracy Wall to launching a crackdown that would set the direction of the country.

Deng's speech in support of the Democracy Wall was never delivered. It is tempting to imagine what was in it. Would it have charted a more rapid course towards even greater opening of the country? Would Deng have embraced democratic reforms – free elections, free media, the rule of law – with the same fervour as his economic program? Maybe not explicitly, but Deng knew his nation had to change: he imagined a future where his country would grow rich and avenge the humiliation of the West. He had seen how backwards China was. He had admitted failure and allowed criticism of the previously infallible Mao Zedong. How America must have appeared to Deng: its cars, its shopping malls and skyscrapers. What would he have made of its free media, its movies, its music, its rebellious youth with their freedom and fashion? However tempted he may have been to allow more open discussion of democracy, he was not prepared to risk the Communist Party.

When Deng did address the Party, he sent a message to those senior figures who were sympathetic to the democracy movement. Deng also closed the door on the growing criticism of Mao Zedong. A rift had emerged between Deng and one of his deputies, Hu Yaobang. In his speech to the conference, Hu had encouraged more free thinking, but others in the party began to suspect him of straying too far into self-criticism. When Deng laid down the law to the party, he was also putting Hu Yaobang on notice – and this was to play out in the coming years in the most spectacular and devastating fashion.

Deng and Hu had shared a commitment to economic reform, Hu implemented Deng's policies that opened up the country. When pro-democracy protests flared again in 1987, senior Party members blamed Hu and pressured Deng to remove him. In the end Hu resigned. Two years later Hu Yaobang passed away, and protesters gathered to mourn him in Tiananmen Square. Between April and June, the numbers grew and Deng Xiaoping said the protesters needed to be sent a warning. We all know what happened next: Deng ordered in the tanks, and Chinese soldiers opened fire on their own people. How many were killed? We still don't know, but estimates have run from several hundred to many thousands.

At the height of the Tiananmen Square protests, just days before the massacre, Mikhail Gorbachev arrived in Beijing. It was the first such visit by a Soviet leader to China's capital in thirty years. It was part of normalising relations between the two communist nations, which had been allies and then bitter enemies. What a time to arrive. Some of the protesters wanted to meet this man Gorbachev, who was opening up the Soviet Union. Gorbachev was troubled by what he saw, especially the hard-line response by the Chinese Communist Party. Some in Gorbachev's delegation said this looked like a revolution; they wondered if they were normalising relations with dead men.

Why wouldn't they think that? The protests in Beijing coincided with similar democracy movements across Eastern Europe: Poland, Hungary, Czechoslovakia. In Romania, the regime of Nicolae Ceauşescu would be ousted. Two years earlier,

Ronald Reagan had issued his famous call: 'Mr Gorbachev, tear down this wall.' In November 1989, the Berlin Wall started to come down. History was moving quickly to its end, just as Hegel imagined.

And so, at this critical moment, in this fateful year, Deng Xiaoping and Mikhail Gorbachev came together, two towering figures of the twentieth century. One who would lift the Iron Curtain that had divided Europe, the other who would massacre his own people to save his Party. Deng had vowed that his country would not go the way of the Soviet Union: his people would get rich but they would not become free. Deng was convinced China had a new model: a Chinese, authoritarian capitalist model that in time would return China – this humiliated, backwards China – to its rightful place at the head of the world order. Its people need only wait. As Deng said, China must hide its intentions and bide its time.

*

The ice age was coming. I was still listening to The Clash, ten years after *London Calling* appeared. Now I was in my mid-twenties and my journalism career was beginning to take shape. I had moved quickly through the ranks, never with any real plan or direction, but with a willingness to work hard and read obsessively. I was making up for wasted time, I suppose; I always felt the loss of those years when my family and I wandered from town to town, never stopping long enough for me to go to school. I started behind and I have been trying to catch up ever since.

But what I lacked in opportunity I made up for in luck: I met the right people at the right time. In journalism new doors kept opening. I had gone from copy boy at *The Canberra Times* to a cadetship with Macquarie Radio Network to a job as a political correspondent in Canberra for the ABC. In a youthful fit of pique I had actually tried to leave journalism a couple of times, but each time it lured me back. At the ABC, the director of news, Ian Macintosh, encouraged and promoted me; more than any other person, he would have the greatest impact on my career. In a future time, as vice president at CNN, Ian would hire me and bring me to China. What Deng Xiaoping set in train for his country would also change my life. I would soon discover that if history ended in 1989, it didn't end for long.

2

THE RETURN OF HISTORY

In the pitch blackness I see them, just the headlights at first, cutting through the teeming rain and illuminating the hills around me. I could soon hear the sound of the trucks, louder as they came closer; from the deep, low hum, I could tell there were a lot of them. The army was coming. This was the moment they had waited for – for over a hundred years. They were still fighting an old war that most of the world had forgotten. But they could never forget. To forget would be to lose who they were. Wars live on in memory well after the guns are silent.

These soldiers were raised on the stories of their parents and grandparents; forged by the bitterness of long, hard winters. Their country had been brought to its knees, pillaged and carved up. Foreigners controlled the sea ports and took the plundered riches back to their home countries. How they despised these devils, these raiders and invaders – but they despised their own weakness more. How corrupt, how demoralised their country had become to fall so low as to be humbled by people they considered barbarians. Wasn't their country the Kingdom of Heaven? But that empire had fallen, and they had watched as others grew rich. They had starved and endured revolution and war. They could not count the numbers of dead. Anyway, what are numbers, when the misery was so complete. But on this night in the rain, these men – and they were men, all hand-picked – would take it all back: they would pour into the city and they would not have to fire one shot.

History began again on this night of teeming rain on 1 July 1997. China's People's Liberation Army – in numbers the single biggest force the world has seen – lined the border with Hong Kong, awaiting the order to cross over and reclaim the territory from the British. The hundred years of humiliation was about to come to an end. Hong Kong had been a symbol of China's descent, its retreat from the world. From the mid-nineteenth century, this once-great global power was overrun. The loss of Hong Kong was the price China would pay for its own decadence. Hong Kong was a scar on China's soul, the British flag that flew over the territory a constant reminder of its disgrace. This night would be a moment of vengeance and vindication: it would announce the return of the Middle Kingdom. The Chinese Communist Party had assembled its finest troops to show the world that China would no more be pushed around.

This handover – such a benign word, hardly fitting of the magnitude and historical significance of the event – had been years in the making. The British prime minister, the 'Iron Lady', as she was known, Margaret Thatcher, and the old Communist Party warhorse Deng Xiaoping had thrashed out the terms of this deal in sometimes tense meetings. In 1982, Deng was running out of patience; locked in negotiations with Thatcher, he leant across the table and said, bluntly, that he could always send in his army and take back Hong Kong in a day. Thatcher replied that, yes, Deng could do just that, and there was little Britain could do to stop him, but it would mean the collapse of Hong Kong itself.

That exchange was recounted in the late Baroness Thatcher's memoir. She went on to say how depressed she was about the future of Hong Kong under China mainland rule. That moment between the two leaders reveals so much about our present: how far the Chinese Communist Party would be prepared to go to take back what it believes is its right. Secret documents of those meetings, later declassified, revealed that Prime Minister Thatcher remained 'seriously disturbed by the Chinese insistence on recovering sovereignty over Hong Kong'. And for good reason. Deng's deputy, Premier Zhao Ziyang, had warned Thatcher that in a choice between Hong Kong's stability and prosperity and China's sovereignty, the Party would put sovereignty first. Hong Kong would be no Singapore.

China's leaders had warned against any move to democracy in Hong Kong. In 1958, a former Chinese premier, Zhou Enlai, threatened Britain that any move to allow the people of Hong Kong to become self-governing would be considered by Beijing as 'a very unfriendly act', with all the unspoken implications that carried. Fast-forward to today and it is clear that anyone who is the least bit surprised at Beijing's crackdown on democracy protests in Hong Kong has not been paying attention. President Xi Jinping is doing precisely what the ghosts of past Chinese leaders have told him to do: he is keeping faith with the Communist Party's authoritarian tradition by imposing on Hong Kong new security laws targeting sedition, treason or secession by pro-democracy protesters.

How many times does the Communist Party leadership have to tell the West that it rejects liberal democracy before we will believe them? Western leaders have stubbornly and foolishly held to the belief that the Party would collapse or become like one of ours.

Successive American presidents and British prime ministers all believed the Communist Party would either reform or vanish. Even Margaret Thatcher, for all her well-placed concern, still believed that Chinese communism would fall just like communism in the Soviet Union. In her memoir, she wrote that the 'Chinese belief that the benefits of a liberal economic system can be had without a liberal political system seems to me false in the long term'.

China's collapse? Deng Xiaoping would not hear of it. He had already shown the world how ruthless he could be by ordering the massacre of his own people; he was reforming his country from a position of strength and fear. The Chinese Communist Party sought to bend the world to its will. Now, in Hong Kong, in front of the world's media, the People's Liberation Army was about to take back what had been taken from its nation.

This was not an invasion; China had no need of that. This was one of those rare moments in world history: a peaceful handover. Not a shot would be fired in anger, yet I think of that moment now as a time when the world turned on its axis. There in the driving monsoonal rain, in an outpost of the old British Empire, we were set a new course. If our worst fears are realised, that night set us on a course for war – and a war that will be so devastating it doesn't bear thinking about. That's what they call it, those military and security strategists whose job it is to think about little else: they call it thinking the unthinkable.

There was no time for such thoughts back then, of course. Oh, there were those killjoys who grumbled about how the Chinese would wreck the place. How it would never be the same. But most were too busy partying to worry about the future. Their minds were in the past. They reminisced about a world that was soon to be gone – of servants and Chinese amahs to take care of the children, of gin and tonic and high tea. Many of those Brits who had sweltered in Hong Kong's tropical heat serving the empire were readying themselves for a return to the old country. They had already packed up their large government-provided apartments. Chinese antiques and revolution-era kitsch were carefully stowed away. The great adventure of their lives was over. Now they watched as the clock neared midnight. The union flag would soon be lowered. To the mournful sound of the Last Post then God Save the Queen, the last British governor, Chris Patten, wiped a tear from his eye. His final duty was to telegram London: 'I have relinquished the administration of this government. God Save the Queen.'

On the border, the Chinese army was already on the move.

*

I had flown into Hong Kong from London, where I was the European correspondent for Australia's Seven Television Network. I had only been there a few months and I had barely spent a night in my new home.

Six months earlier, London was the last place I expected to be. I had been hosting the morning news program *11AM* and a weekend political interview show, *Face to Face*. But I had itchy feet. The studio has never felt like home for me. I have always wanted to be out among it, in the field where stories happen. I liked the long hours, the unpredictability; I also liked the danger. Nothing comes close to that. Nothing ever will.

My news director, John Rudd, stuck his head around my office door one morning and, in his curiously high lilting voice, said 'How would you like to go to Los Angeles?'

'For a story?' I asked.

'No,' he replied, 'for a job. I want you to be our North America correspondent.'

My feet barely touched the floor. This was what I really wanted – to be a foreign correspondent.

My appetite had been whetted earlier that year when I was dispatched to cover what was being reported (erroneously) at the time as a coup against the elected government of Papua New Guinea. What we witnessed was a country's democracy tested, a constitutional crisis that sparked a frenzy of violence and looting that pushed PNG to the brink. A dispute over the handling of the long-running independence war in Bougainville had led to Prime Minister Julius Chan firing his head of military, Jerry Singirok. The general, in turn, demanded the prime minister resign. Chaos ensued. People took to the streets, and there was widespread violence and looting. I recall one reporter doing a piece to camera in the streets looking down to see a severed hand. The army was siding with its leader and everyone was on edge.

My colleague Chris Reason – surely the best name for a reporter – and I drove out to the military barracks, where we were set upon and dragged from our car. One soldier wrestled Chris to the ground and pulled a gun. It is a cliché, but true, that these are the moments when time does stand still. This whole scene played out in what felt like minutes but was likely just a few seconds. Why would this soldier, possibly as jumpy as us right then, act calmly? Indeed, pulling a gun was probably the most instinctive thing he could do.

I responded just as instinctively as he had. In my loudest voice I yelled, 'Stop!' Our cameraman, Justin Okines, who was also now out of the car, kept filming. It was enough to startle the soldier, who relaxed his grip on Chris. It is a mark of the reporter Chris is that throughout it all, he was amazingly calm. He held out his hands to show he was no threat, but did not resist or do anything that might spook the man with a gun aimed at him.

It is often said that no story is worth dying for. I don't believe that for a minute. There are times I have consciously put myself in harm's way to tell a story. The story demands it. When people are risking their lives for truth or justice, I am compelled to honour their courage. It isn't all altruism, though. I admit that the thrill of the chase is intoxicating. Yes, even worth risking death for. I'm sure I can speak for Chris when I say that in those same circumstances, we would do the same thing again.

Reporting in Papua New Guinea reinforced a lesson I had learned very early in my journalism career: always take risks. Make calculations, yes, but never take the safe option. Luck is risk's reward. And I have been extraordinarily lucky. Luck has been my best friend. It is for all journalists. It has never failed me. To be in the right place at the right time makes or breaks careers. At the height of the PNG constitutional crisis, I pulled into a petrol station to fill up, and who pulled in beside me but Sir Michael Somare, the first prime minister of the independent Papua New Guinea and a man considered the father of the nation. The PNG people looked to him for leadership. Here he was right beside me. I asked for an interview and he agreed. (In the strange twists of PNG politics, Somare himself would be forced out of office after reclaiming the prime ministership in 2011 in what his supporters branded a coup.)

But my biggest break in PNG was securing the first interview with the man himself, Jerry Singirok. After Sir Julius

Chan eventually stepped down, Singirok was hailed a hero. The media crowded around the parliament building, where the people had gathered. We had a reporter there, so I decided to take a gamble and try to get into the military barracks and speak to General Singirok. I split from the pack of reporters and drove to the army base. We slowed at the sentry gate, expecting to be turned around, but the guards, likely also caught up in the moment, waved us through. I asked a passing soldier where I would find the general, and he pointed me in the right direction. In minutes, there he was: a man who had brought down a prime minister; a man whose name had been chanted in the streets. But this man I had seen wearing only military fatigues was now clad in T-shirt and shorts; he was out the front of his house washing his dog as though this was just another quiet afternoon.

When good fortune strikes, don't waste it. Careers are made or lost on snap decisions. I had no doubt my coverage of PNG swayed John Rudd to offer me my break as a foreign correspondent. I left work that day already planning my move to Los Angeles. When I came in the next morning, though, I was going to London. Another vacancy had opened up, and the network had decided London was a better fit for me.

I didn't like the idea at the time. London was a bit of a coal miner's shift. I would be working at the opposite end of the day, filing my stories at night. Gloomy London didn't look as appealing as cruising with the top down in sunny California. Yet London had always fascinated me. I was a bit of an Anglophile: I loved the music of the 1960s and '70s, as well as English films and TV detective shows, while the novels of Dickens had shaped my childhood.

As it turned out, John Rudd did me a great favour by sending me to London. London led to Hong Kong, and Hong Kong would lead me to mainland China. It would lead me to witness history.

*

Funny thing, first impressions. What is it that instantly connects you to a person or place? There was nothing about Hong Kong that should have appealed to me. I was a bush kid from rural New South Wales. I was raised in open spaces, and Hong Kong was one of the most densely populated places on earth.

I had first visited Hong Kong in the early 1990s on a stopover. It meant I got to experience one of the great airport landings in the world. The old Kai Tak airport was right in downtown Hong Kong, sandwiched between skyscrapers. Flying in, passengers could virtually see what the local Chinese were eating at their dinner tables. Depending on whether you were a nervous flyer or not, the landing was the most terrifying or exhilarating you would ever experience. There was an old tale that tyre marks from a plane were visible on the rooftop of one apartment building.

My abiding memory of that first trip to Hong Kong, though, was a tiny orange kitten squeezed up against the side of the road as cars hemmed it in. The poor thing had nowhere to go, no way to get across the road. Yet the kitten looked strangely calm. Stalled in the traffic, I watched the kitten for several minutes, but it did not seem bothered. Strange. I checked into my hotel and took a walk down Nathan Road on the Kowloon side. The people, the smells, the chaos, the noise ... I was hooked, and I knew I would be back.

Now, on this night of 30 June 1997, I had just finished my last live report for the late news. Seven was doing special coverage of this remarkable moment. The network had assigned several reporters working around the clock. My old friend Chris Reason was there, as he would be for so many stories to come: East Timor's fight for independence, the death of Princess Diana. I liked working with him; a little healthy competition is good, and we were on our toes whenever we reported a story together. By the time I came off air, the rain had set in. To get to my live broadcast position, I had to catch the elevator to the top of a building, then climb an outside ladder to a ledge where our camera was positioned. It gave us the best view of an extraordinary skyline. With the rain, I had to climb the slippery steps while balancing an umbrella to avoid being drenched.

It was about 9 pm, three hours before Britain would lower its flag and the Chinese raise theirs. I could take a break, get something to eat and prepare for the spectacle – or I could do something else: I could take a risk. A young reporter named Mike Amor was with me – he would go on to his own successful career as a foreign correspondent – and I asked him if he wanted to take a ride. 'Let's go to the border,' I said. 'Let's get a cab and see how far it can take us.' Mike was keen, as was our cameraman, so we hailed a taxi.

Our driver spoke only halting English, but enough to get by and way better than my Cantonese, which at the time went nothing past hello and thank you. We asked him to take us to the border of the New Territories, the part of Hong Kong that led to the China mainland. I told him I wanted to see the soldiers. He was excited, and not just for the hefty fare: he knew this would be a special moment.

The rain pelted down. The taxi's windscreen wipers, even turned on full, could not give the driver any clear vision. He gripped the steering wheel and leaned forward as far as he could, straining to see. We left the city lights behind and wound our way through the hills towards the border. The driver was listening to the radio. I couldn't understand a word but the announcer sounded excited. He was obviously broadcasting the handover. The driver took one road then another, twisting and turning, all the while the radio blaring.

Suddenly, he pulled to the side of the road. 'Out, out!' he yelled.

'What, here?' we asked. There was nothing. Just pitch-black night and pouring rain. Was he leaving us here?

'Get out, get out!' He became more urgent, more insistent. 'Soldiers,' he said. 'Soldiers coming!'

Then I saw the headlights in the distance. The soldiers were coming. Back in the city, around Hong Kong's Victoria Harbour, people would be counting down. Tens of thousands of people. All of them waiting for midnight. Here, we were alone. There was not another television camera or reporter in sight. We rushed out of the car, our camera already recording. At moments like this there is no time to prepare. This was what I had trained for. There would be no take two. The moment would be captured or lost.

As the first vehicles rounded the bend, I started talking. Even now, writing this, I am back there. On that night. In that rain. I can recall almost everything I said. One by one, the soldiers were driven past me, in armoured personnel carriers and trucks. They stood to attention, they looked straight ahead, their guns clutched to their chests. The rain beat down on them. It only added to the moment. I spoke directly to the camera for several minutes, off the top of my head. I didn't have to reach for the words: this drama wrote itself.

At one point I glanced over my shoulder mid-sentence and saw that the soldiers were saluting us. I thought of the famous words of Mao Zedong, that 'power comes from the barrel of a gun', yet tonight there would be no battle. The Communist Party that Mao had founded was pledging to uphold Hong Kong's political freedoms and autonomy. This time, I said, China says it brings not power at the barrel of a gun but freedom and democracy. Today, that sounds embarrassingly naive. But back then we all believed that China would become like us. That the Party itself would embrace democracy or die. Just like Soviet Russia.

We had caught the moment that China had emerged from its great slumber. The Middle Kingdom was returning to the centre of world power. One empire, Britain, had faded, and another was on the rise. To the Chinese, this was the restoration of the natural order of the universe. The emperor was traditionally the Sun King. Their land was the cradle of civilisation. Other peoples were barbarians. Other leaders would travel to pay tribute to China's emperor. How this mighty kingdom had been laid low. Raped and pillaged by foreigners. How humiliated the Chinese had been – but not anymore. Even there, on that night, I don't think I grasped the enormity of the event. News isn't like that. It exists in snapshots, in images and phrases, but it isn't good at reflection. What it is good at is drama.

We were giddy with the thrill of it all. I remember Mike Amor jumping up and down with excitement. I think I was stunned, if anything. We paid our driver extra to race back to the city as quickly as possible. We had caught the moment when Chinese soldiers rolled over the border and we had it to ourselves. But it meant nothing until it was on air. Until we broadcast it, it had not yet happened. Our executive producer, Gordon Westacott, an utterly unflappable man, put our tape into the player, and as he watched I saw him slowly smile. He reached across to the phone and dialled our international editor, Ric Carter. 'Mate,' Gordon said with characteristic understatement, 'we have something here you might want to get on air when possible.'

Reporters live for this, when all comes together – the moment, the training, the luck. God knows I have made enough mistakes or been scooped by rivals, or completely missed a story. You take the good fortune when you can, and savour the moment. But you can't bank it. Tomorrow is another day, and we are always just one failure away from ending our careers. But on this night we went out to the Foreign Correspondents' Club with a story to tell.

What a scene it was, like something from Gilbert and Sullivan or the last night of the proms. It was such a colonial cliché that if I made it up, I would expect to be laughed at. But there they were, the servants of the empire, dancing and singing. Mike and I spotted one man with a handlebar moustache and dubbed him 'The Colonel'. All night we imitated 'The Colonel' in our most ludicrous posh British accents. *How is the colonel? Very well, thank you very much. Would the Colonel like a drink? Well, why not, old man!* On and on we went. Small minds, easily amused. And still full of our earlier adventure. Funnily enough, we found out later that our man with the moustache was in fact a colonel! Then they all sang 'Auld Lang Syne'. And standing there among them, watching some cry, I couldn't help but feel their sadness. Me of all people, an Aboriginal man whose own people had been invaded and colonised by Britain, mourning the tattered glory of Britain.

Somewhere beyond the grave, Napoleon must have been laughing to himself. Two centuries earlier, it is said, he issued a warning: 'China is a sleeping lion. Let her sleep, for when she wakes she will shake the world.'

3

TO GET RICH IS GLORIOUS

Whenever I would come to an intersection in Beijing, I would close my eyes and hope for the best. Cars would head in all directions, each driver looking for an opening; horns would blare but no one would get angry; the drivers would swerve in and out and somehow we would all get to where we wanted. It was a kind of metaphor for China: order out of chaos. Mao Zedong believed in a permanent revolution: under his rule the country was always being made and remade; leaders would be purged from the Party and then rehabilitated. The country itself had come to resemble its Great Helmsman. Luckily, I had a driver who knew how to navigate China in every way – the traffic, the culture and the history.

'No Mao, no China. No Deng, no China open!' Wang would repeat that mantra over and over. Every time I got in the car with him it was an education. I peppered him with questions, trying to learn more about this country and its people. Wang was a patriot, proud of his country's past, but he harboured a deep resentment for the way his nation had been abused. It never got in the way of our friendship; he could separate the personal from the political. But if pushed, he let me know which side he was on.

Wang liked to boast of China's power and how it could take out enemies like Japan and Taiwan. 'Twenty minutes,' Wang would say, 'and no more Taiwan – all finished.' He had been raised with a hatred of the Japanese for their brutal occupation and massacre of Chinese people. Whenever I would raise the subject of Japan, Wang would make an explosive sound and wave his hand dismissively. He had known nothing but the Communist Party, and as far as he was concerned, the stronger the leader, the better.

Hu Jintao was president of China for a period of my time there, and Wang had little respect for him. Hu was a technocrat, the very model of the post-revolutionary leader. He was a product of Deng's reform era, and his job was to keep the ship on course and continue to grow the economy. He was not given to grand ideology. With his dyed black hair, square glasses and mild demeanour, Hu lacked the revolutionary swagger of Mao or the mousetrap instincts and smarts of the diminutive yet imposing Deng. To Wang, Hu was the worst thing a Chinese leader could be: weak. Wang would call Hu a woman (he was not given to Western political correctness) and sniff the air with contempt.

No Mao, no China. No Deng, no China open.

Mao had given Wang and all Chinese people back their dignity. After seizing power in 1949 after a civil war against the US-backed Nationalists, Mao famously told the Chinese people they had 'stood up'. China, he said, had fallen behind the world because of 'oppression and exploitation by foreign imperialists'. China would 'no longer be a nation subject to insult and humiliation'. 'Let the domestic and foreign reactionaries tremble before us,' Mao said. The Great Helmsman's enormous portrait still hung over the entrance of the Forbidden City, in the heart of Beijing, peering down on Tiananmen Square.

If Mao was power, Deng Xiaoping was cunning. He gave people like Wang a future. Deng came to power in 1978, two years after Mao's death. He too had been shaped by a hatred of foreign occupation. Living abroad as a young man, Deng Xiaoping discovered Marxism and became a hardened communist. From the humiliation of history, Deng dreamed of the revival of his homeland. Deng was not blind to the Communist Party's failings: he conceded it had let down the people. He described China's system of government as 'backward'. Once in power, Deng Xiaoping launched an economic revolution to open up his homeland, and declared that 'to get rich is glorious'. Wang was reaping the rewards: the changes he had seen in his country would have been beyond his imagination as a boy in the grey-suited, gloomy China.

I don't know what we would have done without Wang. How would I describe his appearance? A cigarette holding up a man. He was never without a cigarette, and he was so thin that if he leaned against a wall, you'd see more of the cigarette than of him. He billowed smoke and chewed garlic in equal measure. Love him as we did, we could never sit in the car with him without turning our faces to a half-opened window. Even in the depths of a bitter, dark winter, I preferred to breathe in the toxic, polluted, frozen air of Beijing than Wang's garlic and tobacco breath.

Wang was more than a driver – he was a Mr Fix It, a guide, a translator and, beyond all of that, a dear, dear friend. In fact, it is more accurate to say that for me, my wife and our boys, he was family. Wang was the first person my wife Tracey met in Beijing; she called him her guardian angel. Tracey had flown to Beijing ahead of our move from Hong Kong in December 2004, to find a house and enrol our boys in school. She walked out of the airport to find a taxi, and Wang approached her to offer his private car. Wang spoke next to no English, and Tracey even less Putonghua (the official spoken language of China based on Beijing Mandarin), but together they worked it out. Our middle son, Dylan, was with her and had an appointment to sit an entrance test for a prospective school. Wang drove them from the airport and dropped them off; Tracey asked how much she owed him but he waved her away and motioned that he would wait for her. Several hours later, she found him standing patiently beside his car. Wang drove Tracey all over the city to look at houses, and then to her hotel, and he arranged to collect her again the following morning. Before returning to Hong Kong, Tracey had hired Wang as our permanent driver.

Wang was part of our family for the next four years, before we left Beijing for a stint in the Middle East. When we returned again for our second posting in China, we picked up where we left off. This time I had gone ahead from our home in Dubai and tracked Wang down outside the gate of our old housing compound; when he saw me, he started crying and we hugged like lost brothers.

I saw a lot of changes in Wang's life. From spending time with us, he quickly picked up English, and he helped teach us Putonghua. He developed a taste for the Western rock music that I introduced him to. His initial reluctance to discuss politics soon disappeared, and we used the time in heavy traffic to talk about the Communist Party and the rise of China. Wang even became confident enough to discuss the unmentionable – the Tiananmen Square massacre.

The Communist Party had erased this moment from its history. Schoolchildren born after 1989 learnt nothing of it. Wang remembered it as a young man in Beijing. Whenever I broached the subject, he would shake his head – a little in dismay, a little in sadness – and make a gun motion with his hands. Wang was a deeply sensitive man, and I know the memory of the massacre distressed him, yet he owed his life and his prosperity to the Communist Party. For him, chaos and revolution, democracy even, held no appeal.

When we met Wang, he lived in an old rundown *hutong* (a traditional Chinese house) in a ramshackle neighbourhood right behind our plush new housing estate. This was typical of the rapidly transforming Beijing. Old houses sat right next to the new, but they were vanishing. The city officials were in a rush to prepare for the Olympic Games in 2008, and were rapidly knocking down the old and building shiny new apartment blocks.

This makeover was a blessing for Wang. His house had no indoor toilet, no functional sewerage system, no running water, just one communal tap, and no heating or cooling. His family sweltered in summer and froze in winter. Dogs lazed in the middle of the road and chickens roamed loose. We went there a few times to eat in the local restaurants; they would hardly pass our hygiene tests, but this was a real community, and we lived here, so I wanted to be part of it. The food was incredible.

Westerners used to romanticise these *hutongs*, which offered a connection to the old China, walled off from the world. There is no doubt that the city lost some of its character when the neighbourhoods were demolished, and the locals lost their tight-knit communities. But the world would not wait: new shopping malls sprang up; Chinese people were buying new cars (a thousand new cars a day on Beijing's roads during our time there), microwave ovens, large televisions and washing machines;

they took their children to McDonald's and KFC. Visiting the new furniture stores like IKEA was like going to an amusement park: Tracey and I were always amused to see Chinese families lounging over the display furniture, sometimes even asleep on the beds. This was the world that was opening up for Wang.

Within a year of our arrival, Wang and his wife and young son had moved into a new apartment after their old home was bulldozed. The government compensated them, and it was more than enough to afford their new place. Wang's wife had a steady job, and his son was in school. Within a few years, Wang purchased an investment property and became a landlord. This was the new China: as the Communist Party liked to call it, 'socialism with Chinese characteristics'. The Party, under President Jiang Zemin, had only a few years earlier introduced a dramatic shift in its platform, something called the 'Three Represents' (the Party was obsessed with numbering its policies – the 'Two Whatevers', the 'Four Modernisations'): these were economic production, cultural development and political consensus. For the first time, capitalists (now called 'new social strata') were allowed to join the Communist Party. Wang and a billion other Chinese people were riding the crest of this economic wave, unbroken for three decades.

Consider this: China's gross domestic product (GDP) – the measurement of the economy – grew from 360 billion yuan in 1978 to 52 trillion yuan just over thirty years later. In terms of purchasing power parity – that is, what a yuan will buy in China versus what a dollar buys in Australia – China's is now the biggest economy in the world. It has surpassed the United States as the engine of global economic growth. The International Monetary Fund says that between 2013 and 2018, China accounted for

28 per cent of all growth worldwide. Astonishing. And all this in a country that, when I was a child, could not feed itself. What's more, the IMF says China will continue to power the world at the same rate between 2019 and 2024.

Where wealth goes, power follows. Think of the United States, which for all of my life has been the most powerful nation on earth. It has dominated the world – indeed, it wrote the rules for a new world order – since the end of World War Two in 1945. It faced off the Soviet Empire in a forty-year Cold War, and emerged in the 1990s as the world's sole superpower. But the platform for America's dominance was a century of rapid economic expansion beginning in 1870. America's share of global growth grew from just under 9 per cent in 1870 to a peak of 35 percent during the war years of the 1940s. Historian Martin Jacques, in his book *When China Rules the World*, argues that Great Britain's empire was powered by the Industrial Revolution, but even at its peak constituted less than 10 percent of global GDP.

China's economic boom is changing the world, and others are following right behind. Investment banking giant Goldman Sachs forecasts that by 2050, the three biggest economies in the world will be China's, America's and India's, followed by those of Brazil, Mexico, Russia and Indonesia. Is this the end of the West? Some believe so. In any case, as Martin Jacques says, China has led a changing of the guard.

It is easy to get lost in numbers; properly speaking, China's story is a human story. It is a story of people like my driver Wang, whose life was unrecognisable from the lives of his parents. The Communist Party lays claim to having lifted over half a billion people out of poverty, all while maintaining an iron grip on power. This was a high-wire act that challenged everything we thought we knew about human behaviour and political change: as people get rich, they are meant to demand freedom. Wang knew that politics or open criticism of the Party was a no-go, but he now slept in clean sheets, in air-conditioned comfort. He drove a nice car, and had food in his fridge. He was healthier and wealthier than at any other time in his life. Is security not a fair trade for freedom? Wang had certainly made his peace with the Communist Party. Mao had given his country back its dignity, and made the Chinese people strong; Deng had made them rich. Wang could choose where to work, where to eat, where to send his son to school, where to live (within reason). The Party told him that to get rich is glorious; how much freedom did he need?

*

I saw China through my eyes, the eyes of someone who looked at the West from the outside in. I was not born of the West, but the West was certainly born in me. By the time I was born, Australia was opening up for my people. I was always acutely aware that I was a bridge between my parents' lives and mine. They had been locked out, segregated, denied the West's greatest promise: progress. Change was long and hard, and we still walk that road. My people – Aboriginal people – are the most impoverished and imprisoned in Australia.

But how do I explain my life? A boy raised in poverty who now reported the most important story of our times for CNN, one of the biggest news networks in the world. Is it true that the West is a jailer that slips you the key? Certainly I had broken free: I had gained an education and had a thriving career, far more than I could have imagined as a boy.

That's what I saw in China: a people like Wang, brimful of hope and opportunity. And like me, Wang was at the crossroads of the West. Except, as I had to find my way in a Western world, where the West was considered the zenith of civilisation, the last stop on humanity's journey, where I would be measured against how Western – how white – I could be, Wang was Chinese and would never be anything else. China was the Middle Kingdom, the centre of all power, and now it was back. It was turning on its head the idea of what it was to be 'modern': it did not mean liberalism or democracy. It was challenging the very belief that these things were universal. China did not necessarily follow the same path of progress as the West: to be rich did not mean to be free; it could be capitalist and authoritarian; it did not believe – like those in the West – that history was to be buried in the past. China's history was alive, and its people had long memories. China was old but it was also new. It was Mao and Mercedes-Benz.

One of my first assignments as CNN's China correspondent was to produce a documentary navigating this new China. With my producer Tim Schwarz and cameraman Wen Chun Fan, I would travel the length and breadth of the country profiling lives undergoing rapid change. We made for an unusual crew: Tim was an Englishman, frighteningly bright and astonishingly well-travelled and well-read. He spoke English, French, Russian, and both Mandarin and Cantonese Chinese languages. He was a bit grizzled and grumpy at times, but he was loyal and steadfast and we clocked up a lot of miles together, from the most remote parts of China to Afghanistan and Pakistan and the steppes of Mongolia. (Somewhere in Mongolia today there are two horses named in our honour, given to us by a former Mongolian president after we spent two weeks living with him in his ancestral village.) Wen Chun was a six-foot-eight Chinese man whose family had migrated to the United States; now he had returned to tell the story of his homeland. Wen Chun was among the most creative photojournalists I have ever worked with. He was perfect for this trip, not just because he knew the language and culture, but because he brought love and light to every frame of footage he shot. Then there was me, still wondering how on earth I had ended up here.

I woke up on day one of our trip with a fierce itch. I was scratching myself until my skin was red raw. My body was covered in tiny red marks. We had spent the night in a Communist Party hostel – a place set aside for visiting officials – in Guizhou Province. That may give the impression it was somehow salubrious. Far from it. My room resembled a prison cell. There was one small window, the walls were mouldy and stained, and there was an old single bed with a couple of musty blankets. Either the mattress or the blanket was full of fleas and bugs that attacked me all night. We'd been put up here so the local Party officials could keep a close eye on us. In those days, TV crews had to apply for permission to film anywhere in the country; we also had to get clearance for any proposed interviews. The government would assign us a minder, whose job it was to never let us out of sight.

This is how the Communist Party tried to control the media and the freedom of access and information. It was a cat-and-mouse game, as we often tried to sneak away to film sensitive material or do quick interviews. We became very good at it, and it usually involved getting the officials drunk. Getting assigned to an American news team was a prized job, if for no other reason than that it meant long lunches and dinners at the best restaurants in town. In China there is a tradition of raising toasts throughout the meal with a local drink called Moutai – basically bitter firewater somewhat like vodka or gin, but worse and more potent. The Chinese officials took great delight in their ability to drink us under the table. During round after round of toasts, they would knock back the Moutai, while my crew and I, after drinking a few shots, would slyly pour it onto the floor or into our food bowls. Eventually we would feign drunkenness and raise the white flag to head off to bed, leaving our officials to keep drinking and laugh at how weak we *laowai* (foreigners) were. In the morning we would rise at dawn while our minders slept off their hangovers and film whatever we could before getting back in time for breakfast.

Guizhou was one of the poorest provinces in China; it was still trying to catch up to the economic miracle. It is a stunning place, with mountains, rivers and valleys that make you think of a Chinese painting. Its landscape was its curse, though, as there was simply not enough flat, fertile land to grow significant crops. Farmers ingeniously worked the sides of hills, but it never yielded much more than a subsistence living.

I had first visited Guizhou several years earlier with Tim Schwarz, reporting on a mobile doctor service that was restoring the sight of people blinded by cataracts. The doctors would perform operations on trains turned into makeshift surgeries. Tim and I followed the trail of two young blind children as they underwent this life-altering operation. They lived in a hillside village that we could reach only on foot. Their family was dirt poor. Home was a one-room shack where they slept and ate alongside their parents. They shared the space with chickens, and they kept a couple of pigs outside. Without sight, these two children would eventually be destitute. Their parents worried that when they died there would be no one to care for them. They could not work, and they had little education. Their lives would, in all likelihood, be miserable and short.

Meeting this family gave me my first taste of local Chinese hospitality. I did not speak enough Putonghua to carry out a conversation, but Tim was able to translate. What we lacked between us in language they made up for with a beaming humanity. Yes, they were poor, but their hearts were full of generosity. To welcome us, they killed one of their pigs and prepared what for them would have been the biggest meal of the year. We spent several nights with them and they made beds for us alongside theirs.

The father told us how he worked from morning until night to put whatever food he could on the table. Before the children completely lost their sight, they would walk several kilometres down the side of the mountain to attend school. Now they spent their days inside in darkness. This proud man cried several times as he told us of his fears for their future. It was not common for children to be so afflicted with cataracts, let alone two in the same family, but this was a hard land and fate spared no one. Eventually the children made their way to the mobile surgery and the operations were successful. When the bandages were removed after a couple of days, they looked on the face of their father for the first time in years and he cried again.

Now I was back in Guizhou again, this time in the capital, Guiyang, to interview a young tech entrepreneur who had opened an internet cafe. This was a remarkable thing in a country where internet freedom was seen as a threat to Communist Party rule.

The Party had put in place a firewall to control access to the web, but back in 2005 there was still a lot of debate about whether even the Communist Party, with its reach into every aspect of Chinese people's lives, could hold back the tide of this technological revolution. Surely, people would glimpse a world beyond their own, connect with others who took democratic freedoms for granted, and demand the same at home. And in time the web would give many people the ability to mobilise resistance movements that would eventually bring down governments – but not in China. The Party would make technology its friend and use the internet to more closely monitor and control its own people. But the young man we spoke to in Guiyang saw the internet as an opportunity for riches. His cafe became a thriving meeting place for young people who would log on and send messages, talk to people in faraway parts of the country or play online games well into the night.

Over several weeks Tim, Wen Chun and I mapped a changing China. We met the owners of a new youth fashion brand, Sundog, that was selling surf culture and clothes to Chinese kids who had never seen a beach, let alone heard the music of The Beach Boys. We met a young basketball star who idolised the seven-foot Chinese basketball god Yao Ming and dreamed of glory in the NBA. Students who, in earlier times, would have left school and gone to work in the fields were now attending university. Farmers had moved to the cities in search of work in the burgeoning factories that were making China the manufacturing hub of the world.

One man who stood out to me above all else had left his ancestral village to try his luck in Shanghai, a city with a space age skyline and more than 30 million people. He got work in the booming construction sector, and in his spare time collected offcuts of timber, secondhand tools, discarded bricks and other material and set up a stall selling hardware. Within a few years, he had established a mini-empire of several real hardware stores. He was now a millionaire living the China dream.

What was happening was not just an economic upheaval: it was changing the fabric of Chinese society. Old Confucian family values were being shattered as young people chased their dreams. They were not staying behind to care for their ageing parents. During my time in China, a country of farmers – men and women who had raised a peasants' revolution that helped put the Communist Party in power – became a country of factory workers, entrepreneurs, students. What was once a rural nation was now a country of new metropolises: for the first time in China's history, more people lived in cities than in villages.

*

Coming into Linfen was like entering a scene from an apocalypse. There was no horizon here, no sky, nothing to mark the landscape or measure distance. There was just an all-encompassing blackness, pierced only by fires from factory smelters. The whole place seemed shrouded in silence, as if all life had been extinguished. How could anything live here? Dead animals floated in the river. There was no birdsong, just a dense pall of gloom.

Our headlights were on full beam and yet it was the middle of the day. Even then, we could barely make out the road ahead. Whoosh – another streak of fire would shoot from the industrial chimneys into the heavens, just for a moment cracking open the smog like lightning in a storm. Then blackness again. A red coal truck rounded a corner; we heard its horn well before we actually saw it. Our windows were shut tight, but even so I felt the air choke me. Was it my imagination, or was I preparing myself for what would happen when we left the vehicle? I was used to pollution – Beijing seemed always covered in smog – but not like this. Linfen, in the heavy industrial and mining province of Shanxi, was at that time the most polluted city on earth. In fact, according to the World Health Organization, sixteen of the world's top twenty dirtiest cities were in China.

This was the downside of success. China was in the midst of its own industrial revolution, and as in eighteenth- and nineteenth-century Europe, the environment was sacrificed to progress and economic growth. Yes, the lives of hundreds of millions of people were being enriched, but at a devastating cost. Rivers now ran with toxic green sludge. Water was undrinkable. The land had been poisoned, and in some parts of the country crops would no longer grow. Greenpeace estimated that in China half the rivers, a third of all lakes and up to 90 per cent of groundwater were polluted. In the river that ran through Linfen, dead animals floated on the surface. The mountains that had once framed a picturesque valley now served only to trap the smog that all but obscured the city. Car fumes from the clogged roads added to the pollution.

When we parked our car, my crew and I stepped out and took our first breath: it was like inhaling an entire packet of cigarettes in one go. The toxic air stung as it hit the back of my throat. I could feel myself becoming sick. My mind started to wonder about what cancer-causing chemicals I was letting into my body. All those years of taking care of my health, keeping fit, not smoking – it all felt pointless now.

My crew and I could work only in short bursts. We would film for half an hour or so, then retreat to our hotel for respite. Within minutes my eyes would burn and weep. The whites of my eyes turned bright red. Struggling for breath in the dense, heavy smog drained me of energy. Each time we returned to our rooms, I lay down on my bed to recover. How did people survive in this? But survive they did; you could say they even thrived.

Linfen was a frontier town whose people had grown rich. Expensive cars – Mercedes-Benzes, BMWs and Audis (the Chinese favourite) – lined the streets. Fast-food restaurants, sports stores and new shopping malls had sprung up around the city. Trendy locals now wore Armani, Gucci, Dolce & Gabbana, Prada. Many of them were living the dream, and those who were not wealthy – those who had been lured here from the outlying villages to work the factories and mines – were swept along by this progress, believing that their day too would come.

But surely this was unsustainable, I thought. Two decades into China's economic miracle, the cracks were beginning to show. The rich were getting richer but the poor were no longer catching up; people were left behind, others abandoned as families fell apart. Far from the cities, anger was growing as people protested about the impact of pollution or against corrupt officials who abused their power to enrich themselves, flouting the law and ignoring regulations to stoke more and more productivity, generate more and more wealth, which was no longer trickling down to the grassroots. To clear a path for more progress – roads, housing developments, dams and factories – more and more people were forced from their homes.

I met 81-year-old Jiang Mei Ling in her home in an old Beijing neighbourhood, just a couple of rooms and a hard cold floor. She was alone and scared. Mei Ling wept openly, despairing at a life that had left her poor. It was Chinese New Year, a time of celebration and family – a time when the people of this new rich China fanned out across the country, leaving behind the cities to return to ancestral villages and be reunited with family. It is a joyous time, an opportunity to share good fortune, to eat and drink. Fireworks light up the sky night after night. There was a time Jiang Mei Ling looked forward to Chinese New Year. Not anymore. She had no one to share this time with – no family, no friends. She sat alone in her tiny home, soon to be demolished. There was room for a bed, an open fire stove. All her possessions were stacked neatly in one corner. Outside, coal was lined up against a wall. She would burn that for heat. All she had to wear was a tattered old grey Mao-era suit. On her wall was a photo of a strikingly handsome man with jet-black hair and strong jaw – the husband she lost forty years earlier. Everyone she had been close to was dead. Every time there was a holiday or festival, she told me, she felt terribly sad. She was so lonely, she said she would rather die. What was the meaning of life, she asked, if this was what life had become?

Mei Ling's hands shook as she drank from a cup of tea, and she grew frantic telling me she had lost her medical card – without it she could not get necessary medicine. Mei Ling was a proud woman, and despite her age and hardship she carried herself with grace; her face retained the traces of the beautiful young woman she had been.

Hers was an all-too-common story in China. Society had moved so quickly. The old Confucian traditions of family and responsibility had eroded as young people chased their dreams, moving far from their parents. When I met Mei Ling in 2011, China was already becoming an ageing society: there were more than 160 million people over the age of sixty, and half of them lived alone. China did not have time to reach back for those who could not keep up. The country was richer, but more disposable: even people were so easily discarded.

The Yellow River was once considered the cradle of Chinese civilisation, winding its way through the mountains of Gansu Province. I came there to meet a man who would take me on a most unusual fishing expedition. Lun Lun lived in a tiny village along the riverbank. These villages were not just far from the teeming cities of the new China, they were another world entirely. Life here had changed little over the centuries. The people spoke their own language; even my producer Jo Ling Kent – fluent in Mandarin – struggled to understand them. This was 2010, when Hu Jintao was leader of China, yet when we asked one elderly lady about him, she shook her head with no idea who he was. She still had a photograph of Mao Zedong on the wall of her two-room village home. Her life had not moved since the time of the Communist Revolution; China's economic revolution had passed her by.

But it was in places like this that the dreams of the new China were turning darker. The speed of life had overtaken many people; there were bills, the cost of living was rising, unemployment had spiked, and house prices and rent were rising. Families were falling apart under the strain, and there was increasing isolation, anxiety and depression. People who could not cope were taking their own lives, throwing themselves into the Yellow River. It was as though they were sacrificing themselves to something eternal – waters that had flowed forever through that land – to escape a world of unending, grinding change.

Lun Lun had fished these waters all his life. His father was a fisherman and he was raised on the river. Now he had his own boat and supported his family with his daily catch. But when I went out onto the river with him, we were looking for something else – something that would turn an even greater profit. Lun Lun was fishing for human bodies.

He told me he had dragged more than a hundred corpses from the river. They were washed downstream from the provincial capital, Lanzhou, just twenty kilometres away, where desperate people jumped to their deaths from the main city bridge. One person's tragedy was another's industry. Lun Lun retrieved the bodies, but kept them face-down in the water. He then posted photos online; grieving families would get in contact and pay to have their loved one's body returned. Lun Lun charged 3000 yuan – about $500 – just to turn a body over for families to make an identification. If they wanted the body back, they had to pay more. This is how China worked: even in death, a person was measured only by what they were worth on the market.

On this day we patrolled the waters, keeping an eye out for any floating human remains. Lun Lun took us to a bend in the river to show us where he kept two bodies tethered to the riverbank. As we drew closer, I could see the bloated corpses, their heads and limbs bobbing in the water. The police had started to crack down on this gruesome industry, but for people like Lun Lun the potential returns outweighed the risk of being fined. What else would he do? He had little education, and this was his chance to turn a profit.

In China there is a saying '*weiying, neiruan*' – it means 'hard on the outside, soft on the inside'. This is what some China watchers see: a country that is weak at its core. David Shambaugh, a noted scholar of China, wrote an essay in 2015 in which he forecast the end. He said China's political system was broken, and the Communist Party knew it. It was riddled with corruption and was heading the way of the Soviet Union. The shadow of Mikhail Gorbachev loomed over China now, more than the shadow of Mao Zedong. As few people accurately predicted the collapse of the Soviet Union, Shambaugh wrote, so the collapse of China would be a surprise. But it would happen, and when it did it would be 'protracted, messy and violent'. Shambaugh wrote: 'The end game of Chinese Communist rule has now begun.'

Gordon Chang, another student of China and critic of the Communist Party, predicted the same thing in 2001. He said then the Party would not last another decade. He was wrong, but only, he insisted, by the date. The Party, he said, had cheated its way to riches, flouting its international obligations under the World Trade Organization. It was able to call on an army of cheap labour to work in its factories. A decade later, he updated his book, *The Coming Collapse of China*, and repeated the same dire prediction. China's sweet spot was over, he said, the global economy was shrinking, other countries were exporting and stealing China's markets, and its workforce was ageing. China simply could not keep the engines running.

Gordon Chang was wrong again; indeed, China has proved all the doomsday pundits wrong. When the Berlin Wall was coming down and the Soviet empire was disintegrating, China's leaders were told they were on the wrong side of history, but they have bent history – and the democratic West – to their will.

China is richer and more powerful today than perhaps ever before in its history, but the Chinese people are discovering the hard lessons that we in the West have learned: money does not always buy happiness. Ding Xinxang showed me around the one-bedroom his family lived in, in one of the few remaining old neighbourhoods in Beijing. Ding lived only a few streets from me, but our lives seemed barely to occupy the same universe. I used to walk through the streets near his home to eat at a local noodle restaurant: it was strewn with garbage, and mangy dogs lazed on the ground. Ding introduced me to his family, his wife and a son who was intellectually disabled. Children with issues like this were often hidden away in China. Some were abandoned because their families could not carry the burden. I had done a story about children with autism, and visited one village where a child was chained and bound inside a small wire cage that he shared with a dog. To my eyes it was heartbreaking – it was harsh by anyone's reckoning, really – but as I had learned over and over in China, this is a harsh land, and sentiment, even love, is secondary to survival. Ding Xinxang and his wife had a faith beyond money or the Communist Party, and it kept them strong. He was a driver and work was in short supply. In a good month, he told me, he might make a few hundred dollars, but that went quickly on rent and the necessities of life. It was hardly enough to plan for the future, or to build any security for his son. 'I don't think about the future,' he told me. 'I don't have the strength. It is useless.'

Din Xinxang was among the hundreds of millions of people who had missed out on the boom times. The gap between rich and poor in China grew ever wider. Ding did not blame the government; he told me that life, even for the poor, was better than it used to be. But he said he knew the rich looked down on him. Ding's way of life was vanishing before his eyes. Around him, houses were being flattened to make way for new apartment buildings. Unlike my driver Wang, who was a local resident, Ding was a migrant worker and not entitled to any local government assistance. He wouldn't get a new home. He and his wife and his son would be homeless and poor.

Happiness was not a word I heard a lot in China. America's Academy of Sciences had tracked China's happiness index for twenty years: predictably, it found the poor had little joy in their lives, but the rich too were far from content. But Ding Xinxang told me he had something many of the rich had lost: family, and (in an officially atheist country) a belief in God. 'Without God we would be in despair,' Ding's wife told me. Christianity sustained her in ways the Communist Party never could, she said. They only had one bedroom in a rundown house, but they had faith and they had each other.

4

HISTORY, HOMELAND
AND HARMONY

As relations between the West and China continue to plummet, and talk of a new Cold War intensifies, how much do we really know of the nation that is set to define the twenty-first century? We know that China is an authoritarian country ruled by the Communist Party, and that it rejects the liberal-democratic values of free speech, the rule of law and democracy. Yet it is also an indispensable nation, on track to become the world's biggest economy. Right now, most analysis of China veers between hawkish predictions of war, containment, decoupling, and finding some diplomatic accommodation.

But we have surely dropped the delusion that China will become like us: that economic freedom will lead to political freedom. Whilever the Communist Party is in power, its trajectory is set. When I was living in and reporting on China it became ever clearer to me that if we are to understand this vast, heaving, contradictory, complex, inspiring and maddening country, we need to grasp three things: history, homeland and harmony. And we need to see these things through modern China's three most powerful leaders: Mao Zedong, Deng Xiaoping and Xi Jinping.

Mao was the revolutionary communist leader who saw his mission as reviving a fallen, humiliated nation. After seizing power in 1949 following a civil war against the US-backed Nationalists, Mao famously spoke to the Chinese people, telling them that they had 'stood up'. Mao was avenging history. China would be humiliated no more.

Deng Xiaoping came to power in 1978, two years after Mao's death. He had fought alongside Mao, forged by the same resentment at foreign occupation and vowing to avenge China's humiliation. Deng biographer Ezra Vogel describes how Deng as a young man travelled to France and during a layover in Shanghai 'saw white people treating Chinese, in their own country, as if they were slaves'. Working in France he saw how 'European imperialists were humiliating China ... and Chinese workers were treated worse than local workers.' Living abroad, Deng Xiaoping discovered Marxism and became a hardened communist. From the humiliation of history, Deng dreamed of the revival of his homeland.

By the time he came to power, Deng was prepared to reckon with the failings of the Party, particularly Chairman Mao's failed Great Leap Forward – a fast track to high production and modernisation that had triggered the Great Famine of 1958–62. Upwards of 40 million people died in those few years. Chinese journalist Yang Jisheng, in his book *Tombstone*, describes how starving people ate bark from trees, droppings from birds and rats, and most horrifyingly the bodies of their dead children just to survive. Deng conceded his nation had to change, and set it on a course of economic revolution, but at the same time doubled down on Communist Party power. The Party and the homeland would be inseparable.

❊

Before Xi Jinping took power in 2012, he visited migrant Chinese workers in Mexico and told them: 'There are some bored foreigners with full stomachs who have nothing better to do than point fingers at us.' He had learnt well the lessons of history. Xi reminded the Chinese people of the 'hundred years of humiliation' by foreign powers stretching back to the Opium Wars of the mid-nineteenth century. Xi was determined to complete the rejuvenation of China and return the nation to the apex of global power.

To history and homeland, Xi has added harmony. He speaks of the 'harmonious society', an idea he has inherited from his predecessor, Hu Jintao – but where Hu saw harmony as political reform and social justice, Xi means stability. In the name of harmony he has cracked down on dissent, jailed dissidents, rivals, lawyers and journalists, enacted harsh new laws to stop protests in Hong Kong, and locked up over a million ethnic Uighur Muslims in what human rights groups have called 're-education' – or brainwashing – camps. It is harmony by force. Xi is reaching back to Mao, who sought to distinguish the real people from the enemies of the people, those Chinese he called 'the running dogs' of the imperialists. Mao spoke of freedom and democracy, but it was 'freedom with leadership' and 'democracy under centralised guidance'.

Xi Jinping is often described as China's most powerful leader since Mao; some analysts see him as a break from past Communist Party bosses, a man taking the country on a more dangerous authoritarian path. Yet Xi is an extension of the past. Xi is a party princeling, the son of one of Mao's revolutionary lieutenants. He embraces Deng Xiaoping's vision for the homeland and the Party. Let's not think that Xi is any more brutal than his predecessors: Mao was responsible for the deaths of tens of millions, and while Deng is remembered as a reformer, he is also the man who ordered his soldiers to shoot citizens protesting for democracy in Tiananmen Square in 1989.

Xi is everything his party and the ghosts of leaders past have made him. Yes, he is more assertive – even aggressive – but China is also more powerful. This is always how Mao and Deng saw their country's future. The Party is what it has always been. It is we in the West who are constantly surprised. China's most dominant leaders – Mao, Deng and Xi – have told us how they see the world and China's place in it, how that is rooted in history, homeland and harmony. That's where diplomacy begins: with a clear understanding of what we are dealing with.

The question, then, is whether – or how – we can live with it.

*

In 2012 the world was introduced to Xi Jinping. He was about to be crowned the new leader of China. He had been earmarked years before, and represented a new era in Party leadership: the first president born after the Communist Revolution. But what did the world really know about him? Long-time China watcher and former CNN Beijing correspondent Mike Chinoy said Xi had risen to the top by being calculating; he was very careful about disclosing what he truly believed. CNN assigned me to go in search of this elusive figure. Xi had spent a year travelling the world in a charm offensive, meeting leaders including US President Barack Obama. He vanished at one point for over a week, and rumours swirled that he may have had a heart attack.

Xi was deliberately dull, with his slicked-back black hair and dark suits and a permanently fixed half-smile that concealed what was truly going on in his mind. What charisma he had came from his wife, a famous Chinese folk singer, Peng Liyuan. But Xi sang from the Communist Party songbook. Analysts I spoke to warned that Xi would be no reformer: he would not weaken the Party. Nor would he be a traitor to his class. Chinese historian Zhang Lifan told me that Xi was a 'safe choice', a consensus candidate who would keep the Communist Party as the only ruling party. Any reform or 'liberty', Zhang Lifan said, could happen only on condition of the survival of the one-party dictatorship.

When Xi took power, China's fault lines were widening: a growing wealth gap, a slowing economy and an angry population protesting about everything from unemployment to poor health care, environmental damage and government corruption. The China dream was fading as more and more people were left behind. Inequality was growing. Academic and writer Gerard Lemos witnessed this first-hand as a visiting professor at Chongqing University. He detailed the unravelling of China in his 2012 book *The End of the Chinese Dream*, a devastating portrait of a society adrift; drowning in despair; addicted to drugs and alcohol; defenceless against the power of the state, which could with impunity seize the land and homes of poor Chinese people.

I witnessed this myself, reporting on entire villages washed away in the building of the massive Three Gorges Dam. I spoke to people whose homes were being demolished to make way for lavish new apartment blocks. Despite being threatened with arrest, many refused to be silenced. During one interview in

Shanghai, the police smashed down the door and dragged us away. The woman we were interviewing was detained for several months, during which time, her family told us, she was beaten. Lemos wrote at the time: 'A long, dark shadow of fear and trauma has spread across Chinese society.'

The Party was at a point of deep existential crisis, afraid of its own people, nervous about revolutions abroad that may spread to China, and rotting from the inside. At the same time the geopolitical plates were shifting: China was locked in an increasingly volatile stand-off with its bitter historical enemy Japan over disputed islands in the East China Sea, while relations with the United States were worsening over everything from trade to defence. Still, there was optimism that Xi Jinping would steer China to a safe harbour. None other than former Australian prime minister Kevin Rudd – in an earlier life a diplomat in China – told me that he believed Xi 'was someone you could do business with'.

To uncover Xi Jinping, we have to go to the mystical place called 'Yellow Earth'. It is the dusty plateau of Shaanxi Province, in north-west China, alongside the fabled Yellow River – considered the cradle of Chinese civilisation. It was here that Xi was banished as a young man during the Cultural Revolution. Xi's family was in disgrace. His father, Xi Zhongxun – a revered figure in the years before the Revolution – had been purged from the Party. It is extraordinary to think that Xi senior had been one of Mao's most trusted figures – he was the youngest man appointed to Mao's cabinet, and someone Mao said had been 'tempered by fire'. Now he was banished. One of Xi Jinping's older stepsisters is said to have committed suicide during this time, humiliated and taunted. Xi was sent to work the farms, like so many other children of the elite. He needed re-education in the truth of the Party.

Foreign Policy magazine, in an article titled 'The Creation Myth of Xi Jinping', spoke to people who remembered the 'tall, slight lad' carrying two bags of books. They said at first he lacked the strength to work in the fields. One elderly woman remembered him as having 'holes and patches in his pants like the rest of us'. He was 'really skinny' and handsome, she said, and she remembered him singing patriotic revolutionary songs that proclaimed 'if there was no Communist Party, there would be no China'. The village of Liangjiahe today is a shrine: the façade of Xi's old mudbrick home still stands, and the kerosene lamp by which he would read into the night.

Xi calls himself a 'son of Yellow Earth'. In a short autobiography, he describes arriving in Shaanxi 'anxious and confused'. He recalls living in lice-infested caves and toiling all day. It toughened his body, fortified his spirit and hardened his hands. Xi attended daily 'struggle sessions' and had to denounce purged Chinese revolutionary leaders, including his father. Yet rather than turn away from the Party, Xi Jinping grew ever more devoted. By the time he left Yellow Earth, Xi writes, 'my life goals were firm and I was filled with confidence'. Yellow Earth is a state of mind as much as a place. China scholar Geremie Barmé has described Xi's years in Shaanxi as the Chinese version of the American 'log cabin' story – the tale of the politician who rises to power from humble beginnings. According to Barmé, it is a powerful narrative of hardship that binds Xi to the struggles of the ordinary Chinese people.

*

There is a photo on a wall outside a small wooden hut in Yan'an, in Shaanxi Province, showing two men, tired, a little bedraggled, with a faraway look in their eyes. These men are battle-hardened: they have seen years of war and walked a long hard road. Their green army shirts are unbuttoned; there is an undeniable air of danger about them. They look like the revolutionaries they are.

I had come to this place in search of Mao Zedong. Here at his hut I see him as I had never really seen him before; this isn't the stout, balding, decadent figure fixed in our imaginations, but a leaner, hungrier man, someone who was rewriting history, who would loom over the twentieth century and whose image shapes China still.

Standing alongside Mao is his lieutenant, Zhou Enlai. Zhou would be the diplomatic face of the Communist Revolution. He was debonair and handsome; there was always a touch of French elan about Zhou, and he had spent time living and studying in France. He had also studied in Japan, and like the other revolutionaries was well schooled in the history of ideas. The photo of Zhou and Mao was taken at the end of the Long March, as the Communist Party regrouped its forces and prepared to take the country. Here the myth was born, in the place now considered holy to many Chinese true believers: the place of Yellow Earth.

Mao had fought a bitter power struggle within the Communist Party that had pushed him to the limits of his health and his sanity. In the early 1930s the Party was fighting on multiple fronts: a war against the Japanese occupation, a civil war against the rival Chinese Nationalist forces, and a war within its own ranks. Senior communist figures had unleashed a hailstorm of criticism on Mao, particularly his military tactics. He was removed from leadership positions. Mao knew how high the stakes were: his closest friend and fellow revolutionary Cai Hesen was executed by a Nationalist faction in Guangdong. In their book *Mao: The Real Story*, Alexander Pantsov and Steven Levine describe Cai's killing: 'The Butchers subjected him to inhuman tortures, and then crucified him on the wall of his cell. Then finally they pierced him through the chest several times with a bayonet.' Mao was facing his own battle to the death.

At his lowest, Mao grew deeply depressed. He would sit in darkness high in the mountains, playing a mournful tune on his flute. He was flanked by his wife, He Zizhen, and his closest and most trusted supporters. Zhou Enlai – the future ally – was working against Mao. At one point, he wrote to the Party leadership that 'Mao is physically weak; he remains at work in the high mountains and suffers from insomnia and a poor appetite'. Mao was accused of being a counter-revolutionary and a 'rightist opportunist' – the same language Stalin had used in expelling his rivals in the Soviet Union. Mao was challenging the Party's strategy of trying to seize major urban centres; he preferred a guerrilla campaign, building a stronghold in rural areas. He wanted to use the anti-Japanese sentiment swelling amongst ordinary Chinese against the Nationalists, who he said had not defended the key Chinese region of Manchuria from Japanese invasion. Manchuria was now in Japanese hands.

The communist forces attacked the city of Ganzhou but failed to take it. It was a turning point for Mao. As Pantsov and Levine say, Mao's rivals 'had to swallow their pride'. None other than Zhou Enlai was dispatched to ask Mao to return to the field. Mao did so with strategic brutality, raiding and pillaging villages and towns, slaughtering the rich, and landholders and even peasants who opposed his forces. Pantsov and Levine write that Mao's army 'left a wasteland in their wake'. The Soviets had sprung to Mao's support, further strengthening his position. Within the Party, Mao adopted a 'divide and rule' strategy. Zhou – ever attuned to the twists and turns of power – now aligned himself with Mao.

But the Communist Party infighting continued, and Mao was again sidelined. His life then has been described as a 'living hell'. Mao himself said he 'was immersed in a cesspool ... not only a single person, but not even a single devil dared to cross the threshold of my house ... At least they did not cut off my head.' While this internal struggle continued, the Nationalist Army, under its leader Chiang Kai-shek, gained the upper hand, eroding communist-held territory. There was a bounty on the heads of communist leaders, including Mao. Revolution, Mao said, was not a dinner party, and his family was paying an enormous cost. He and his wife had a baby boy, whom they had to abandon and would never see again. Now, with the communists on the run and the Nationalists in pursuit, Mao and his troops and supporters began what would be celebrated as the Long March.

For a year from October 1934, the communist Red Army beat a retreat, escaping to the north and west of China, covering more than nine thousand kilometres under constant attack. They usually travelled at night to evade the bombing by Nationalist planes. The Red Army was devastated. By some estimates, a hundred thousand people started out on the march and only eight thousand survived. Otto Braun, a German Communist Party adviser, catalogued the daily death toll. He wrote: 'More and more our route was lined with the bodies of the slain, frozen or simply exhausted.' The Long March demanded enormous sacrifice. Mao and his wife had another child, this time a daughter, whom they left in a village house. Mao never saw her, and no one knows what became of her.

Mao's legend was forged on the Long March, and during that year he finally claimed control of the Party. That's what I saw in the photo on the wall of Mao's hut in Yan'an: a man exhausted, yet exhilarated, and ready for the final push to victory. He had sacrificed his family and led what remained of his troops to safety. As Mao wrote: 'Has history ever known a long march to equal ours? No, never. The Long March has proclaimed to the world that the Red Army is an army of heroes.' He had also won the power struggle within the Party. Zhou Enlai, who had plotted against Mao, now stood beside him. Two men with a thousand-yard stare and a thousand miles ahead of them.

I have to admit to being captivated by the image of Mao and Zhou. Standing where they had stood, I could imagine what it must have been like. If there is a period of history I would like to magically be transported to, and cover as a journalist, it would be China of the 1930s and '40s. This was where World War Two truly began – not in Hitler's Germany, but in the Japanese invasion and the bloodlust of China's civil war conflicts, which killed tens of millions of people. So much of what we now see as the modern world was created on China's blood-soaked ground.

I had come to Yan'an to meet the last of the Long Marchers. They were old women now living in a special home. Here their every need was met. They were heroes of the nation. Age had robbed them of their mobility, and they moved more slowly than they had in those years of struggle and sacrifice. Their skin was like tanned leather, and their eyes misty and wet. But their minds were as sharp as ever. One young woman took us to see her great-grandmother and sat beside the old lady as she recounted her adventure. She had been a young woman when she followed Mao on that epic march, and now she was in her nineties. What a China she had seen. From war and revolution, bloodshed almost beyond imagining. And she had seen Mao Zedong stand in Tiananmen in 1949 to proclaim the Communist Revolution and tell the world 'the Chinese people have stood up'.

*

The world champion heavyweight boxer Mike Tyson has a saying: everyone has a plan until they get hit. He could have been talking about television. On 15 November 2012, as the air began to turn bitterly cold in Beijing and the chill wind swept in from the Gobi Desert, I stood outside, waiting to go live for CNN to announce China's new leader. This was the day Xi Jinping would take the helm and introduce a new generation of party leaders.

We had a plan: Xi was expected to arrive on stage at 11 am and make a speech that would be heard around the world. He would set out his vision for China, how the country would take its next step to global power. I would go live on air at 10.45. I would speak for fifteen minutes backgrounding Xi – who he was, his path to power, his ideas – and then we would take the speech. I would come off the back of it to analyse what he had said. We were expecting to be on air for no more than an hour. I always enjoyed live reporting: I like working without a net. Anything could go wrong and I had to be prepared. But this day was something else.

Eleven am came and went and there was no sign of Xi. Because CNN had committed to live coverage, there was no alternative but to stay the course. I was on air alone, being asked questions by a news anchor broadcasting from our headquarters in Atlanta, Georgia. In circumstances like this, I just had to keep 'padding', as we say in TV: keep talking, trying to keep the audience informed and interested. The biggest crime was to be boring. Easier said than done when there is nothing happening. But this is what I lived for.

I have always been a very calm person, and I'm blessed with a photographic memory that has never failed me. I can only describe it as like a filing cabinet in my mind, and with each question I reach into another file to retrieve information: dates, facts, anecdotes. On this day, as the minutes ticked by, I could feel myself smiling inside. I filled the hour before Xi Jinping appeared and we got the first real glimpse of a man who would soon be called the most powerful person on the planet.

In the months leading up to Xi's coming out, CNN had sent me to Fujian Province to see where he had cut his teeth as a Party leader. I wanted to get as close to him as possible, to meet people who had spent time with him. Crystal Wang was a young entrepreneur who had struck up a friendship with Xi that made her phenomenally wealthy. Crystal had started a tech company, Newland Hi Tech Group, with nothing more than a single desk and one employee: herself. In twenty years she had turned it into a worldwide mini empire worth hundreds of millions of dollars. Xi Jinping, she said, was a very kind person who supported her business. She described Xi – who at the time was vice president of China – as 'a good listener'. In his time as governor of Fujian, Xi championed high-tech and green industries. Crystal Wang got lucky: her rise mirrored his. Xi's father had been a reformer, and his son embraced the Deng Xiaoping revolution, opening China's economy to the world.

Like other parts of China, Fujian had rapidly transformed. The capital, Fuzhou, was an enormous metropolis of more than seven million people. It was considered one of the fastest-growing cities in the world, and was at the heart of China's transition from a rural to an urban society. It had made people like Crystal Wang phenomenally wealthy, while others were left behind. Xie Yingling was a thirty-two-year-old unemployed welder, and he told me he had a message for the man who would be China's new leader: 'I want a job.' Xie told me the local economy was 'just bad'. Everywhere I went, I saw more evidence of the growing gap between rich and poor. The streets were crowded, there was pollution in the air – choking industrial smog – and rubbish on the roads. When Xi was governor he provided housing for local fishing families, but too many others now felt they were being abandoned. And they were growing angrier.

This was Xi's heartland, and if the Communist Party was to survive, it would have to keep faith with ordinary Chinese people. Xi would have to stand up to the world, particularly the United States, which was ramping up the pressure on Beijing, accusing the Communist Party of manipulating trade to make China richer and America poorer. China watcher James McGregor told me that Xi would need to be tough, but he would need to be tough 'with a smile on his face'. Xi would need to be democratic – in a Communist Party way – but he could not be pushed around. He was inheriting a country at the crossroads: it could take the next step to becoming a true superpower or the Party itself could crumble under its own corruption – or even be overthrown by a people who no longer believed that it represented them.

When Xi Jinping spoke to the Chinese people as their new president, he vowed to complete the renewal of his country. His first target was corruption. Xi would take a lead from Mao Zedong and clean out the Party. Xi put senior figures on notice that he was coming after them if they were taking bribes or were out of touch with the Chinese people. The outgoing Chinese premier, Wen Jiabao, had warned that corruption was a cancer that could kill the Party, even as Wen's own family was implicated in allegedly crooked business dealings. Far from 'serving the people', Wen's relatives had helped themselves to extraordinary wealth, controlling businesses worth billions of dollars. Decisions Wen made had profited his own family. Xi Jinping would make corruption public enemy number one. In the coming months, he declared war on what he called the 'tigers and flies' – the big and the small. In a speech in 2013, Xi warned: 'All are equal before the law and Party discipline.' No one was immune: 'anyone who violates Party discipline and state laws, whoever he is and whatever position he holds, will be fully investigated and severely punished. This is not empty talk.' To Xi, power must be 'caged by the system'.

*

When Xi Jinping took power, the Chinese Communist Party was already turning on its own. Before his elevation to president, one of his great rivals was eliminated. Bo Xilai was powerful, handsome, tall and charismatic. Like Xi, Bo had modelled himself on the great revolutionary hero Mao Zedong, and as Party chief of the sprawling city of Chongqing, he had overseen reform that had outstripped most of the country. Economic growth had galloped way ahead of the national average, while the city's infrastructure – roads, office towers and shopping malls – had rapidly modernised.

Bo married new-style Chinese capitalism with old-style Maoist rhetoric. He fashioned himself as 'redder than red'. Communist slogans sprung up around Chongqing, and people were urged to sing Cultural Revolution–era songs. So successful was Bo that a former US secretary of state, Henry Kissinger, visiting Chongqing, said he 'saw the vision for the future'. But it was a future Bo himself would not share in. He had gone too far, too fast, and it had all come crashing down.

In 2012 I travelled to Chongqing to look behind the veil of Party secrecy – to try to get as close as possible to the greatest Communist Party purge in a generation. I met a man named Wu Dengming who had seen it all. As a boy he saw his country torn apart by war and revolution. He watched Mao Zedong's communists claim China for themselves. Later, Wu served in the People's Liberation Army. But this was a man who did not toe the Party line.

He was seventy-two when I met him, but he had lost none of his vigour, or the impish grin that had challenged authority for decades. Wu was a hero of the environmental movement, one of the fathers of 'green China'. He had been beaten, persecuted and threatened in his fight against big business and officialdom. He bounded down the stairs to greet me at his office in the leafy surroundings of a university in Chongqing; after extending a firm handshake, he began talking rapidly. Wu was an old man who'd seen too much to bother with caution. If he thought it, he said it. 'This is a fight between gods, way beyond the reach of ordinary people,' he told me.

The fight he referred to was a political conflict that in 2012 gripped the entire country. The gods in question were the secretive inner circle of the Communist Party. This drama read like a big-screen political thriller, and had thrust Chongqing – a city of more than 30 million people – into the spotlight. In the week before I met Wu, the Communist Party had sacked Chongqing's chief, Bo Xilai. Bo's father was a revolutionary icon, a hero of the fabled Long March, but Bo was a political star in his own right. He was widely expected to become one of the nine members of Xi Jinping's new and all-powerful politburo standing committee.

Bo Xilai styled himself as the people's champion, and the poor flocked to Chongqing from rural villages looking for a better life. When I travelled there, most people I spoke to on the streets were glowing in their praise for him. 'I felt lost and my heart was heavy when I heard the news [of his sacking],' one man told me. A woman who worked up to fifteen hours a day shining shoes in the city centre said life was better for the elderly and the poor because of the ousted Bo. 'The city is greener and safer,' she said.

Bo had also cracked down on crime. Under his orders, police busted gangs and locked up corrupt businessmen. While this won praise in some circles, critics said he used it as a means of persecuting rivals. The crackdown ultimately led to Bo's downfall. His former top cop and right-hand man, Wang Lijun, spectacularly sought refuge in the US consulate, claiming his life was in danger. The city was a hotbed of rumour and innuendo, but the truth was lost in Chongqing's famous haze.

'No one can know,' another local Chongqing man told me. 'We know nothing!'

To Wu Dengming, the man who had seen it all, this was a politburo power play. Wu had watched Bo up close for years, and said he was too ambitious, too desperate for success.

'Bo made enemies,' he told me, adding that he had taken his 'neo-Maoist' campaign too far. But, he continued, this was about more than just Bo. This was about a system that had strayed too far from the people. 'Bo Xilai thinks like a feudalistic dictator and treats ordinary people like his subjects,' Wu said. 'I think only when communist officials start treating people as their masters will people start wholeheartedly supporting the Party.'

As the Party's gods tried to manage the transition to a new generation of leaders, they were looking all too human.

Like Wu Dengming, Wang Kang had spent much of his life caught up in the internecine strife of the Communist Party. Wang looked every bit what he was: a Chinese scholar. He had a Confucian beard, greying hair and a deep, resonant voice enunciating Putonghua tones; he epitomised gravitas. Wang was one of the few insiders who dared to speak publicly about Bo Xilai. But even he admitted to me that he was taking a risk by agreeing to my request for an interview.

'Several foreign media have told me they cannot find one single person to speak in the vast city of Chongqing,' he said. 'No one dares go public. This is sad.'

Wang was a well-known identity, plugged into local politics and personally familiar with the people at the centre of this scandal, which had grown to encompass a murder investigation, allegations of spying and rumoured sexual affairs. Wang peeled back the layers of intrigue, revealing how the Party bosses got to Bo Xilai through his wife, Gu Kailai. She had formed a business relationship – some believed also a more intimate bond – with a British Mr Fix It, Neil Heywood, who linked British firms with Chinese companies. Heywood even did some work for a firm run by former British spies. Heywood was described as elusive and mysterious and he played up to his glamorous 'man of mystery' image, even driving a James Bond–style sports car with the number plate 007. Heywood was married to a Chinese woman, and had formed deep business and political relationships in China. He identified Bo Xilai as a rising powerbroker, and wrote a personal letter of introduction when Bo was mayor of the large port city of Dalian.

Bo and Gu were a formidable couple. Both were steeped in the Party, Bo through his father, Bo Yibo, while Gu's father was a People's Liberation Army general. Both fathers had fallen foul of the Party hierarchy. Bo Yibo was jailed for opposing Mao, accused of being a capitalist and counter-revolutionary. Bo Xilai and his brother were also imprisoned during the Cultural Revolution. Those years have been described as leaving an 'evil mark' on Bo. But as is the way in China, the Bo family had been rehabilitated. Bo Yibo was named one of the 'eight immortals' of the Communist Revolution. His son was on track to emulate his father, perhaps even surpass him. Gu Kailai was the perfect wife for an ambitious politician. Her family too had been restored to its glory, and she was a successful lawyer dubbed by some – not always kindly – as an 'empress'; to others she was China's answer to Jackie Kennedy. Bo and Gu were 'devout' communists, but that did not stop them currying favour with the rich and powerful. And they had big plans for their son Bo Guagua. That was where Neil Heywood came in useful. He appealed to the couple by offering to open the door for their son to attend Harrow, the exclusive English boarding school.

Australian journalist John Garnaut, who was reporting from Beijing at the same time as me, chronicled this dramatic power struggle in his book *The Rise and Fall of the House of Bo*. He says Bo and Gu were creating their own dynasty. Their son – who had gone on to study at the prestigious Harvard University in the United States, drove sports cars and cultivated an image as one of China's most eligible bachelors – was crucial to their plans. Garnaut even outlines an attempt at parental matchmaking to link Bo Guagua and the daughter of the American ambassador and presidential hopeful John Huntsman. But the marriage of Bo and Gu became strained amid gossipy rumours of affairs, treachery and greed.

By 2012, Bo Xilai had been detained and was under investigation. Gu Kailai was accused of murder, and Neil Heywood was the victim. As John Garnaut writes: 'They had all grown up in a world where winners took everything and those who were not constantly accumulating power lived in constant fear of having it stripped away.'

Bo Xilai had launched his crackdown on criminals and political rivals, which was popular with the public but made him mortal enemies. As Bo grew more consumed by his quest for ever greater power, Gu drifted into a deep depression. She withdrew from work and was described as living more like a hermit, sinking into drug addiction. Gu had connected Neil Heywood to lucrative property deals in Chongqing. When the deals soured, Heywood tried to extort money from Bo Guagua. In written testimony, Gu said she 'must fight to my death to stop the craziness of Neil Heywood'.

Gu arranged to meet Heywood at a rundown hotel in the hills outside Chongqing. She had concocted a plan to kill the English businessman. She would get him drunk and then slip him a poisonous cocktail. According to court testimony, as Heywood lay intoxicated on the bed, Gu dripped a lethal dose of cyanide into his mouth. Gu arranged the room to make Heywood's death look like suicide. Then she phoned Wang Lijun, Bo Xilai's trusted police chief, to tell him her plan had succeeded.

From here things unravelled: Wang became fearful of being betrayed by Gu, and confided in Bo Xilai that Gu had killed Heywood. Bo removed Wang from his post, and soon after, Wang made his escape, dressed disguised as a woman, to the American consulate. He sought political asylum and provided evidence that Gu had killed Heywood. The American consulate turned Wang away, but his attempted defection and his allegations against Bo Xilai and his wife stunned the Party. It prompted a diplomatic incident. This scandal of murder, drugs, sex, power and money captivated the Chinese people.

As a reporter, I was immersed in the story. I retraced the last day of Neil Heywood's life, travelling from Beijing to Chongqing, and to the hotel where he was poisoned. I first glimpsed the sprawling complex, nestled into the lush hills on the outskirts of Chongqing, from a distance. The air was fresher here, the temperature several degrees cooler than in the sprawling metropolis of more than 30 million people below. In its heyday, this was a high-end resort area, but as we drove along the windy road towards it I could see it was well past its prime. There were rundown buildings, dogs sprawled on the concrete, and a smattering of restaurants, massage centres and karaoke bars that clearly hadn't had a facelift in decades.

In November 2011, Neil Heywood, this British businessman with seemingly rare access to the rich and powerful in China, made this same journey. He would never return. His body was found, and a murder investigation began that shook the foundations of power. My crew and I checked into the grimy and dilapidated Nanshan Lijing Holiday Hotel. Other TV crews had been turned away at the gate – the traditional hand-over-the-camera-lens shot – but we managed to find rooms on the same floor as the room in which Heywood was poisoned, and with key in hand I walked in the footsteps of Heywood. The corridor was musty and there was a stale smell of damp carpet mixed with years of cigarette smoke. It was hardly the salubrious establishment befitting Heywood's high-flying image.

When I opened the door – the lock itself was jammed and took several attempts – the room was hardly an improvement. The furnishings were old and chipped: there was a faded, flimsy lounge and a double bed with a garish purple-and-white vinyl bedhead. A bug was fighting for its life on the floor, the skirting boards were busted, and power points had been dislodged from the walls, the electrical wires exposed. The air conditioning switch was old and faded yellow. When I turned on the fan, it spluttered before rattling to life. The only decorations were faded plastic flowers, and – appropriately for this story – a jigsaw puzzle on the wall. At night, mini-skirted call girls wandered the corridors, furtively knocking on doors as they touted for clients. I was reminded again how unlikely such a setting was for this baffling story that had captivated the country and thrown open the secretive doors of the all-powerful Chinese Communist Party.

There were police everywhere. Patrol cars parked in the driveway, and plain-clothes investigators moved around the grounds. I wished I could be a fly on the wall in the hotel staff rooms, but publicly they would say nothing. Over lunch we pressed waitresses for any morsel of information, but they were practised at keeping their mouths shut.

'There are lots of police here – what's happening?' I asked.

'Nothing, they're just having lunch,' one waitress replied, before vanishing the moment after our plates hit the table.

Yet behind closed doors, this was all anyone was talking about. With each passing day, more details were emerging of Heywood's business and personal links to one of China's most powerful families, and how it had all allegedly gone so terribly wrong. Bo Xilai was still a hero to many ordinary working Chinese. But now he was in disgrace, stripped of his titles and hidden from view. The investigation had yet to reveal its findings, but all the major players were either dead or silenced. Dozens of people connected with the case had been arrested.

I finally got one man to talk, and he wouldn't condemn Bo. 'He should be remembered for the good things he did,' he told me. But like everyone, he was fascinated by the twists and turns of the case.

Wang Kang – the old insider – told me that Bo had flown too high. His crackdown on crime, popular as it was, had gone too far. 'Extortion of confessions through torture was commonplace – too many unjust and mistaken cases were made in the process. That is for sure,' Wang said.

Bo had revived the spirit of Mao Zedong, and this made some in the Party nervous. Wang said it frightened the reformers, who wanted to get rid of Bo.

'He's been playing the role of Mao's successor,' Wang argued. 'He was visiting PLA camps and giving the soldiers Mao's bust as a gift. None of the other politicians has ever done that. I think it has been a huge misjudgement of Bo. Going back to Mao's path is definitely not an option. That has proven to be a dead end. Mao led a road to ruin.'

Now it was Bo Xilai facing ruin. This murder scandal was all the opportunity his enemies needed to oust him. He would pay for the crimes of his wife. 'It somehow became impossible for Gu to end this relationship with Heywood,' Wang said. 'My guess is both factors exist. They were involved both financially and romantically.'

Wang Kang had little sympathy for Bo Xilai. Back then, as China moved into a new era – that of President Xi Jinping – the Party was in crisis, locked in a battle for its soul. It was losing the trust of the people, and Bo Xilai would be sacrificed. As Wang told me, one leader had fallen, but China may have taken big steps to saving itself in the process.

The big winner was a man who was more ruthless than Bo; who came from the same privileged Communist Party background; who had suffered the same rejection and disgrace during the Cultural Revolution; who had learned that survival meant 'kill or be killed'; who was even more of a Maoist than Bo – who was more Maoist than Mao. When Xi Jinping took power, he condemned Bo Xilai to life imprisonment.

The path was clear for Xi: a man who could have been his great rival was gone, and Xi himself would be the heir of Mao and Deng. He would complete the great rejuvenation of the Chinese nation. History, homeland and harmony would be his priorities. He would avenge the history of humiliation, renew the glory of the homeland, and impose harmony by removing any opposition. The Party reformers may have been glad to see the end of Bo Xilai, but they were getting a new president who would turn back the clock – who would crack down even harder, lock up even more people, silence any dissent. He would be smarter than Bo Xilai, and more ruthless.

If this was the war of the gods, then now there was only one god standing. As political scientist Li Weidong said, Xi Jinping was henceforth free 'to follow Bo Xilai's political line without Bo Xilai'.

5

ENEMIES OF THE PEOPLE

By 2012 I had reported in China long enough to gain a sixth sense. Every China-based journalist would know what I'm talking about – an inner voice that says: 'You're being watched.' I heard that voice while I was sitting in a Starbucks in the Chinese city of Chengdu with cameraman Brad Olson and our producer who for security reasons I will call Mei-Mei. Brad and I had spent enough time together to read each other's thoughts. He tilted his head and averted his eyes, drawing my attention to two men who had positioned themselves just off to our right. I nodded back.

We had been expecting this. We were in Chengdu to speak to Buddhist monks hiding out from the authorities. Several monks had set themselves alight in recent weeks – ritual self-immolation – to protest the Chinese Communist Party's crackdown on their homeland, Tibet. Chengdu, in Sichuan Province, bordered Tibet. Indeed, old maps showed it as part of Tibet. Tibet was off limits to us: the last thing the Party wanted was foreign journalists reporting on what went on behind the wall of state-enforced censorship. So we took another approach. Brad, Mei-Mei and I had flown here from Beijing to try to smuggle ourselves behind the lines.

We hired a car and began the drive through the mountains. We left at night in the driving rain, thinking it might offer good cover under which we could avoid the authorities. Passing one small town after another in the pitch blackness, we got to within touching distance of the border – and then we saw it: a light and sentry box with a boom gate. We considered pulling into a side road and trying another way across, but there was no avoiding it: there was only one way across. We decided to try our luck and see if we could bluff our way through.

We pulled up at the roadblock, and Brad and I slumped down in the back seat to look less conspicuous while Mei-Mei sat in front to do the talking. The guard pointed his flashlight at the car, waving it around as Brad and I tried to hide our faces. Mei-Mei told him we were tourists. The guard asked for our passports; this would not be good. I worried that he would cross-reference our names and details, see that we worked for CNN and arrest us. For the briefest moment, we considered turning the car around and making a run for it – but what would we do without our passports? I put my faith in Mei-Mei to talk our way out of this.

The guard was gone for about ten minutes, and when he returned he spoke briefly to Mei-Mei. I could hear her remonstrating, speaking more quickly and waving her hands around. The guard handed back our passports, and our driver put the car into reverse. We wouldn't be going to Tibet, but it seemed we would not be arrested either. Not yet, at least.

Tibetans, Uighur Muslims, political dissidents, artists, lawyers, writers – during my years covering China, I reported on the Communist Party's crackdown on all of these groups. They were enemies of the state: those the Party wanted removed or brainwashed or eradicated. The Party cannot stand any rival. The

Party is about power: its projection and its appearance. The Party reaches into every corner of life in China. It is the all-seeing eye. Despite the appearance of change, with its markets opened and freer movement allowed, the Party retains a tyrannical heart. Former China correspondent Richard McGregor says in his book *The Party: The Secret World of China's Communist Rulers* that it has 'eradicated or emasculated political rivals; eliminated the autonomy of the courts and press; restricted religion and civil society; denigrated rival versions of nationhood; centralised political power; established extensive networks of security police; and dispatched dissidents to labour camps'.

The Party has a volunteer army of spies and informers that monitors the movements of people. I have seen this. My crew and I would arrive for an interview, sometimes unannounced, only for the police to come crashing in within minutes. Neighbours are only too eager to blow the whistle on those who dare to talk to foreign media. Yet astonishingly I met people time and again who were prepared to risk their freedom and their safety to speak out. Often it was the people with the smallest voices who spoke the loudest. In reporting these stories, we became enemies of the state too.

I had no sooner arrived in China than the Chinese secret police sent me a warning that they had us under surveillance. It was deep winter and the lakes in the centre of Beijing had frozen over, turning them into large open-air skating rinks. We took our three boys to the lake, and as our eldest boy, John, was pushing his two younger brothers on a sled, I looked up and saw two men in black (the clothing of choice for plainclothes Chinese cops) suddenly throw John across the ice and take off at speed with the two younger boys. I chased after them and they tipped over the sled, sending my sons skidding across the ice. They were unharmed, and the two men raced off the ice and jumped a fence.

Were they cops? I have no doubt. Plainclothes police regularly followed my family and me around. We were photographed having lunch with friends. Unmarked cars parked outside my house. Our phones were bugged. At work we would leave the office and use other phones to make sensitive phone calls. It didn't work. Interviewees would be often warned off speaking to us. The police knew our movements ahead of time and would intercept us. Our Chinese staff would be visited by police at dead of night and interrogated.

*

Brad, Mei-Mei and I had stopped at that Starbucks in Chengdu to view our footage and send some vision back to our bureau in Beijing. This was our regular plan of attack to outwit the Communist Party censors. We would shoot vision for our story and send our material in, just in case we were detained by cops and had our tapes confiscated. Starbucks was always a good spot. It had some of the best internet speed in China, and we would get a coffee into the bargain. On this day, though, with the Chinese secret police watching us, we could not hang around. We hatched a plan for Mei-Mei to take our footage and leave; Brad and I would follow soon after. We would get into separate taxis and regroup at our hotel. Hopefully this would throw the police off our trail.

After failing to get across the border, we had made contact with Buddhist monks in Chengdu. They had agreed to speak to us, despite the threat of arrest if discovered. We arranged to meet them in a nondescript apartment in a poor neighbourhood. The monks were conspicuous with their shaved heads and saffron robes. They were being hidden by supporters, and they wanted to get their message out about how they were being persecuted. They were Tibetan independence activists, and loyal to the Dalai Lama. They supported their fellow monks' campaign of self-immolation. If this was what it took to win freedom, they told me, they would do the same.

Tibet is one of the many fault lines in China. Previously a contested independent state, it was annexed by Beijing in 1951, and the Dalai Lama fled into exile in 1959 after a Tibetan uprising. Tibetans see China as a cruel occupier destroying Tibetan culture and overrunning the local population. According to some estimates, more than a million Tibetans have died under Chinese control from violence and starvation. The Chinese Communist Party, though, calls its presence a 'peaceful liberation' of the country. China has brought wealth and development, it says. Former leader Deng Xiaoping said Tibet was part of the modernisation of China. To the Party, Tibet was always part of China, tracing it back to 1792, when the Qing Emperor sent his army to push back Nepalese forces. The fall of the Qing ushered in a new era: Tibet became part of the great humiliation narrative, with the Party seeing itself as avenging the invasion of Western forces like Britain, which moved on Tibet in the early twentieth century. The party sees Tibet as part of the reunification of the motherland, just like Hong Kong or Taiwan.

Any reporting of Tibet is scrutinised and censored. Stories that I filed to CNN were blocked: the TV screen would immediately go black. It was the same for all sensitive issues. In a room somewhere an army of censors would watch every minute of a broadcast with a finger on the button. When the story was finished, normal transmission would resume. It became a game for us to see if we could slip through this wall of control. Sometimes a snippet of my stories would make it to air before quickly vanishing from the screen. In the field, we played a cat-and-mouse game to film our stories and evade any interference; we were successful more often than not, but on this day we were not so lucky.

Brad, Mei-Mei and I met at our rendezvous, convinced we had shaken off our pursuers. We knew we did not have any time to waste, and if we made it to the airport we were confident we could board the plane and return to Beijing, mission accomplished. It was usually like this – the local authorities would try to stop us but once we were out of their jurisdiction, they would throw up their hands and we became someone else's problem. Not this time.

As we approached the airport, our driver stopped at a toll gate and we could see a car speeding up behind us; it looked like they were determined to hit us. We urged our driver to accelerate, and he got us to the entry of the airport. We flung him some money and tossed our things out of the car, then rushed inside hoping we could disappear into the crowd. We told Mei-Mei to go ahead with our camera discs and try to get through security – she had a better chance of looking like a tourist. Brad and I would follow and hope for the best. We didn't get to check in before we felt arms around us. Several police now marched us through the airport and back outside and into a car. We were taken to a local police station and put into separate lock-ups. The police wanted to confiscate our belongings and our phones.

This had happened on several other occasions and I had developed a routine. I demanded to make a call to my embassy –

but in fact I called my wife, Tracey. 'Hello, is this the Australian embassy?' I said.

Tracey knew this was code that I had been arrested. She would then make contact with CNN to try to secure our release. She was always very calm. Tracey knew the risks of my job and had dealt before with my long absences, especially in dangerous places. There was a time she thought I may have been dead. I was working in Pakistan during an earthquake, and a military helicopter that I was meant to be on crashed, killing several people. Hours went by and no one heard from me or my cameraman, Wen Chun Fan. Fortunately for us, we had missed the ride and flown on a later chopper. We arrived back in Islamabad oblivious to the concern our colleagues and families were feeling.

Brad and I were interrogated for hours, about who we had spoken to and where. The police searched our belongings, looking for any camera discs. Brad regularly swapped discs while we were filming. Sometimes he would shoot 'dummy' footage – useless vision that he would leave in the camera just in case of circumstances like this. The police played the vision and pocketed the disc. The real footage was with Mei-Mei, who we believed was now on her way to Beijing. Then I heard Mei-Mei's voice through the wall and my heart sank. They had found her. Now we would lose all of our material – the entire trip would be a waste.

After about five hours of detention, the police released us. CNN had been reporting that we were arrested and it had become a minor international incident. Dissident Chinese media and activists posted our news on their websites. Satisfied that they had confiscated our material, the cops told us we were free to go.

I can't say incidents like this were not distressing, but Brad and I had been here before – and we had reported from far more dangerous places. But Mei-Mei had never endured anything like this, and understandably it shook her up. She told us that she had made it on board the plane, but the cops came to her seat and forced her back into the terminal. Mei-Mei was tiny – there would have been no need for any heavy-handedness – yet she said they dragged her by the hair and frog-marched her through the airport like a criminal. Mei-Mei is a Chinese American, but to the cops she was a traitor. She said they made threats against her family and called her a 'running dog' – a traditional insult reserved for Chinese people working for the West. I don't think Mei-Mei ever truly recovered from the ordeal; she left CNN not long after.

The police had confiscated all the material Mei-Mei had been carrying, but Brad had a surprise for us: he had hidden one of our discs – the most crucial one, with the interviews with monks and critical footage of the police pursuing us – inside his underwear. The police had never thought to search there. He retrieved the disc with the goofy, self-satisfied smirk Brad would get when he did something well. One of the beautiful things about Brad was his desire to please. He would endure any hardship to get the job done. This time he had saved us. For all of the efforts by the authorities to stop us we had our story.

I lived for moments like this, when I could give voice to the struggle of others. Part of me enjoyed the cloak-and-dagger nature of our work, and even the risk we were running, but the story was everything. The Buddhist monks were killing themselves to be free. They wanted to make sure the world could not look away. Now I could put their story on screens around the world. The Communist Party censors may blacken the screen in China, but millions of people elsewhere would see behind China's wall of secrecy.

※

China, for all its power, sometimes seems to me like the Wizard of Oz: a small man hiding behind a loud voice. It is the illusion of power, and the Party must maintain that illusion or it will crumble. The Party needs a permanent enemy. If one does not exist, it must create one. It rules by fear because it knows it cannot rule with love. As Mao Zedong said: 'Communism is not love. Communism is a hammer, which we use to crush the enemy.'

Despite all the talk of 'serving the people', the Party gives every sign of being afraid of the people. Its hold on power is tenuous. It has made a bargain with its people: we will make you rich but you will surrender your freedom. It has lived up to its side of the bargain but the yearning to be free is undeniable. The Party stands astride history; there is no inexorable drift to freedom. But it knows it is pushing against a tide. The Party has confronted catastrophe throughout its existence: during the Cultural Revolution, in the Tiananmen Square protests of 1989, and with the collapse of the Soviet Union in the early 1990s. As Richard McGregor reminds us, '[T]he Party has picked itself off the ground, reconstituted its armour and reinforced its flanks.' It has been prepared to sacrifice its own people to ensure the Party's survival. But it is nervous: it is forever looking over its shoulder, scared of shadows.

A decade ago, the Chinese Communist Party cracked down

on a girls' TV talent show, accusing it of corrupting the morals of the nation. *Super Girl* was styled on *American Idol*, where girls would compete for a shot at stardom. At its peak it pulled in an astonishing 400 million viewers. To the Party chiefs, this was worrying: they described it as 'poison for your youth' and had it pulled from air. It was the second time it had been banned; the first came in 2006 after criticism from the then Chinese culture minister. Why? Because it was importing Western values of individualism. What's more, its format of voting for contestants came too close to democracy. When *Super Girl* was cancelled, one distraught fan posted on Weibo (China's version of Twitter): 'Maybe we need another revolution.' No wonder the Party was worried.

The lengths the Party will go to defend itself against 'Western decadence' are sometimes laughable. In 2011, I reported on President Hu Jintao's own 'cultural revolution': he had declared 'war' on Lady Gaga! Yes, the American pop star was deemed enemy number one. She was seen as infecting Chinese youth with poor morals and eroding traditional Chinese culture. Hu wanted out with scantily clad Western pop stars and in with demure, conservatively dressed Chinese folk singers. I spoke to Beijing-based social commentator Jeremy Goldkorn, who said Hu's culture war indicated a weakness: a fear that the centre could not hold in China. Hu recognised that Party propaganda was no longer working, he told me. Lady Gaga was seen as infiltrating China and poisoning young Chinese minds.

The President even went as far as publishing an essay in the official Party magazine, *Seeking Truth*, accusing the West of using ideology and culture to divide China. Hu wrote: 'We must clearly see that the international hostile forces are intensifying strategic attempts to Westernise China.' China already limited the publication of foreign books and movies, and heavily censored information. Yet the internet threatened all of that. Young people were flocking to internet cafes, finding ways to break through the great firewall and swapping ideas. At the same time, the Arab Spring was in full bloom. Young people in the Middle East were protesting for democracy and ousting strongman leaders. Hu was nervous. What if Chinese youth turned on the Party? Lady Gaga must be silenced!

These are just some examples of how the Communist Party, for all its power, is fearful. China scholar Susan Shirk coined the phrase 'fragile superpower' to describe a nation that spends more on domestic security than external security. Between 2007 and 2019, domestic security spending tripled to more than 1.24 trillion yuan (more than $200 billion). In areas the Party considers 'hotspots' – like the north-western province of Xinjiang, home to the ethnic Uighur Muslim population – security spending increased more than 90 per cent between 2017 and 2018. China is on track to become the world's biggest economy, and it is building a military it says can fight and win any war. So why is it so fearful at home? Because the history of China is one of violent revolution.

Modern China was born of revolution: first in 1911, with the end of the Qing Empire, and then the bloody civil war that led to the victory of the Communist Party in 1949. The memory of violent revolt is what spooked the Communist Party in 1989, when pro-democracy protesters took over Tiananmen Square and Deng Xiaoping called in the army to massacre its own people.

The Communist Party likes to give the impression of order,

but beneath the surface China is roiling with anger. Each day there are hundreds of protests across the country: from pent-up frustration over things like corruption, land seizures, pollution, economic stress. Exact numbers are difficult to ascertain, but analysts have estimated that between the 1990s and 2010, mass protests grew from fewer than 9000 per year to 180,000 annually. I have seen these protests erupt spontaneously and violently in the most unlikely places. In 2011 I found myself in the middle of a riot outside an Apple store as people queued for the release of the latest iPhone. Frustrated that they had to wait for the store to open, someone in the crowd began throwing eggs; quickly the anger spread until people rushed forward, smashing windows and viciously attacking security guards. This was less about waiting for a new phone and more a release of pent-up anger. Materialism can feed the ego, but I had spoken to enough disenchanted Chinese people to know that they also felt something was deeply broken in the soul of their society. People told me they were angry with the Communist Party, which they said was too quick to use force to impose order. There was also a strong anti-American sentiment in the crowd that suggested an identity crisis: this was a country that wants what the West has but rejects what the West is.

Protests about phones, however explosive, are one thing, but protests for democracy are another. If the Party cannot stomach girls voting for pop stars, what chance is there for a vote for real leadership? In 2019 Xi Jinping came down hard on the unrest in the streets of Hong Kong that captured global attention. For months people had turned out in their hundreds of thousands, setting the streets alight, smashing shop windows and clashing with police. Initially they were angry at new extradition laws that allowed Hong Kong residents to be handed over to the mainland Chinese courts. These protests were a catalyst for demands for greater freedom and democracy. The Party had steadily encroached on the 'One Country, Two Systems' deal after the handover of Hong Kong in 1997. Hong Kong was meant to retain the vestiges of its British inheritance – free press, free elections – for fifty years before being fully merged with the mainland. But Xi Jinping had grown increasingly impatient, and the sight of Chinese youth rioting and demonstrating raised fears of a contagion that could spread throughout China.

Xi's determination to create a 'harmonious society' means locking up dissidents, writers, artists, lawyers and political rivals. It explains in part the sweeping detention of Uighurs and Tibetans. In 2020 human rights groups revealed that hundreds of thousands of Tibetans have been held in military-style 'education camps', to be trained as rural labourers and schooled in the dominant Han Chinese language and culture. Human rights groups say a million Uighurs are locked up in similar conditions. The Communist Party says it is for education, and also part of a crackdown on Uighur separatists whom the party calls terrorists. The Australian Strategic Policy Institute has released a study of satellite imagery that it says reveals 380 detention facilities in Xinjiang. And more of these camps are under construction.

The Communist Party knows it cannot appear to be weak. It especially cannot show weakness to the world. The memory runs deep of what happened to the Qing at the turn of the twentieth century, when China's rulers were seen as feeble and corrupt, humiliated in the Opium Wars with Britain and then brought down. As Susan Shirk wrote: 'Any Chinese government that looks weak in the face of foreign pressure is likely to be overthrown.' This is the price authoritarians pay for power: they rule the people, but they must rule with an iron fist: they inspire fear, often loyalty and devotion too, but they can never rest. As China scholar David Shambaugh has said, the Party is 'insular, paranoid and reactive'. It is a leadership that fears a talent show like *Super Girl* but needs to convince the world – and its own people – that it is a superpower.

*

The phone rang in our Beijing bureau. My producer Steven Jiang answered and I could see a puzzled look on his face. He put the phone down and turned to me and nodded for us to go outside. 'I don't believe who that was,' he said. It turned out it was Christian Bale, the Hollywood star best known for his role as Batman. He was in China making a movie and wanted to meet us.

Christian called again the next day to talk to me, and I was taken aback by his English accent. I had never really thought of him as English – I was more used to him playing American characters. Christian had been watching a lot of CNN during his down time and said he liked my reporting, especially our work on the detention of a blind Chinese civil rights activist named Chen Guangcheng. Chen – known as 'the barefoot lawyer' – had been a long-time campaigner for the rights of women forced into abortions as part of China's one-child policy. Chen was being held under house arrest, and human rights groups said he was regularly beaten and starved; he was growing weaker and sick and they were concerned for his life.

Chen was being held in a village in Shandong Province, about eight hours drive from Beijing. In 2011 we set out to try to interview Chen. Our chances were always next to zero, but in trying to get to the activist we could reveal the ring of steel that was locking him down. When we arrived in the village it was obvious that the authorities would never allow us to contact him. The entire place was shut down; roads were blocked and police cars everywhere. We parked our vehicle and hired a local car and driver to get as near as possible to Chen's house. We got to the dirt road leading to it, where we parked and got out. My cameraman Brad Olson began rolling immediately.

As we walked, a group of burly plain-clothes cops came towards us; they looked menacing and were clearly determined to stop us. As we filmed, they ran towards us, throwing punches and trying to wrest the camera from Brad. We turned to flee and they began pelting us with rocks; I was hit in the back which forced me into a ditch. When we made it back to our car, they came after us. Brad filmed the car chase as our driver tried to outmanoeuvre them. He was nervous, and after dropping us at our vehicle he quickly sped off. We managed to evade arrest and made it back to Beijing. We had not met Chen, but in a most dramatic way we had alerted our viewers around the world to his plight.

It turned out Christian had seen our story and wanted to try to meet Chen. Christian has a deep social conscience, and he told us that he could not work in China without also using his profile to shine a light into human rights abuses in the country. It was a way of paying down a debt: he had earned money but it would not buy his silence. We told him that it was highly unlikely we would get to Chen, but he wanted to try anyway. He was aware of the risks and accepted we would likely be physically attacked. Of course, we knew that this would become an international incident – a Hollywood movie star being beaten by Chinese secret police while trying to visit a blind activist who was being tortured and held under house arrest sounded like a movie in itself.

The first problem was how to evade Christian's minders. He was being housed in a luxury hotel surrounded by police. His email account and phone were tapped. But he had used an alternative phone to call us, and we set up an email account with a false name. We hatched a plan to meet him in the early hours of morning in the basement of his hotel and whisk him away in our car. It worked. Christian was waiting in a dark corner with a hoodie over his head; we drove in and opened the door, and he sprinted to the car and dived into the back seat.

When you spend time with someone for hours on end, you bond. Christian was incredibly serious, a deep thinker and a reader. As we drove, we talked about ideas and politics. He was fascinated by China, and wanted to know what I thought of the country and what its rise might mean for the world.

China, I told him, was where the limits of the idea of Western modernity were tested. Communist China was a product of the twentieth century, a creation of the West yet deeply antagonistic to the West. To understand China was to grapple with contradiction. Mao Zedong talked about the unity of opposites. As Mao said, 'One thing destroys another, things emerge, develop and are destroyed; everywhere is like this. If things are not destroyed by others, then they destroy themselves.' The struggle of opposites is absolute. There is constant movement and change. Before there is unity there is struggle: a process of alienation and dis-alienation, and out of that something new – and then the struggle begins over again. In the synthesis of capitalism and communism we get what the Hegelian philosopher Slavoj Žižek has called 'the poetic justice of history'.

When we arrived in Chen's village, security was tight. As I expected, and had warned Christian, we were not going to meet the dissident. But we had come this far, and Christian was determined to see it through. As on my last visit, we got out of our car – only to be met head-on by the same thugs who had attacked us previously. This time they were even more forceful. One was a hulking figure wearing a long green army coat and hat, its woollen sides pulled down tight. He would soon become a national cult figure after his run-in with the Hollywood actor. He flung himself at us, knocking cameraman Brad to the ground and kicking at him; others were flinging punches at me and Christian, who had taken out his mobile phone to film the altercation. We got Brad to his feet and rushed to our car, only again to be pursued, this time relentlessly. We raced down narrow lanes and across fields, trying to get away and avoid losing our footage. This was going to be explosive – Christian's profile would see to that – and would draw attention to Chen Guangcheng's plight like never before.

After another marathon drive into the night, we arrived in Beijing as the news cycle was kicking into gear. We had sent our vision to the newsroom and I had written and edited a story in the car. It was leading all news bulletins, although predictably the Chinese censors blocked our broadcast. CNN programs were all requesting to speak to Christian, who stayed on air well into the early hours of the morning. This was a public-relations nightmare for the Chinese Communist Party. They were not only having to defend their treatment of a blind activist, but were now wondering what to do with a Hollywood star who had gone rogue.

Within days, Christian left the country. Then, remarkably, Chen Guangcheng staged a dramatic escape, itself like something out a movie. It was actually compared to the prison escape movie *The Shawshank Redemption*. At night, this blind man slipped past his sleeping guards, climbed a wall and somehow made it across an open field, to be met by the supporters who had plotted his getaway. He was put into a car and driven to the American embassy in Beijing. Now a story that had started with secret phone calls and emails between Christian and ourselves was a full-blown diplomatic crisis.

China and the United States were in a stand-off. The Communist Party had been embarrassed. At the time, it spent $111 billion on domestic security, and yet it could not hold a man blind since birth. It also showed that for all the Party's power, it could not control everyone. Now the world was asking harder questions about China's human rights record. Chen's escape came ahead of a visit by the US secretary of state, Hillary Clinton, who had previously spotlighted Chen's case. The Chinese authorities wanted Chen back, and the US embassy had taken him to a hospital to seek treatment from injuries incurred by months of abuse by his security guards.

I heard Chen's voice for the first time down a static-filled phone line. I had managed to get through to him in hospital, where he had a secretly hidden phone. It was 3 am and Chen told me that even in his hospital bed, he feared for his life. There had been mixed messages coming from the US embassy, who said Chen had told them he wanted to stay in China, yet now he was telling me a very different story. Down the phone line, Chen Guangcheng spoke to the world and made a direct appeal to President Obama.

'Please do everything you can to get my whole family out of here,' Chen said.

Chen said US officials had driven him to the hospital and then abandoned him. And now the Americans and the Chinese had seemingly struck a deal: Chen and his family could live safely in China. The activist did not believe that for a moment. 'I am very disappointed with the US government,' he said. 'The embassy promised they would be with me at the hospital but soon after we got here they were all gone.'

Chen told me he was worried about his family: in his words, they were 'being terrorised'. He said his wife had been tied to a chair by police for two days, and they had threatened to beat her to death. If he didn't leave the embassy, Chen said, his wife would pay the price.

To the world, Chen Guangcheng became a symbol of courage in China: of those people who would stand up to the worst of the Communist Party. In China itself, there was silence. The party blocked all coverage of Chen's plight, fearing it would spark a wider uprising. When I spoke to ordinary Chinese people on the streets, they were oblivious to the drama. Out of forty random people I spoke to, only two even knew who Chen Guangcheng was.

The Chinese Communist Party was nervous. Chen's escape coincided with an anti-corruption crackdown inside the party. There were too many firestorms at once for a secretive, paranoid regime to control. I spoke to long-time China analyst James McGregor, who told me he had not seen the Party this nervous since the 1989 Tiananmen democracy protests. He said they were busy pouring water on anything that might set fire to the country.

This was truly Kafkaesque: a bizarre world of alternative reality, where the Chinese Communist Party tried to pretend that what the world was watching unfold simply wasn't happening. Its only weapon was an information blackout and more arrests of dissidents. The censors targeted Weibo, blocking search terms that could relate to Chen. At the height of the drama, Chen released a video aimed directly at China's senior figures. He asked Premier Wen Jiabao whether the thugs who had held him captive and beaten him were acting on their own, or whether they were directed by the Party itself. It was a question to which Chen already knew the answer.

It is part of the paradox of China that while the Party shut down coverage of Chen's escape, it stoked anger against CNN and Christian Bale, and we went viral across the online community. Our foiled attempt to meet Chen had captured the Chinese imagination – we were the enemies defeated by Chinese authorities. One meme became hugely popular: the huge, green-coated Chinese secret policeman – now dubbed 'Pandaman' – was shown crushing Christian Bale, Hollywood's Batman, underfoot. Pandaman quickly became a national cult figure. For anti-West Chinese patriots, Pandaman was a hero and Batman was the symbol of American weakness. Cartoons showed Pandaman towering over Batman and glowering back at the world: 'The Legend Ends', said one poster. It doesn't take much to stoke Chinese anger. The Party plays that card well, whipping up xenophobia whenever it suits. Now we were the target.

After weeks of drama and backroom negotiations, Chen Guangcheng finally fled China. He was whisked to Beijing airport in a special diplomatic motorcade, and onto a flight bound for the United States. We were at the airport trying to evade security, but we could not get close to Chen. We asked Chinese passengers if they knew who they would be sharing the flight with. One woman waved her hand and said, 'No, I don't know,' clearly unwilling to say anything. Another passenger said he was confused about the case: he'd heard too many different stories, he said, and he didn't know who or what to believe.

What a moment this was for Chen. He had spent four years in prison, and then another eighteen months in confinement in his village, where he'd been tortured, beaten and starved. Now he was free. We couldn't take any credit for this, but our wild ride across China with Christian Bale had helped bring his case to global attention. After arriving in America, Chen Guangcheng was given a special award at the United Nations. Christian Bale presented it to him.

6

THE SHADOW OF MAO

Xi Jinping was sworn in as president of China in the shadow of Mao Zedong. Mao's face peered down from an enormous portrait that framed the entrance to the Forbidden City, the old imperial palace in the centre of Beijing facing Tiananmen Square and the Great Hall of the People. Mao looms over China like an emperor. His body lies in state, visited daily by thousands of pilgrims. At times there have been shrines to him throughout the country that depict him as a god. They would draw tens of thousands of people every day. For the Communist Party, Mao has been like the burning sun: impossible to look at for too long, yet without which there is no light.

How should the Party remember him? This is the man who delivered the Party to power, defeated the Nationalist Army and restored the glory of China but also oversaw violence and famine that killed tens of millions. Mao tore down China to remake it. There is a line that he was 70 per cent right and 30 per cent wrong; the Party has never formally said this, but it sounds so convincing that it has taken on the sheen of truth. When Deng Xiaoping was changing course, opening China to the world, Mao had fallen from favour. Powerful figures spoke against him, even as Deng himself was careful not to denounce the Great Helmsman. But thirty years after his death, Mao was back, reborn in a new generation searching for identity.

To many in China, Mao Zedong is the country's eternal father – 'No Mao, no China,' as my old driver and friend Wang never tired of telling me. This was a mantra I heard everywhere I went. Mao's picture held pride of place in every house in every village across China. To these people he remained a symbol of strength, a man born a peasant – albeit a somewhat comfortable one – but who rose to lead the people's army of the Communist Party and unite a warring country. Mao has re-emerged as the face of resistance and defiance, a symbol of the rejection of Western dominance that has accompanied China's resurgent power. In the weeks leading up to Xi Jinping's inauguration as president in 2012, young Chinese protesters took to carrying Mao's image aloft during protests against Japan over disputed islands in the East China Sea. I met one young woman from Mao's home village in Hunan Province who lamented how weak she thought her country's leaders had become; if Mao were still alive, she said, China would just take the islands.

But for all those who saw strength in Mao, others remembered fear: revolution, paranoia, famine, brutality and tens of millions of deaths. They reminded me how China suffered during high-profile campaigns introduced by Mao such as the Great Leap Forward, where millions of people died through starvation or persecution during a catastrophic attempt to modernise China between 1958 and 1961. Many people still carried the scars of the Cultural Revolution. When I took to Beijing's streets, I found some still wary when I mentioned Mao's name.

'Why are you asking me this?' asked one woman as she scurried away from our cameras. 'Where is your identification? You shouldn't be talking about this,' she warned.

Another young woman was more forthright: China had no more need of Mao. 'I think that Chairman Mao is a rather extreme person. We don't really need those who are too extreme; instead, we need people who can connect China with the international community. In the long run, this would be best for China,' she said.

But overwhelmingly I found peopled wrapped up in a nostalgia for revolution.

'The current leaders should be as strong as Mao,' one Beijing resident said.

'For the Chinese people, he represents belief – a great man,' said another.

The country that once couldn't feed itself was now the world's second-largest economy and an emerging superpower to rival the United States. Mao's peasant revolution has given way to 'socialism with Chinese characteristics'. Yet Mao remained inescapable, not just in the minds of ordinary people nostalgic for the past, but at the heart of the party itself. Mao had feared that, like Joseph Stalin, he would be buried twice – once in death and again in memory, posthumously purged by the Party he led. But the Soviets always had Lenin as a lodestar, which meant they could afford to bury Stalin; Mao, by contrast, is the Chinese Communist Party's founder and saviour. And now, standing where Mao once stood, Xi Jinping sees the spirit of Mao as China's future.

When Mao died in 1976, for a moment there was the real prospect of civil war. He had presided over the Cultural

Revolution, which had trashed the country's history, persecuted its elites and let loose an army of angry youth. Mao had systematically severed connections to those he once kept close. It was one of the many things that bound Xi Jinping to his vanquished, disgraced rival, Bo Xilai: both their fathers had been ousted from Party leadership. Now, with Mao dead, the army was placed on high alert and sections of Beijing were shut down.

Mao's widow, Jiang Qing, jostled for power with her three key supporters, together known as the 'Gang of Four'. The Gang had overseen the mayhem of the Cultural Revolution. Jiang Qing had been a movie actress named Lan Ping, but she became a revolutionary who liked to boast of creating order from chaos. Mao had protected her, but now that her husband was dead, senior Party figures turned against Jiang, among them Deng Xiaoping, who called her 'evil'. She was soon arrested and denounced in the media as a 'swindler' and a 'maggot'. Jiang Qing had once said that she would bite 'whomsoever Chairman Mao told me to bite', but now the Party was using Jiang's arrest to preserve the memory of Mao. Jiang was the one with blood on her hands, while China's new leader, Hua Guofeng, declared that 'Chairman Mao will always live in our hearts'.

Mao was a poet, a revolutionary and a philosopher. He rewrote the rules of guerrilla warfare and gave birth to a new movement, 'Maoism'. He was also, along with Stalin and Hitler, one of the tyrants of the twentieth century; his vision and his decisions condemned tens of millions of people to death. Yet more than Stalin and Hitler, Mao's image has become a staple of popular art and Chinese communist kitsch. In Beijing, Mao's *Little Red Book* is for sale in every street market. His face adorns T-shirts and coffee mugs.

I admit that I have a Cultural Revolution-era bust of Mao and a ceramic image of his famous 'Red Flag' car in my home. I would never have anything of Hitler. Why Mao? I can't really say. I think these images are less about Mao the man or what he stood for than a memory of China, the place that was my home for many years. It is a connection to the country and its history that I still want to keep close. And he is endlessly fascinating. I could not report China without trying to understand this man who gave his name to a whole mode of thinking: Mao Zedong thought.

> The East is Red, the sun rises,
> In China a Mao Zedong is born.
> He seeks the people's happiness
> He is the people's great saviour.

The anthem 'The East Is Red' captures the cult of Mao Zedong. It was written during the hard years in Yan'an after the Long March. Mao was elevated to the pantheon of communist thinkers, alongside Marx, Engels, Lenin and Stalin. He declared China the centre of world revolution, and revolution would come only from violent struggle. He famously wrote: 'A revolution is not a dinner party, or writing an essay, or painting a picture, or doing embroidery ... A revolution is an uprising, an act of violence whereby one class overthrows the power of another.' Power, Mao said, came from the barrel of a gun, and 'the Party commands the gun'. Only with guns, Mao wrote, can the whole world be transformed.

China scholar Julia Lovell, in her magnificent history of Maoism, reminds us that the Chinese Communists had learned the brutal lessons of the power of the gun. The rival Nationalists, in 1927, launched a brutal search-and-destroy mission to wipe out the Communist Party and its supporters in their stronghold of Shanghai. It ignited years of violence that, Lovell writes, left millions dead, 'disembowelled, decapitated, soaked in petrol and set alight, branded to death with hot irons, tied to trees with grit rubbed into their mutilations'. The massacre of 1927 turned Mao from thinker to fighter.

*

I remember once driving through Shaanxi Province in northwest China – the fabled 'Yellow Earth' – during a drought that had cracked open this rock-hard soil. My news crew and I had gone in search of survival stories, to see how people were holding up in one of driest periods in more than fifty years. Between 2010 and 2011, lakes had emptied, crops had failed, and millions of people were without water. From my car window, across a parched open field I saw a man chipping away at the ground. It intrigued me. I have always followed my instincts and they told me now that there was a story here.

We parked and walked closer to him. He was digging a well, searching for just a drop of buried water. Right then, it was as precious to him as gold. All day he had hacked away at the ground, but it gave him next to nothing. The man's wife showed us a bucket that held only a few centimetres of water. That was all they had to show for their toil. Yet he didn't stop – not even to talk to us. As I interviewed him, he kept on digging, his shirt off and his wiry muscles clearly aching, dripping with sweat. That image has never left me, because it tells me how these people will endure. It captured a maxim I had heard over and over in China: to eat bitterness.

These are the people who looked to Mao Zedong, and look now to Xi Jinping. They have lived through monumental change; those old enough still remember famine, revolution and death. China is again a powerful country, but it is still in search of its identity: what it is to be Chinese. What is China? Empire or nation-state? Is there such a thing as Chinese civilisation, or has 5000 years of culture been obliterated by a century of revolt? Has China triumphed over foreign domination or is it a victim, never to be healed of its hundred years of humiliation?

The Chinese people have lived at the crossroads of modernity; they are haunted by chaos and burdened by history. This is what I found so intoxicating about China; it is what spoke profoundly to me, and inspired me as a reporter. I was never just telling the story of China; I was looking for some part of myself. Because China stands in for so many of us who have felt the West wash over us like a tsunami, leaving us to cling to the wreckage of our lives. We are caught in the undertow of the West, which drags us to a future that the ideas of the West created. As French historian François Hartog wrote, '[T]he West has spent the last two hundred years dancing to the tune of the future – and making others do likewise.'

When I looked into the eyes of that man digging in vain for water, I knew him. I had seen that look in my father and grandfather. His wife, standing beside him, was my mother. I shared with them the journey from the past to the future. It is a journey those born truly to the West don't truly understand. How could they, when the future – when progress – is their invention? But I have spent so much of my life reporting the stories of people on that same journey as me: people from Palestine and Iraq and Afghanistan and Pakistan and North Korea and, of course, China. And we outside the West have to ask ourselves harder questions. Existence itself is something we cannot take for granted. What can we carry on that journey from then to now? What do we leave behind? How much of ourselves do we get to keep? Or does the West demand that we put all aside to become indistinguishable from one another?

How many of us even get to make that journey? The West came to China as it came to the land of my ancestors, in gunships, with flags and money and progress. It littered the ground with our corpses but told those of us who were left that the West was freedom. Freedom was the gift of modernity, transported by empire and colonisation and violence. And for all of that, it is so alluring. Desperate people will risk their lives to get on leaky boats to travel to freedom. For all America's sins it still draws the world's tired and poor.

Mao Zedong studied the West and he drew on the great thinkers of his own country. He is the nexus between the post-Qing Empire China and the nation that today has returned to global power. The humiliation of the Opium Wars plunged China into a dark night of the soul. The Qing Empire was corrupt and weak, and China was occupied by the British, the French and the Japanese. The fall of the Qing triggered rebellion, civil war and revolution. For China, the arrival of the West shattered thousands of years of culture and assumed Chinese superiority. Western imperialism forced change. From the 1890s, Chinese thinkers wondered how they would respond to the West. What would they keep and what would they discard? Darwinian biology and Newtonian physics threatened to usurp more traditional Chinese views of the world: the spiritual East versus the material West. Historian John Fairbank wrote that a 'dominant majority civilisation' now found itself 'in a minority position in the world'.

A new generation of Chinese scholars, writers and philosophers wrestled with the very nature of time and being. The collapse of the Qing Empire punctured the view of China as the centre of world civilisation. Western ideas of linear progress and individualism increasingly appealed to younger Chinese as they looked to throw off traditional Confucian beliefs in community, patriarchy and hierarchy. Indeed, some blamed Confucianism for stunting China's growth. One nineteenth-century writer, Yan Fu, was influenced by European liberal thinkers such as John Stuart Mill and the father of economics, Adam Smith. Historian Charlotte Furth points out that Yan Fu 'advocated the infusion of Anglo-Saxon liberalism into Chinese politics'. These were radical new ideas, and shook the society to the core. As Yan saw it, people 'were the true lords of the world'. Perhaps the most influential thinker of all, Liang Qichao, looked to the Western idea of history as a march of progress – and progress meant modernisation.

Liang is the thinker who paved the way for those to come, including Mao Zedong. China historians Orville Schell and John Delury have called Liang 'the godfather of Chinese nationalism'. He looked at his nation, defeated and humiliated, and saw weakness. Liang coined the phrase 'the sick man of Asia' to describe China's fallen state. Being crushed by Japan in 1895, Liang said, 'awoke our nation from its four-thousand-year-long dream'. China was no longer the centre of the world.

Like Yan Fu, Liang set about inventing a new nation. He especially began to sow the seeds of what would become a national consciousness. As Liang embraced Western ideas, he also advocated the unity of the 'yellow race'. He coined a term, *minzu*, to describe the people of the nation – even then, well before Xi Jinping, China was grappling with ideas of harmony in a nation so ethnically divided. A Han – the majority ethnic group – consciousness developed, especially in opposition to the Qing rulers, who were despised Manchu – a distinct ethnic group the Han considered foreign invaders. There is much of Georg Hegel in Liang. He believed in revolution as a force of change, and that history was forward-leaning. He began to talk of what he called *hsin min* – a 'new people'. Humanity, he said, 'is the pivot of evolution, the inexhaustible source of its transformation'. Liang saw democracy and public rule as alternatives to empire. But as much as Liang imagined a future liberated from China's past, he believed Chinese people were 'morally backward'.

By the early twentieth century, the 'new people' ideology was giving way to 'national essence'. This was strongly racial, a pro-Han ideology and vehemently anti-Manchu. As Charlotte Furth writes, there was a 'strong undercurrent of solidarity with China's common people'. It was a 'victim' mentality that would grow into the narrative of national humiliation. In today's terms, we would call it a populist movement that fed on fear and anxiety and was racist and anti-elite. We might even say its aim was to 'make China great again'. Furth says the movement 'offered a definition of the Chinese people as a "nation" – an organic collectivity based upon common ties of place, blood, custom and culture'. They still recognised history as an engine of change and progress, but also affirmed the essential nature of Chinese 'identity'. Not unlike the explosion of thought in Europe in the seventeenth and eighteenth centuries, Chinese thinkers were challenging each other, trying to write a new nation and a new people into existence. While some embraced the West and ideas of progress, others were vehemently anti-Western and saw progress as superstition. These are the same fault lines that run through China today.

World War One was critical in China's turn away from the West. The Chinese had watched as Europe tore itself apart. All its ideas of liberty, freedom and progress had failed to avert the most brutal war the world had seen. Then the Treaty of Versailles added insult to China's grievances, handing Japan control of former German-occupied territory in China. There could be no greater insult. China was seen as weak and impotent – now it could not even control its own territory.

It was in these moments that the seeds of Chinese resentment were sown. This was the great humiliation, the century of dominance and ridicule of China by the West. As historian Jerome Ch'en writes, 'from 1842 to 1942, China had been treated by the West with distrust, ridicule, and disdain, mingled from time to time with pity and charity, only occasionally sympathy and friendliness'. Liang Qichao, who championed progress and modernisation, now turned sour. He had been sent as an official observer to the Paris Peace Conference, and now condemned Western civilisation. Following Western faith in science and progress, Liang now believed, would lead China to catastrophe.

*

History is full of quirks, and so it is that revolutionary China is connected to the election of the first black president of the United States. Barack Obama walked the same school halls as the man who would be the first president of the new Chinese republic, a man revered today as the 'Father of the Nation'.

Sun Yat-sen was a young boy when he was sent from his village in China to live with his older brother, who had travelled to Hawaii to seek his fortune. It was a pivotal moment, one that can truly be said to have altered world history. In Honolulu, Sun attended the private Oahu College, later renamed Punahou School, where Obama would be educated a century later. There, Sun took his first steps on a journey of faith, philosophy and history that in time would turn him to revolution. He fell under the sway of a teacher who not only converted him to Christianity, but also planted the seeds of a deep mistrust of the West and America. Sun saw how the United States had annexed the Hawaiian islands, stealing them from the indigenous people.

Living in America, Sun was torn between his exposure to new ideas and new culture – he admired the strength of the West – and the roots of his Chinese identity. He was deeply influenced by Liang Qichao, and also saw China as inherently weak. When Liang returned to his village, he could no longer live among his own people, whom he considered inferior. Yet he was also fired by a passion to rescue his country and overthrow the rotting Qing rulers. Like Liang, Sun believed in the unity of the Han race and began to develop his own ideas about what a new China might look like.

After studying to become a doctor in Hong Kong, Sun returned to Hawaii and built support for armed revolt back home. He was banished from China and spent sixteen years in exile, travelling between America, Japan and London, and visiting cities like Sydney. The West was strong, he said, because it had power and wealth. He believed that the West bullied China, and that 'Westerners are ready to pounce like tigers on the rest of the world'. More than ever, Sun was convinced the corrupt Qing rulers must go.

Battered by war and rebellion, and occupied and humiliated by foreign powers, its territory carved away, the Qing Empire fell in 1911, and Sun Yat-sen was anointed the first president of the Republic of China. He didn't last long in office – just forty-five days – before handing over to Yuan Shikai, who had been prime minister in the imperial cabinet and commanded the strong military forces of China's north. But Sun would set the course for the nation. He laid out his guiding principles for the rejuvenation of China: nationalism and the struggle of the people. For Sun, this wasn't just about saving China as a nation; he believed he was saving the Chinese people from extinction.

From the time of the Opium Wars, a new generation of Chinese had seen themselves as locked in a battle against white Western dominance. As much as they admired the West's strength and studied its great thinkers, they knew that the West held China in contempt. As Sun said, 'The rest of mankind is the carving knife, while we are the fish and meat … we face a tragedy – the loss of our country and the destruction of our race.'

Two men would emerge from Sun's shadow to finish what he had started: Mao Zedong and Chiang Kai-shek. Chiang not only fought under Sun, he later married the sister of Sun's wife. Chiang had also spent time in Japan and studied in Moscow, and like Sun was torn between a grudging admiration for the West and a desire to rescue his own country. He was ruthless and ambitious. He was described as aloof and charismatic. Chiang, alongside his glamorous wife, entranced the West, particularly the Americans, who backed his Nationalist Army in its war with Mao's communists. Mao and Chiang had fought together, but in 1927 Chiang unleashed the 'White Terror': the slaughter of communists in Shanghai, which quickly spread around the country and helped spark a ten-year civil war that ended with Mao's communists taking control.

Although they fought on different sides, Chiang and Mao were united in their view of the white Western world. Chiang felt deeply the shame of China's defeats by foreign and Western powers, and of those treaties that had carved up Chinese territory. The treaties, he believed, kept the Chinese in 'bondage'. Schell and Delury write that 'a smouldering anti-foreignism' is everywhere in Chiang's writing. In one diary entry he wrote that 'the stupid British regard Chinese lives as dirt'. The intensity of China's shame and anger can never be underestimated. Chiang and Mao, like Sun Yat-sen before them, never forgot that they were fighting on multiple fronts. They fought the enemies at home and the enemies abroad.

Mao Zedong's Communist Revolution was a peasants' revolution. He wrote that China's peasants would 'rise like a fierce wind' that no power could suppress. China's peasants would accomplish, he said, what Sun Yat-sen had failed to do: they would 'send all the imperialists, warlords, corrupt officials, local bullies and bad gentries to their graves'. Mao fought with the gun and the pen. He had been a librarian and had spent his days lost in words, reading the classics. Close friends say he was obsessed with the histories of ancient China and with Western philosophy. Like the other emerging leaders of China, Mao revered Liang Qichao. Mao biographers Alexander Pantsov and Steven Levine write that 'Liang Qichao's book, *On Renovation of the People* ... was a treasure trove of knowledge for him'. As Liang wrote, he 'wanted to search for the primary cause of the decay' of the Chinese people, to avoid future disaster.

Mao's exhaustive reading did not lead him to a more liberal or democratic view of the world. 'There is no universal human morality ... we have a duty only to ourselves, and have no duty to others,' he wrote. To Mao, China had fallen because the Chinese people were ignorant and weak. He famously compared them to a blank sheet of paper. Mao would write the future, and the people would follow. There was no moral law from on high: 'You are God,' he wrote. 'Is there any God other than yourself?' Mao fashioned himself as the tiger and the monkey king. In China, the former represents power, and the latter is a supernatural being. As China scholar Roderick MacFarquhar wrote, Mao believed China needed to be destroyed to be rebuilt, and he 'would be the monkey king to lead that destruction'. First it was the peasant armies that drove his Communist Revolution, while in the 1960s the Red Guard youth led the destruction of the Cultural Revolution.

Mao Zedong gave China back to the Chinese people, but at a cost of blood and misery. His was a permanent revolution, government by chaos. The death toll of Mao's war and revolution is immeasurable. Just between 1958 and 1962 – the period known as the Great Leap Forward, Mao's vision of mass industrialisation – at least 40 million people are estimated to have perished. Most starved to death. Mao stands with Hitler and Stalin as one of the great mass murderers of the twentieth century. Historian Frank Dikötter called it a 'catastrophe of gargantuan proportions'. It was not merely the extent of the catastrophe, he argues, but the way in which people were killed that was so shocking: 'between two and three million victims were tortured to death or summarily killed'. Dikötter cites one case in which a father was forced to bury alive his son because the boy had stolen a handful of grain.

For Mao, the revolution could never end. If some revolutionaries, such as Vladimir Lenin, read Hegel and imagined that out of the struggle of thesis and anti-thesis – the destruction of the old – would come the synthesis of the new, then Mao saw only contradiction. As Mao said, 'A drama begins with a prologue, but the prologue is not the climax.' This set Mao apart from other Marxists: there would be no end point, no final communist utopia, no 'end of history' moment. Struggle, to Mao, held priority over unity. While Mao fought the imperialists abroad, he also fought the enemy at home: first the Nationalists, and then, after unifying the country, those he termed 'reactionaries'. In his famous essay *On Contradiction*, he wrote that the purpose of his 'people's democratic dictatorship' was 'to suppress the reactionary classes and elements and those exploiters who resist socialist revolution, or in other words, to resolve the internal contradictions between ourselves and the internal enemy'. In the Cultural Revolution, 'resolving contradiction' meant the destruction of the enemy.

Yet Mao, for all that the Chinese see him as the redeemer of the nation, did not deliver China to global power. Instead, it was Maoist communism's embrace of capitalism that powered the great Chinese revolution: the economic revolution. It was Deng Xiaoping who, after Mao's death, opened the country to the world and set China on a course to usurp the United States as the most powerful economy on the planet. As philosopher Slavoj Žižek says, this is 'the true Hegelian synthesis'. It is what Hegel would have referred to as the negation of the negation: not capitalism overthrown by communism, but capitalism and communism in an unlikely alliance. The Chinese communists, he says, have presided over 'arguably the most explosive development of capitalism in history: *we can do it better.*' There is, writes Žižek, 'a kind of poetic justice in the fact that the final result of Mao's Cultural Revolution is today's unprecedented explosion of capitalist dynamism in China'.

Xi Jinping is the embodiment of this synthesis. He is where Mao and Deng meet. He is their heir, and in many ways now their superior. He is more powerful because China is more powerful. Xi is poised to lead the country back to its place as the greatest power in the world – the place it lost after the fall of the Qing Empire. This is Xi's dream. Each Chinese thinker, from Yan Fu to Liang Qichao to Sun Yat-sen, Mao and Deng, lives in him. He is a product of the Cultural Revolution, the son of Yellow Earth. Xi straddles the fault line of modernity: where the West meets the world. He knows what the West is, and wants what the West has to offer, yet rejects much of what the West stands for.

The West believes history is something to be vanquished, or sometimes commemorated or mythologised. History is a story – a fable – more likely told in Hollywood films. This is the great virtue of the West – that it can free people from the chains of their past, and that each generation can write their history anew. But it blinds the West to the most fundamental fact of modern China: that China is scarred by humiliation. It has been mocked and conquered, and the memory will not dim. It is who they are. The Chinese will die before they are humiliated again.

In an article published in 2016, 'Xi Jinping: History Cannot Be Denied', President Xi writes: 'To destroy a state, one must first erase its history. The hostile, foreign or interior forces that often write about the Chinese Revolution and the new China never cease to attack, slander, and tarnish: the principal objective is to confound people.' Xi portrays China as a victim of the West. He knows that this narrative has a powerful hold on his people. I have no doubt he believes it, but it serves another function: in a country that is fraying at the edges, where many are left out of the China dream and are angry and alienated, Xi knows that he can always exploit a toxic nationalism. He will never let fade the memory of the Opium Wars, and he knows that to win the hearts of the people he must inhabit the spirit of Mao. Xi Jinping has a tiger by the tail: he presides over a schizophrenic nation that is neither communist nor truly capitalist, that is strong but paranoid, rich but not free. The fall of the Qing Empire haunts China still; and a modern-day emperor, Xi Jinping, knows how quickly kingdoms can fall.

*

In a small village in Guangdong Province, in southern China, I caught a glimpse of an alternative future. It is Xi Jinping's worst nightmare, a people's revolution that overthrows the Communist Party leadership.

For several months in 2011, in one small part of the country, that nightmare looked terribly real. The people of Wukan rose up against corrupt local officials, who the locals say had illegally seized villagers' land. Thousands of people attacked government buildings and the police station, chanting, 'Give us back our farmland!' Things turned even nastier when one of the village leaders died in police custody. At CNN we received video of people being viciously beaten by police. But the villagers were not deterred. For a period the protesters forced the entire local government out of the village. In the end, the government relented and allowed the local people to run their own elections and choose their own representatives. Perhaps even more remarkably, the foreign media was allowed in to tell the story. It was very different from when I had sneaked into the village months earlier and hidden in the home of one of the villagers. We almost succeeded in evading the police before we were discovered and run out of town. Now I was back to witness something I never thought I would see: democracy in China.

Xue Jianwan ran for election to honour her father. He had led the village protests but was arrested and died in police custody. The family believed he had been murdered. I met Xue in her home, which was now a shrine to her late father. What he had started Xue was determined to finish. On election day I watched her walk proudly to the ballot box and place her carefully folded ballot sheet. Xue had joined in the protests; now she told me she hoped this display of people power would be the start of a new future in her country.

But while the locals were optimistic, others were more cynical. To the critics this was all for show – the Party would still pull the strings. Undoubtedly so. But the Party was nervous too. China's history told them that an angry people could topple empires. In earlier times these villagers may well have joined the rebellions against the Qing Dynasty; they could have been part of the 1911 revolution that led to the founding of the Republic of China; perhaps they would have marched with Mao Zedong as he took back the country. While the protesters in Wukan were voting, a new generation of Maoists were gathering strength.

Historian Julia Lovell says the People's Republic of China 'is held together by the legacies of Maoism'. Mao is the 'invisible hand' reaching into the judiciary and politics, silencing dissident voices. In the lead-up to Xi Jinping's presidency, the new Maoists had used social media to build an influential base. The 'internet Maoists', as Lovell dubbed them, were vehemently anti-West. They established a popular website they called 'Utopia'. It was a vehicle for attacking the United States and championing anti-American movements in the Middle East. Utopia idealised North Korea, which had defied the United States and remained in a declared state of war with America. They refused to hear any criticism of Mao Zedong, and denounced anyone who spoke against those they saw as traitors to Mao's vision, including members of the Party itself.

According to Lovell, Mao became 'a symbol of a more equitable time'. The internet became the neo-Maoists' greatest weapon against the Party. They tapped into the frustrations and fears of the people, who now spoke openly and circulated petitions online. Utopia became a mouthpiece for the disaffected, the disenchanted, those who had likely never experienced the extremes of Mao Zedong and who romanticised the Cultural Revolution. As Lovell writes, 'Utopia and an increasing cohort of competitors and copycats would embrace a worldview that saw global conspiracies of Western domination, the infiltration of China and the party by traitors and "hostile forces", and a belief in an inevitable and unavoidable conflict with the United States.' The neo-Maoists 'saw Mao Zedong as their magic weapon'.

When Bo Xilai fell, the neo-Maoists lost a champion – the person they believed could lead a Maoist revival in China. For a time, these new revolutionaries themselves were in retreat.

Government authorities descended on the headquarters of Utopia and other like-minded organisations. They were temporarily shut down. But when Xi Jinping came to power, they were back. Xi may have orchestrated Bo's demise, but he knew the power of Mao. He would not tolerate criticism of Mao: to Xi, it was 'historical nihilism', and if unchecked it would destroy the country. He married a renewed sense of Chinese pride with a narrative of historical humiliation. Those few foreign commentators who saw in Xi a reformer, someone who would open up the democratic future, were terribly wrong. Xi was shrewd; he dressed like Mao but thought like Deng. He purged his rivals and revived revolutionary slogans, but continued to open up his country's economy. Xi made pilgrimages to the resting places of both Mao and Deng, part of a populist play for the hearts of the Chinese people. Some neo-Maoists began to refer to him as the 'great hope' of their country.

I arrived in China, in Beijing, in 2004, as this new Mao movement was taking hold. It wasn't just limited to the angry youth on the internet – this strident nationalism permeated society. We chose to live in a typically Chinese neighbourhood far from the expat enclave. If we were going to live in China, we wanted to live with Chinese people.

Our youngest son started school in Beijing, the only foreign student in his class, where all lessons were taught in Chinese language. He quickly began to speak like a local, with much better Mandarin than anyone else in the family. Sometimes, if we were struggling to be understood, he would translate for us. He had local friends and we got to meet other people; we were invited into their homes, or ate together in local restaurants. We had been in our new home only a few weeks when my wife and children were invited to a local film night. They didn't know what to expect – perhaps a children's film or a comedy. What they got was a violent anti-Japan propaganda film. After one scene where a group of Japanese prisoners were lined up on a hillside and executed, to the cheers of our new neighbours, Tracey thought it best to make a quiet exit.

A few years later, we moved to another neighbourhood, again living predominantly among locals. Near our house was a small children's playground with a few amusement rides. One of the most popular was a ride that featured small mock fighter planes. Every few seconds an alert would sound and the children would press a button to open fire. A warning voice would shout, 'Meiguo, Meiguo, Meiguo!' – American, American, American. These children were learning very young who the 'enemy' was. It was harmless enough, I suppose, but it was another indication of a turn in the country.

During my years covering China, I saw it go from the policy of 'hide and bide' favoured by Deng Xiaoping – hide your capacities, bide your time – to Xi Jinping's aggressive nationalism. Relations with the United States turned increasingly sour. In 2011, CNN was invited along on a rare up-close tour of Chinese military facilities with the US defense chief, Admiral Mike Mullen. Mullen had been very blunt in his assessment of China's military build-up in the Asia-Pacific. A couple of years before, he said China was 'developing capabilities that are very maritime focused, maritime and air focused, and in many ways very focused on us'. Mullen was warning that America and its allies needed to work together to meet the China challenge.

During one quiet moment at a Chinese army base, I quietly asked the admiral about the state of the US–China relationship.

'What relationship?' he replied.

Each year, old Chinese men would parade in the main streets of Beijing proudly wearing their military medals. These were the veterans of China's victory over America. We know it as the Korean War, but in China it is celebrated as 'The War to Resist America and Aid Korea'. China's intervention in the Battle of the Ch'ongch'on, against the advancing forces under US World War Two hero General Douglas MacArthur, caused what is still today the longest retreat in American military history. MacArthur had launched what he called a 'home by Christmas offensive', to push out the Chinese forces who were aiding North Korea. On 25 November 1950, hundreds of thousands of Chinese forces launched a series of surprise attacks against MacArthur's men. The American general had bet on the Chinese soldiers not striking, but he had walked into a trap. As journalist David Halberstam writes in his book *The Coldest Winter*, 'The bet had been called, and other men would now pay for that terrible arrogance and vainglory.'

The Chinese, using a strategy devised by Mao Zedong, had waited patiently, watching every move MacArthur made. Mao had made his own bet – that MacArthur's ego would inspire him to cross the thirty-eighth parallel marking the separation of North and South Korea, to try to capture the North. In just one month China had moved 300,000 troops into North Korea completely undetected. MacArthur had drastically underestimated the Chinese, telling the US ambassador in Seoul that there were only 25,000 Chinese soldiers. Halberstam quotes military historian S.L.A. Marshall, who said the Chinese divisions were 'a phantom which cast no shadow'.

It was a disaster for the United Nations–allied forces, and thousands of troops died or were wounded. The battle turned the tide of the war, locking the opposing sides into a grinding stalemate. British historian Max Hastings likened the rout by the Chinese to 'the collapse of the French in 1940 to the Nazis and the British at Singapore in 1942 to the Japanese'. Only a year before, Mao Zedong had established the new People's Republic of China; now he could proclaim a victory over the American imperialists.

The Korean War has never ended. An armistice was signed, but there has never been a peace treaty. China and North Korea forged their relationship in blood. As China has re-emerged as a global power, the victory over the Americans has taken on mythical dimensions. The battle is seared in public memory. Schoolchildren study the war, which is described as a 'just war against aggression'. In 2010, when he was vice president of China, Xi Jinping marked the anniversary of the battle with a speech. 'The imperialist invaders imposed this war on the Chinese people,' he said; China was 'driven beyond the limits of forbearance'.

America has tried to erase the memory of Korea. It is often referred to as the 'forgotten war'. The Battle of the Ch'ongch'on does not capture the imagination like Gallipoli or Normandy or Stalingrad or the Somme, yet it can now be seen as a turning point of the twentieth century. The United States emerged from World War Two in 1945 as the world's predominant power. We talk about the 'American century', yet how long did it truly last? Just five years after victory in the Pacific and helping to liberate Europe from the Nazis, American soldiers were humbled by an army of Chinese volunteers. Mao Zedong had earlier defeated the American-backed Nationalist Army in the Chinese Civil War, and now had triumphed over the Americans themselves. If we're looking for a moment that would shape the twenty-first century, then the Battle of the Ch'ongch'on is a good place to start. The trajectory of the twenty-first century was set. Mao's China would face violence and revolution, starvation and mass death, but it would also emerge as a genuine threat to American dominance. Ahead for the United States lay more war, economic strife, political scandal and terrorism, all of which would make it a fractured nation no longer sure of its place in the world.

After Korea, America was soon embroiled in another war, in Vietnam. Again it faced the spectre of Mao Zedong, this time in the Viet Cong leader Ho Chi Minh, who had studied in China and Moscow in the 1930s. The Russians and the Chinese had variously supported the Vietnamese communists, even as they at times clashed with each other. Ho returned home after the Japanese invasion of Indochina in 1941 and founded the communist independence movement, the Viet Minh. After World War Two, war broke out between Ho's Viet Minh and the French. The war reached its climax in the battle of Dien Bien Phu in March–May 1954. The victory by Ho Chi Minh's soldiers marked the first time a European army had been defeated in the history of colonisation. It was the end of the French empire. In the years ahead, Ho would mastermind the defeat of another Western power, dragging the United States and its allies into a quagmire that eventually forced a US withdrawal and the fall of Saigon to the communist forces in 1975.

In 2004 I travelled to Dien Bien Phu, as Vietnam marked the fiftieth anniversary of the victory over France. On the hills around the city were the relics of war: old tanks and weapons. The French trenches were still there. I climbed down into one, and it was like I was transported in time. Chairs and desks and fold-out beds were still there. I could imagine the French general, Christian de Castries, dug in and convinced that he would prevail over Ho's forces. But he faced another military leader, Ho's general, Vo Nguyen Giap, who like Mao in Korea moved his forces into place backed by weapons largely from Mao's China. Giap assembled 40,000 troops for what he expected to be the battle to end all battles. General Castries, displaying the hubris of MacArthur in Korea, underestimated Giap's numbers. The French were overrun.

CNN assigned me to visit Hanoi to meet General Giap. He was an old man, well into his nineties, but still sharp and immaculately turned out. He greeted me in his beautiful villa, surrounded by a wall and lush gardens, wearing his green military uniform festooned in medals. This man who was dubbed the 'Red Napoleon' was tiny in stature but his charisma filled the room. I spent more than an hour talking to him as he recounted the Battle of Dien Bien Phu and how he had vanquished the coloniser. Giap's name should be as familiar to us in the West as Napoleon or Patton or any of the great generals of history. Yet when I have mentioned his name to people – well-read otherwise informed people – they have looked at me blankly. This tells me about the arrogance of the West, that it is too easy to see the world through Western eyes. The Battle of Dien Bien Phu presages the unravelling of the West. Its dominance, its power, is not immutable.

But Giap was not just the hero of the first Indochina war – he then masterminded the victory over the Americans in Vietnam. Giap told me that a nation that stands up and knows how to unite will always defeat a foreign invader. Giap perfected what he had learned from the Chinese. This was Mao's playbook, and it would be emulated by insurgent movements around the world. More than two million Vietnamese died in what Giap called the 'War against American Aggression'. Giap told me that the Vietnamese sacrifice was the price of freedom. His people, he said, would never be slaves to anyone. 'Nothing is more precious than freedom,' he told me.

At the time I was in Vietnam, America was still at war: this time in Afghanistan and Iraq. Again, despite its enormous firepower, the United States was bogged down in a conflict against local insurgencies. America had been fighting the same war, in different countries, for more than half a century. It was already drained and tired. Almost two decades later, as I write this, American troops are still on the front lines of these wars without end. The long retreat after the defeat in the Battle of the Ch'ongch'on presaged the slow erosion of American power and prestige. War haunts Americans, just as it haunts the Vietnamese, the Koreans and the Chinese.

The Vietnamese writer Viet Thanh Nguyen says war exists first on the battlefield and then in memory. So true. I carry the memory of war, of how a war against my own people by foreign invaders more than 200 years ago still weighs on my soul. I carry the memory of trauma. It is part of what draws me to report the world. I could not begin to understand China without understanding the memory of war. The Chinese are still fighting the Opium Wars of nearly two centuries ago. The fall of the Qing Empire displaced China from the centre of the world; Mao Zedong told the Chinese people that they had 'stood up'; and now Xi Jinping promises to restore the nation to greatness.

*

The shadow of Mao still looms over China. He not only changed the course of his country, he helped shape the world. He perfected new ways of war that have been employed from Korea to Vietnam to Iraq and Afghanistan. Smaller forces have shown that they can bring down great powers. After Mao's death, some Chinese leaders wanted to bury his ideas along with him, but there is no China without Mao. His legacy has grown where those of others are barely remembered, and his influence has extended into a new century. From where we sit today, Mao Zedong, of all the great and horrific leaders of the twentieth century, perhaps exerts the greatest influence. It has been a long and brutal journey: from the disgrace of defeat in the Opium Wars, to foreign domination, to the massacres of the Japanese occupation, to civil war and revolution, and to the return of China as a great power. This history links powerful figures: Sun Yat-sen, Mao Zedong, Deng Xiaoping and Xi Jinping, each of them seething with resentment at foreign humiliation and betrayal, and each waging war on their own people.

Each day in Beijing, I would pass by Mao's giant portrait. Through the sun and rain and snow, through all seasons he has stared down on his people. For they are still *his* people in a way that they will never belong any other Chinese leader: not Deng, not Xi. Mao is the eternal president, still lying in state.

When we talk today about a struggle with China, we must realise the dimensions of that struggle: it is with a myth, it is with memory. We are wrong to think this is just about economics or diplomacy or even firepower. This struggle is deeper. It is existential: for the Chinese it is about who they are. I have come to believe that we in West no longer know what that even means. We believe we are masters of the universe, that our science and logic can answer all questions; we think we have vanquished history and killed God. This is what scares the West, I think, making a folly of all that we have been led to believe about time and power. What scares the white West is that Mao may be right: history does not bend to freedom; it bends to might.

7

THE HERMIT KINGDOM

What do an obscure opera and the nineteenth-century German philosopher Hegel tell us about North Korea? Everything. Let me start with the opera, *Sea of Blood*. Yes, it is ominously named, and deliberately so. Here's the plot: Japan has occupied North Korea. A poor tenant farmer named Yun-seop joins others to fight the invaders. All are soon killed, but Yun-seop's wife raises an army of resistance and defeats the might of the Japanese forces.

Sea of Blood is revered in North Korea as the perfect representation of Korean spirit. The opera was adapted from the play *Blood Sea*, written by North Korea's founding father, Kim Il-sung. It is the artistic representation of what North Koreans call Juche. You cannot possibly understand North Korea without grasping Juche – it is the key to the 'Hermit Kingdom'. It was the guiding philosophy of Kim Il-sung, and underpins every aspect of society – politics, economics and culture. It essentially means 'self-reliance'. Under Juche, individuals determine their destiny, and the North Korean people are 'masters of the revolution'. The North Korean regime used music to deliver this philosophy to the masses. In a thesis for the University of Pretoria, Kisoo Cho looked at how the revolutionary opera became the embodiment of this idea. 'It is no exaggeration to say that all the arias and songs performed in the opera ... contain political messages,' Cho wrote.

Indeed, Kim Jong-il – who inherited power from his father in 1994 – said: 'Music must work for politics and music without politics is the same as flowers without scent.' Enter the German philosopher Georg Hegel. Korean scholar Hyun-Joo Lee studied the transformation of North Korean music, and drew a direct link to Hegel's ideas of history. 'North Korean music cannot break the bounds of Hegel's philosophy,' she wrote.

I have returned again and again to Hegel in this book: for me, he is the thinker who unlocks the door to so much of our world. He has been the inspiration for despots and tyrants, and he is seen as the philosopher who promises to free us from the chains of our history. He is widely considered the philosopher most difficult to read, yet his ideas continue to resonate. Remember, it was the American political scientist Francis Fukuyama who famously drew on Hegel at the end of the Cold War and the collapse of the Soviet empire to ask if the world was witnessing the end of history.

For Hegel, world history was driven by the battle of ideas. As Fukuyama drew on Hegel to celebrate the triumph of liberal democracy, a century earlier Karl Marx was equally influenced by Hegel when he wrote about the fall of capitalism and what he imagined as the birth of a socialist utopia. Marx saw Hegel's concept of history – with a beginning, a middle and an end – as culminating in the 'workers' paradise', with the proletariat having overthrown the capitalist bourgeoisie.

As the Soviet Empire fell, triggering a collapse of one communist regime after another, North Korea remained; in its secretive capital, Pyongyang, Fukuyama's view of history did not prevail. North Korean specialist Bruce Cummings has written about North Korea's take on Hegel and history. 'The Kim dynasty put Marx on his head, or Hegel back on his feet, by arguing that "ideas determine everything",' Cummings argued. Where Marx saw the overthrow of monarchy on his march to history, the North Koreans seized on Hegel's belief in the state as being 'of one mind' – in this case, the mind of Kim. Juche, then, is a curious amalgam of Marxist-Leninist ideas, ancient Korean belief and selective readings of Hegel. North Korea is a state forged in war – liberated from the Japanese, carved out of the Cold War, and in a state of enduring, unending conflict with the United States and its allies.

Juche – self-reliance – locks North Korea out of the West. It combines with Jawi – self-reliance in defence. This is a paranoid regime in a constant state of war and determined to stand on its own, so it is little wonder it has so relentlessly and provocatively pursued nuclear weapons. Victor Cha, long-time North Korea watcher and author of *The Impossible State: North Korea, Past and Future*, once revealed that during nuclear negotiations with the United States and other countries in 2005, a Pyongyang envoy said: 'The reason you attacked Afghanistan is because they didn't have any nukes. And look what happened to Libya. That is why we will never give up ours.'

North Korea has been popularised as a laughing stock, and its leaders mocked as comic buffoons. I get it – there is something decidedly wacky about North Korea that makes it easy to lampoon. But behind the bouffant hairdos and platform shoes of generations of the Kim family, there is something far more deadly, calculating and dangerous. The lonely, misfit leader depicted in the film *Team America: World Police* may get a laugh in Hollywood, but the stakes here are serious.

Any credible North Korea analyst will never dismiss the Kim dynasty as 'irrational' or 'unpredictable'. Brutal? Yes. The stories of defectors escaping the death camps are beyond frightening. Petulant? No doubt. North Korea hates being ignored. But the regime's rulers are not stupid. It is a murderous regime, but it is not suicidal. It has nuclear weapons, but to use them would risk annihilation.

Current leader Kim Jong-un has learned the lessons of his father (the late 'Dear Leader', Kim Jong-il) and his grandfather Kim Il-sung: survival is all. While he threatens to unleash disaster, a first strike would be truly mad. Writing in the journal *Foreign Policy* after a nuclear test in 2013, David Kang and Victor Cha said authoritarian rulers do not survive if they are truly out of touch with reality. 'If Kim moves beyond the political theatre of the past 60 years – chest-thumping, name-calling, threatening to turn Seoul into a "sea of fire" – and actually risks a major military strike … he's putting his own neck, as well as his country's, on the line,' they wrote.

The North Korean regime is about survival. It holds a gun to the world's head; it appears crazy enough to use it, but it is smart enough to know not to. North Korea's presence makes our world unstable. Even its great patron, China, at times cannot control its little brother. Although the countries have been previously described as being 'as close as lips and teeth', there are real questions about just how much influence the Chinese still have.

In the meantime, the music continues to play. Like his father and grandfather, Kim Jong-un sees music as the language of the people, the path to indoctrination. He has formed his own all-girl band, the Moranbong Band, which scholar Kisoo Cho says 'plays the role of spokesman for the Kim Jong-un regime'. It performs at all official functions, playing songs of war and victory perpetuating the philosophy of Juche.

The world waits and wonders how or when this music will stop.

*

I'm so close I feel I could almost reach out and touch it. In the distance I see disused smoke stacks from abandoned factories, grey stark buildings; the odd old truck. Set against an austere, cold, ice-blue sky and bare trees, the few people visible walk slowly in small groups, speaking among themselves. This is my glimpse of the 'Hermit Kingdom': strange, secretive, forbidding North Korea. I have come to Dandong, a Chinese border town, home to North Korean officials, workers and some terrified defectors.

Dandong is every inch a bustling, booming small city on the move, but it is almost as much Korean as Chinese. Even street signs and billboards are in Korean characters. I have walked the pedestrian 'Broken Bridge' out to the middle of the Yalu River. This stretch of water, maybe a kilometre wide, is what separates China from its close ally. Suddenly the bridge stops; pylons mark the remaining distance.

If I were able to keep walking, in another two minutes I'd be not just in another country but in a different world. And it is a world now in official mourning after the death of Kim Jong-il. North Korean state media have broadcast images of a grief-stricken nation, with people openly weeping. That's the official image at least – but an image that, for me, is about to be shattered by a random meeting with a North Korean man who is living in terror.

We meet him by chance; our crew is out filming in the freezing pre-dawn light, and he wanders over, intrigued. It is what we have been waiting for: a chance to speak to a North Korean away from what could so easily be the choreographed tears of Pyongyang. What does he really think? What is life in his country like? What will become of it without the so-called 'Dear Leader'?

But this fit and affable seventy-year-old man suddenly makes to escape from our questions. He can't talk, he says; he can't even be seen with us.

'There are many North Korean spies here.'

'Everywhere?' I ask.

'Exactly, many, many. There are hundreds of spies,' he says, walking quickly away.

This was in 2011. Even across the border in China, North Koreans feared the reach of the Kim family. When Kim Jong-il died, the always impenetrable country shut down even harder. CNN, like other foreign media, could not get a visa to enter the country, so we did the next best thing and came to the booming Korean towns that dot the border. In many ways it was better: in North Korea we would be constantly monitored, while here we could at least try to get close to people. Getting them to trust us was another thing.

I could not identify this man we had found – he wouldn't even give us his name. We called him Mr Lee. He spent part of the year in Dandong, part of the year in North Korea. He told me that speaking out risked death. 'North Koreans don't speak openly. If anyone knows I'm talking I would be sent to prison, and there's no mercy there. I would be shot dead,' he said. But after our assurances, quietly, warily, he opened up a little more, painting a picture of a harsh life across the border, where people were starving, aid was scarce and the only operating factories were for making weapons. At that moment, he said, he feared the country was desperate, facing a potential power vacuum that could easily see it lash out. 'Before Kim Jong-il died, he was preparing the country for war and death and to hand power to Kim Jong-un,' Mr Lee told me.

Other North Koreans I met were in mourning. We'd seen busloads of women workers crying, too distraught to speak. Flowers continued to be delivered to the North Korean consulate. Korean businesses and restaurants, normally flourishing, closed their doors.

Mr Lee shed no tears for Kim Jong-il. He held no hopes for the now much heralded 'great successor', Kim Jong-un. This man knew too well what had happened under the Kim family rule. To him, it was a regime obsessed with pumping money into its military while desperately poor people went hungry. 'Pig feed, that's all we can eat,' he told me. 'Corn, we grind it into a porridge. No one can get full on that. There is no food, not even food from China. It's been blocked for three years.' Even if you had money there was nothing to buy, he said; any possessions were traded for what little food remained.

Mr Lee was not a defector or a refugee. His story was even more compelling because he was one of the 'lucky ones'. He was well off by his country's standards; he had relatives on the Chinese side who ran businesses. This was a financial lifeline for his family back home. Lee was able to work there himself, on a limited visa that restricted him to Dandong. But he crossed the border every six months just to keep his family alive.

'I can't not go back, I have to,' he said. 'I have a son and daughter. If I don't go back, they can't survive.'

This was just one man's story. A story of fear and horror under what, by most accounts, is one of the most repressive, paranoid regimes on earth. It is a story borne out by human rights groups, which report the deaths of millions during past famines, and of hundreds of thousands of dissidents locked up in brutal gulags.

In Dandong, we are ushered up the stairs of a concrete apartment block and into a small apartment to meet a woman who fled North Korea and now lives in constant terror. This small, frail woman reaches out to shake my hand, but I don't dare grip it too tight for fear that I might break her delicate bones. Her skin is jaundiced and her shoulders rounded; she is slightly stooped and her stomach looks bloated and swollen. Again, we cannot identify her, so we call her Miss Kim, a common name in Korea.

We sit in her living room and she tells me of her desperate escape from her homeland. Miss Kim was married and lived in a small village outside Pyongyang. This was during the famine in the 1990s, when millions of people are estimated to have died. (I say 'estimated' because the secretive North Korean regime maintains the number of dead was 250,000, but no serious observer believes that.) The famine has been described as the least understood humanitarian disaster of the period. People starved while the Kim regime lived in luxury and poured money into its war machine. The famine was government-induced: crazily, food production went into reverse. Floods and droughts made a bad situation worse.

Miss Kim says she was reduced to stripping bark from trees to boil down into a soup. She developed a serious kidney disease, and her husband and family deserted her. This was the harsh reality of life in North Korea: Miss Kim was a liability. People who were starving could not carry another hungry mouth, especially someone who was sick and could not work. She decided to risk all and flee the country. In the dark of night she waded into the Yalu River and crossed at its narrowest point, fearful that at any stage she might be spotted and shot.

When she made it to the other side, she was snatched by people smugglers – Chinese organised crime gangs that preyed on Korean defectors and sold them into what amounted to slavery. Miss Kim was traded to a Chinese farmer looking for a 'wife'. When he discovered how ill she was, he demanded his money back and dumped her. Miss Kim was rescued by a Korean Christian group, who paid for her freedom, if that's what it could be called. When I meet her she is hiding out in her apartment, unable ever to return home, and too scared to go out for fear she will be kidnapped again and sold back across the border, where she would certainly be executed.

Throughout our interview, Miss Kim stares intently into my face. I notice throughout how she picks nervously at her hand, digging her fingernails deep into her skin. Before we leave she asks my producer and interpreter if she can touch my face. Why, I ask. She tells me Miss Kim cannot believe how old I am. She thinks I must be much younger. Where she is from, people in their late forties do not look like me. They are old before their time; many die before they reach fifty. Miss Kim is still alive, but she will never be free, not while North Korea remains under the control of a totalitarian, murderous regime, suspicious and closed off from the world, which keeps its people locked down and cowed into submission.

As evening falls from the Chinese side of the border, Dandong becomes a city of light, while North Korea fades into darkness. Only the occasional dim glow faintly illuminates a black sky. Some more poor people are straggling along the riverfront. I can't help but think of the role fate plays in our lives. I could easily be one of those people I am watching in the distance; where I stand, on the other side of the border, is a mere accident of birth. We are separated by water, history and fate.

Mr Lee, for a while, stands on the lucky shore. But he shares the fear of his countrymen. He knows the reach of the North Korean regime. He is spied on, so he watches what he says and who he speaks to. He has taken an enormous risk even in the few minutes he allows me to walk alongside him. For all his privilege, he is as much a prisoner of the Hermit Kingdom as those whose lives are trapped within its borders.

*

As we leave our bus, we can barely hear a sound. We have stopped near a public square in the centre of Pyongyang. Our government minders whisked us here with just a moment's notice. In a country obsessed with secrecy, we are told where we will be taken only at the last minute. Our schedule can change even mid-trip. We'd started our day at the birthplace of the man North Koreans call the 'Great Leader' and the father of the country, Kim Il-sung. It is 2012, the centenary of his birth, and North Koreans are flocking here to pay homage. To these people, Kim is more than a leader – according to the constitution, he is 'president for eternity'.

Several months after I stood on the bridge at Dandong staring into the darkness of the secretive country over the border, I am in Pyongyang as the country prepares to crown a new leader. On my arrival in the North Korean capital from Beijing, I have to hand over my mobile phone and computer. From now on, every call I make, everything I write, every move, every meal, every person I speak to will be monitored by the Kim regime. This is all a PR stunt. I am being allowed into the country because the government wants to send a message to the world: that the Kim family remains in control, and that this nuclear-armed nation is still at war and will kill and die to defend itself. It is also a message to the North Korean people: look how strong we are that the world's media bows before the image of the great Kim family.

This is the price of reporting in North Korea. If this is what it takes to get a look inside this closed-off world, we will take it. Even if we catch just a glimpse of what is really happening here it will be worth it. I ask our government minder if we can speak to some people. In North Korea, it is forbidden for us to simply approach someone unannounced. He selects a group for us and then asks me to choose. They are young women, probably only in their twenties, and all from the same Pyongyang factory. They are clearly nervous, wary of our intentions.

'President Kim Il-sung is our father,' one lady says. 'We are one family, and because of his birth he has given us a powerful socialist state.'

Others here still mourn the loss of the Great Leader's son, the man they call the 'Dear Leader', Kim Jong-il, the previous December.

For one woman we meet this day, the tears have not stopped. 'We used to come here with happiness, but not anymore,' she says. 'My heart is breaking. This is why I can't stop crying.'

This is the power of the Kim cult. These men are dead, but in every other respect they are still alive. Here in an atheist communist country, it is no exaggeration to say they are godlike. The drab concrete skyline is brightened only by the splashes of colour of the countless thousands of portraits, paintings and statues of the leaders.

'Quickly, on the bus,' our minder orders us.

We are being rushed from our birthplace pilgrimage to what we are told is a great surprise. We race up a hill, and there before us is a sea of people. Everyone stands in rows, silent, not moving. Then a thunderous roar; before them two massive mosaics, the smiling faces of the Great Leader and his son materialise. The people rise as one, holding flowers and chanting. This is the adulation the regime demands.

Human rights groups and defectors claim that people can be sent to brutal gulags for not showing enough deference, or for the crime of having dust on one of the leader's portraits. In this way, the personality cult continues. And now the power is passed to a new generation. The youthful Kim Jong-un is now the Supreme Leader.

*

For just a moment we can hardly believe what is happening. The boyish leader takes a step towards the microphone, the massed ranks of the huge army he commands poised before him. And then he speaks. The adoring crowd who have been chanting his name fall silent. I am standing there at the very moment when these people hear their new leader speak for the first time. Some of them perhaps did not even know he existed; that's how secretive the Kim regime has been.

Kim Jong-un, not yet thirty years old, appears slightly nervous. His voice doesn't waver but his body moves back and forth restlessly and his eyes dart around. If his nerves betray him slightly, his words stay strong. He stands atop the shoulders of the men who have gone before him, his grandfather and father. Directly below him hang their huge portraits. The third generation of the Kim dynasty pledges to build on his family's legacy. But already, just with making this speech, he is veering from their path. It is something his father never did. The North Koreans I speak to say they can't recall ever hearing their leader's voice. To be here now is 'the greatest gift I have received in my life', one man says.

Kim Jong-un is speaking to two audiences: his people and the outside world. The newly crowned Supreme Leader vows to try to unite the fractured Korean nation, still separated after more than half a century.

'We have suffered the pain of separation for nearly seventy years,' he declares. 'We have lived as one people on the same land for thousands of years. To suffer like this is heartbreaking. Our party and our government will work with anyone who truly wants reunification.'

But this is not a day for talk of peace. This is a military parade, with all the menace this isolated nation can muster. To North Koreans, the display says they can defend themselves. To their enemies, especially the United States, there is a deadly message.

'Our military has become a powerful military able to handle any kind of modern warfare, with complete offensive and defensive capabilities,' Kim says. 'The foreign powers are not the only ones with a monopoly on military supremacy, and the days of their threatening and lying to us with atomic weapons are forever gone.'

It is 100 years since the birth of the founding father of the nation, Kim Il-sung. Installed as leader by Russia in 1945 after the liberation of Korea and the separation of the region into North and South Korea, he is still revered as a freedom fighter and hero. To honour his birthday, the military, one of the largest on earth, shows off its arsenal. Soldiers – men and women – goosestep with precision, while columns of tanks bearing the message 'We will smash the United States imperialists' roll across the great parade square.

The latest high-tech weapons then follow, including drones and missiles that have the potential to strike targets thousands of miles away. This is a battle-ready army, in a country still technically at war, and with soldiers determined to follow any order.

'With the strategy of the Great Leader, Kim Il-sung, the dear Kim Jong-il and Kim Jong-un, and with our bombs and weapons, we will destroy them,' a group of soldiers tells me.

In North Korea the army comes first, and no expense is spared. While it shows off its guns to the world, many people go hungry. The military is well fed, but aid agencies say the country's rural population suffers from chronic malnutrition and stunted growth as they scrounge for food. In a rare concession, Kim says his regime will not allow people to suffer any more – which is as close as he can get to admitting the government has failed the people in the past.

'Our fellow citizens, who are the best citizens in the world, who have overcome countless struggles and hardships, it is our party's firmest resolve not to let our citizens go hungry again,' he says.

Across the capital, people watching on are alive to this moment. When I approach one group and merely mention the name Kim Jong-un, they explode into chants and loud clapping. One man, beaming at our camera, says, 'We want to tell the world how proud we are to have such a man to lead us.' Kim has inherited the power, adulation and responsibility few people could possibly be prepared for. The world is watching, and wondering if he will be different from his forefathers – and whether he will even survive.

When the parade has passed Kim will face the reality of ruling this poverty-stricken pariah state.

*

North Korea exists in a time warp. It is modern, no doubt: the ideas that created the nation – Stalinism and Marxism, Hegel – emerged from the great explosion of Western thought in the eighteenth century. It is forged in war, a product of the bloody twentieth century. Yet in the twenty-first century it appears archaic, a relic of the Cold War. North Korea, perhaps more than any other nation on earth, has been sealed off from the West for decades.

This hits home to me one day sitting alongside the river in Pyongyang chatting to my government minder; it is one of those rare moments when we drop our guard and speak to each other like friends. It is his job to follow me everywhere I go. That's how it works in North Korea – the government monitors everything I do or say. But as the days pass, we slowly develop a bond. We share meals and hours in the back of a car, and he tells me that he is a musician; in his previous job he was responsible for chaperoning visiting orchestras. He much preferred that, he tells me, as musicians were less trouble than journalists. I am an amateur musician, and there's nothing I enjoy more than spending hours playing my guitar, so we talk about our shared love of music.

'Do you like The Beatles?' I ask. Then it hits me, this gulf of time and culture between us. He looks blank. 'You know, John Lennon, Paul McCartney – The Beatles?' He has never heard of them. This man whose passion was music has no idea about the most influential popular musicians of the twentieth century.

Veteran North Korea watcher Andrei Lankov says the secretive country can only be understood by going back in time. I found in North Korea what I searched for everywhere I reported: history, and how it bends us or breaks us, how it works its way into us and how the ghosts of our past whisper into our ears. It can poison us, history. It is an open wound. All the things the West thought it had buried in the twentieth century remain alive in this small, secretive country. To a West full of hubris, North Korea is baffling. How can it still stand? How could this regime have not been swept aside in the global triumph of liberalism? It is the undead, a ghost of the twentieth century that haunts a new century.

North Korea was born when the world was putting itself together after the devastation of World War Two. In 1945, Korea was liberated from three decades of Japanese colonial rule. But it became a nation divided, as the superpowers, the United States and the Soviet Union, carved up the post-war world. The Republic of Korea was established in the south in August 1948; a month later, Kim Il-sung was installed in the north as the leader of the Democratic People's Republic of Korea. Within two years the Korean Peninsula was at war, separating families, brother against brother. As Korea historian Bruce Cummings says, 'Koreans know this war in their bones.'

Why do the people not rise up? How can one family hold an entire country in fear? When people are starved, when they live under the constant gaze of a tyrannical state, when the world is shut out and information tightly controlled, surely they would say 'no more'. But I have long stopped being surprised at what people will live with. Something strange happens when you spend any time in a country like North Korea. Inside my hotel room, I settle into a routine: work, sleep, eat. It becomes, in its own way, so normal. I laugh, I listen to music, I go for walks in the hotel grounds, even finding beauty along the river, just as I would do anywhere else in the world. I even become used to working under government control: I find myself bonding with my state minders, enjoying our conversations, finding out about their families. We go for dinner in a local Korean barbeque restaurant and it just feels so utterly mundane. And I am someone who cherishes his freedom, who has spent a lifetime reporting many of the world's most brutal places. I am hardly one to be complacent, but day after day I find the outside world slipping from my mind. Imagine what it is like to know nothing else, to see your leaders as gods, to see the outside world as hostile and to live in a permanent state of war. 'Normal' here has an entirely different meaning.

This is the real North Korea, a world I see from a train. Visits to the country often don't get beyond Pyongyang, but this time we are travelling across the country to one of North Korea's missile sites. The Kim regime has invited foreign media there to show off the country's military might. North Korea has assembled an arsenal of nuclear weapons, as many as sixty, and now has the capacity to strike as far away as the United States or Australia. As we leave the capital, we are transported to a different world. Pyongyang is a show city, North Korea's face to the world. I keep hearing The Beatles telling me about living with eyes closed and misunderstanding all you see: that's Pyongyang. There are tall apartment blocks and shopping centres; I even visit an amusement park. The train station looks like a hive of activity, with people shuffling back and forth, dressed in business suits – the very model of a bustling world capital. Can I trust my eyes? I have been told that it is common here for actors to play roles – even just getting on and off buses or working in shops – for the benefit of visiting media. But outside the city limits, the harshness of life cannot so easily be hidden.

This land is poisoned and parched. Nothing grows here anymore, as pesticides and fertilisers have killed the earth. It is brown and cracked. As the hours go by, nothing changes, just a relentlessly austere landscape, and I find myself drifting into a deep melancholy. I can feel the hurt here, it is just a touch away. As dusk falls, I ask my cameraman, Scott Clotworthy, to film me speaking directly to camera: I want to convey what this moment means to me, to capture this feeling of being caught between worlds in this cloistered, shuttered kingdom of fear. Scott, in a stroke of genius, films my reflection in the train window, which adds an eerie quality, like a photo negative: there is reality and the trace of reality. I talk about the hold this country has on me, how I have peered over its border and shared the lives of those who have dared to escape, and how now I am here on this train, looking out on a land where people move more slowly.

Movement is meditative to me. Since I was a child, I have been entranced by the dancing light, as the moon strikes the water or the early sun brings the colours of the earth to life. My eyes would follow the headlights of our car bouncing off the trees, splintering the darkness. There's something in this, something primal. It is light that drew our ancestors to move forward to other lands. We have warmed ourselves by the light of fire and spun stories that explain who we are and what has brought us here.

The Greek god Prometheus created humans from clay and then stole fire to give us civilisation. But he was a trickster: his gift of light was also a curse. Prometheus, we are told, is the rebel who stands against tyranny; he is the spirit of revolution. Western civilisation worships the light; it is the path of progress. Christianity is described as the coming of the light. But Prometheus warns us too of over-reaching, and the dangers of knowledge. He has inspired great art and writing: Mary Shelley's *Frankenstein* was subtitled *The Modern Prometheus*.

Yes, that's what I have seen as I have followed the light on my own journey in the world: we are our own monsters.

8

CALL HIM IMRAN

Evil can be beautiful. It is a strange thing to say – or so I would have thought a long time ago, before I saw evil, true evil. Now I know what I didn't know then: that evil's beauty can be its power. Evil seduces us, it touches us in the places we keep covered. It knows our secret, that thing we dare not confess even to ourselves: that it dwells within us. No, more than that: given time and circumstance, we find it so easy to commit the most barbarous of acts. Evil need only whisper the right words and we will stop at nothing.

These things I have seen give me nightmares. Sometimes I think I have shaken those memories, and for a time I will sleep peacefully and I won't gasp for breath – but then the bad dreams return and I am back there, running from a faceless enemy, fighting off an imagined knife attack, smelling blood or the stench of burning flesh. Sometimes my wife will wake me, worried; at other times, she says, she just watches me and waits for it to pass. I wake up tired after those dreams, my body sore. It is always the face of evil I see, and it is so familiar because this evil is human. That's the truth – it isn't a thing with horns, it is you and it is me.

I saw the power and the beauty of evil in the mountains of Pakistan, and it spoke with the sweetest voice. If you can imagine the taste of a voice, it was like honey on my tongue. This voice was so soft; it was gentle and humble, and the sound of that voice seemed to come from somewhere and sometime so far away. It was a voice that could only be heard in some place open, windswept and desolate. It wasn't a voice that could come from a city; it had never strained to be heard because it spoke to the silence. When I think of that voice now, I hear it coming from a cloud, the sound filling the empty space, its echo bouncing off the trees and the rocks. If I were to die, I may be comforted that this voice was the last thing I would hear. And that is what it was meant to sound like, because this was the voice of death and this was a place of death.

The headless bodies were dumped in the town square. The severed heads themselves were left on doorsteps or impaled on posts. You might think that here was a place beyond grace, a place without God – except the men who did this killing called themselves God's warriors. They prayed five times a day; they read only the word of God. They grew their hair and beards long to honour God. Their god was to be feared; theirs was not a god of love; they had no place for forgiveness. There was no love. There was just God's law – at least, what these men determined that to be – and the promise of death for those broke it.

Violence like this strips life of everything that is precious. Decapitating heads and limbs is a ritual act of erasing the humanity of the victim. They no longer even look human: just dismembered bodies like discarded animals left to rot. At times like this, you have to remind yourself that these were people – fathers, sons, husbands – and they loved and were loved and laughed and cried. Their lives mattered. You have to cling to that, because these killers want to take that from us; they want us to stop seeing ourselves in each other. We must be bent to the will of God – the God without mercy.

In the worst places, I have seen the glory of the human spirit. It has never failed to fill me with awe how people find the will to go on: to give life meaning in spite of what we may see as senseless violence. So we owe it to these people never to forsake their humanity. We should never forget that these were shopkeepers, barbers, farmers, truck drivers, teachers or doctors, people who would have filled their days with dreams, thoughts, jokes, lies. They would have talked about what they planned for dinner, what would they watch on television, all that banality – the stuff that makes a day go slow, folding into a week, a month, a life – and all of it gone. That's what happened here: those little things, those things we might ordinarily complain about but that lend our lives meaning, were replaced by public floggings, empty streets and the absence of music or laughter. Children stay inside, girls can't go to school, women wrap their faces and stare at the ground and men grow longer beards because if they don't, they will hang from a lamppost as a warning to others.

They gave this town centre a new name: Zibahkhana Chowk, in English 'Slaughter Square'. It was now controlled by a band of Islamist militants whose name means 'students'; we know them as the Taliban. They had been formed in the madrasahs – Islamic schools – that spread rapidly throughout Pakistan from 1979 onwards: that year when the world tilted on its axis. The Islamic revolution in Iran and the Soviet invasion of Afghanistan would be a prelude to the end of the Cold War and the rise of a new sectarian terrorism. The madrasahs would provide the foot soldiers for what some would cast as a new holy war. These Islamic schools had been set up by General Muhammad Zia-ul-Haq, who ruled Pakistan as president from 1979 until his death in a plane crash – later ruled a criminal act of sabotage – ten years later. Some students were orphans of the war over the border in Afghanistan. These children didn't study literature or art or science and mathematics; they would just recite the holy Koran over and over, their bodies swaying in a trance.

The spread of these madrasahs corresponded with the growing jihad of the 1980s: the schools were funded by both predominantly Shia Iran and its rival for dominance of the Muslim world, Sunni Saudi Arabia. Iran and Saudi poured money into Pakistan, competing for influence. At the peak of the schools' influence, up to two million children attended them, according to estimates by the Pakistan government. Pakistani journalist Zahid Hussein, who has devoted his career to reporting the country's militant groups, says they developed links with international terrorism. In his book *Frontline Pakistan*, Hussein says that 'the trail of international terror led to the madrassas and mosques'.

By the mid-2000s, with the war on terror raging, I was spending more and more time in Pakistan. I fell in love with the rugged beauty of the country. It reminded me of Australia: much of it was dry and parched, and the eucalyptus trees made it smell like home. I have to admit I was drawn to the danger of the country too. In fact, at times when I was there it was dubbed the most dangerous country on earth.

It wasn't just that it was terrorist central; Pakistan was also nuclear armed, and locked in an existential stand-off with neighbouring India that at any moment threatened to ignite into all-out war. Unlike in other war zones, I was free to travel in Pakistan wherever I wished. It was an ally of America – technically Pakistan was on our side, even if only fools believed that – so I could attach myself to the Pakistani military and go right into the heart of battle. Much of the country was like the Wild West – you could go in but there was no guarantee you would get out. I pushed my luck on too many occasions. But I had willing compadres.

That was another thing that drew me to Pakistan: my heart skipped whenever CNN posted me there because I knew I would be working with the toughest, most resilient and beautiful people I could ever wish to work with. I was always among friends, local Pakistani people who worked alongside us and my TV crew who became like family to me. CNN – a company I would bleed for – asked a lot of us: long hours, sometimes days without sleep. The network had high expectations, failure was never an option and excuses were a weakness. For some it would be too much to handle, but it was fine by me.

On this trip in 2009 my cameraman, Sarmad Qaseera, and I had piled into a Pakistani Army helicopter in the early hours of the morning. We were flying from Islamabad to the Swat Valley in the northern part of the country. The Pakistanis pronounced it 'sir-wat' – impossible to spell, really, but make an elongated s sound and then slide into the final syllable. 'Ssseeer-wat', that's it. It is an extraordinarily beautiful place, what the locals called a little Switzerland. Soaring mountains and clear flowing streams made it a haven for tourists, but that was before the terror came. Now it was the place where the bodies were dumped in Slaughter Square.

The Pakistani Taliban had overrun Swat, forcing the army to flee. A madman had taken control. He was an imam – an Islamic preacher and scholar – known as Maulana Fazlullah. He rode a white horse and wore long flowing robes, like one of the horsemen of the apocalypse, and death followed soon after. He was dubbed the FM mullah because he had taken control of the local radio station, from where he would announce his daily decrees. He had outlawed music; women were ordered inside; girls were banned from school; men must not shave. He ruled by fear and violence. His daily sacrifices were a warning to others: submit or die. He would video executions and ritual whippings. These videos were sent to me and my crew; we would have to sit through them to decide what we could include and what we must leave out in my daily television news reports. In my mind I can still see men and women held down while another man repeatedly lashed them with a whip for breaking one of the mullah's laws. Fazlullah's right-hand man used to call me regularly on my mobile phone to give me the latest message the Taliban wanted broadcast.

Fazlullah waged war on the Pakistani forces for months, and he had the upper hand. He would orchestrate massacres across northern Pakistan, sparing no one, not man, woman or child. In the city of Peshawar, then a Taliban stronghold, Fazlullah's forces slaughtered 150 people at a local school. It was his men who in 2012 had shot into the face of a young schoolgirl, Malala Yousafzai, who became a global activist for the rights of girls and women in Pakistan. This was all still to come when I boarded the chopper to Swat.

After months of intense fighting, the army had pushed back Fazlullah's forces. Thousands of militants were killed, but there were hundreds of civilian casualties too. This battle forced more than two million people from their homes: they fled the area and sought shelter in makeshift refugee camps. The Taliban had retreated into the caves in nearby hills. The army held a shaky peace. Mingora was a shelled-out city of shattered buildings, and those people who remained were terrified; I saw them shivering in dark alleyways as I drove by with Pakistani soldiers. They didn't trust the army, thinking – not without some reason – that the military would desert them and the feared Fazlullah would return.

The Pakistanis wanted to show off the trophies of their war. Sarmad and I were taken to a barracks where weapons – guns, grenades, knives – where laid out on several tables. One of the army officers explained what the weapons were and where they'd been discovered. As an indication of just how organised and well-armed the Taliban were, the weapons had come from (among other places) Russia and China. There was distinctive Chinese writing on some, and notebooks were inscribed with Russian. The officer said that the Taliban had recruited Chinese Uighur Muslims and Chechen fighters from Russia: 'some pepper sprinkled in the salt', as he described it to me. But this was just a prelude to the Pakistanis' real prize. I was led to a man chained to a chair in the blazing sun. This was when I heard the sweet voice of death.

His name, I was told, was Imran – nothing more, just Imran. He was very tall, as Pashtun men often are. His skin was light, with a golden-reddish tinge, and his hair and beard too were red. His blue eyes – again not unusual here – only added to a picture of serene beauty. Beatific, in fact, in the full meaning of the word radiating a holy bliss. For Imran, I learned, was a holy man, an Islamic preacher. He had been one of Fazlullah's men, now captured by Pakistani soldiers, and I was brought here to interview him.

Imran was no simple preacher, nor just another of Fazlullah's henchmen; he fashioned himself as a holy man but he was in a very real sense the devil incarnate. I can think of nothing else to call him. If indeed it is the devil who tempts us, who offers us the gift of eternity in return for doing his work here on earth, then yes, Imran was the devil.

The army officer who brought me here told me that Imran – if in fact that was his real name – was the man who identified and trained suicide bombers. Boys would be kidnapped and brainwashed, turned into walking bombs and then turned loose. It was Imran's job to break down the boys, then convince them that it was their divine duty to kill. He knew what to say to them; he knew how to reach that part of them – perhaps, in other circumstances, the very best part of them – that so desperately wanted to believe in something, anything. This was the part of their soul that yearned for God, and in that need, Imran knew, these boys could not tell salvation from damnation. In return for giving their lives and taking the lives of others, he told them, Allah would offer them the fruits of heaven. How many lives had Imran destroyed in this way? This man before me, bound in chains, seemingly radiating heaven: what was I to think of him?

He spoke so slowly and softly that I had to lean forward to hear him. Close, close enough that I could feel his breath. I could see now how he used that power to draw people in, to bring them under his spell so that he could enter their hearts and their minds. Closer ... lean in closer ... then he's got you.

Imran's English was very good, and I wondered if he had been educated overseas. It wasn't unusual to find among the Taliban men who had studied at universities in Europe or the United States. The man I was in regular contact with – Fazlullah's media spokesperson, Muslim Khan, spoke in a broad American accent. He had lived in Boston and spent four years working as a painter in the United States. Khan had been a left-wing student activist in his youth, but like so many in search of an identity had drifted to Islamic fundamentalism.

We fool ourselves if we think that living in the West or receiving a broader education inoculates people against radicalism. It can have the opposite effect. Studying abroad can leave some feeling isolated, rejected, humiliated. For the first time, they experience racism or a clash of values and culture that leaves them disoriented, unsure of their place in the world. Their beliefs are often challenged, they are tempted by the freedoms of the West, and they can become self-loathing. The study of Enlightenment philosophy, liberalism, democracy doesn't open them up to the world but turns them against it.

One of the founders of modern Islamic radicalism, an Egyptian named Sayyid Qutb, studied in Colorado and read voraciously of science, literature and philosophy. When he left he wrote about 'The America I Have Seen', lamenting the West's individualism, racism, even its 'poor haircuts'. He was appalled at what he saw as the loose morals of American youth of the 1940s, what he described as 'the animal like mixing of the sexes'. Not that Qutb completely averted his eyes: he recognised the 'seductive capacity' of American girls with 'expressive eyes, and thirsty lips'. To Qutb, Americans were 'primitives' living amid 'deviant chaos, and the endless means of satisfying animalistic desires, pleasures and awful sin'; he returned to Egypt rejecting everything he had seen and became a leading figure in the Muslim Brotherhood.

Qutb published widely and advocated violent struggle. He was later convicted of plotting the assassination of Egypt's secular nationalist president, Gamal Abdel Nasser – a man Qutb saw as having betrayed him – and was executed. In death, Qutb became a martyr, and his stature grew among a new generation of angry young Muslims, among them an Egyptian doctor, Ayman al-Zawahiri, who became a founder of al-Qaeda, and another rich young Arab, someone the world would soon come to know, Osama bin Laden. Bin Laden was the son of a billionaire construction tycoon. His family was close to the Saudi royals and lived the life of the jet set. The many Bin Laden siblings – his father is believed to have had up to 50 children – holidayed in Europe. They attended universities in England. But Osama from a young age was different. He stayed behind in Saudi Arabia and entered university in the tumultuous year of 1979. He studied alongside members of the Muslim Brotherhood, and among his teachers was Abdullah Azzam – a man who would become known as the father of global jihad – and Sayyid Qutb's brother Mohammed.

The young Osama watched the events in Afghanistan closely. He met Afghan fighters during the Hajj and within a few years joined the fight against the Soviet Red Army himself. Inspired by Islamist teachings, he led a group of fighters in the struggle against the Soviet invasion. By then Pakistani and Saudi intelligence agencies were working with the CIA to support the Afghan resistance. As Steve Coll points out in his book *Ghost Wars*: 'Working together they purchased and shipped Afghan rebels tens of thousands of tons of weapons and ammunition.' Coll says by 1985 CIA funding topped US$250 million, with the Saudis matching it dollar for dollar. Saudi Arabia was also funnelling money into the madrasahs in Pakistan that became a breeding ground for jihadists. The anti-Western ideas of Sayyid

Qutb spread like a virus. The man in front of me, Imran, was directly connected to the ideology that had brought violence to the streets of New York, London, Paris and Sydney, and sparked a never-ending war that had cost so many innocent Muslim lives.

'I am sorry,' Imran whispered. Over and over he repeated it: how sorry he was, how he could see now the wrong he'd done. He told me how we should all be brothers, not enemies. Of course the world looked very different now to Imran, chained to a chair facing his own imminent death. The man who had sent others to do his killing, who had promised them a martyr's paradise, was now facing his own mortality – and failed his own test. He was no man of God; he was a weak man who lacked the conviction of his own twisted version of his faith.

I had seen the evil Imran had done. I had stood in bloodied market places in Pakistan and watched as grieving mothers picked bits of smouldering flesh out of shrapnel-marked holes in the walls to put into plastic bags because it was all they had left of their children to bury. What this man represented, what he had let loose in the world, sickened me. Yet with this defenceless, hollowed-out figure now before me confessing his remorse, I couldn't help but feel pity, even sadness. Not just for Imran as a human being, but for all who had died and suffered – for everything that had brought us to this place, all of the hatred and vengeance in our world that pits us against each other. And there was that voice: a soothing, healing voice, a voice that sounded like the sweetness of heaven, yet had poisoned the minds of so many young men and turned them into killing machines.

I had my story – this was what the Pakistani Army had brought us here for. They wanted a PR coup: to show that they were pushing back against a militant force that had come within a couple of hours' drive of the nation's capital, Islamabad. As we boarded the helicopter to return to our bureau, I could see that my cameraman, Sarmad, was as troubled as me. He was a hard man, Sarmad, but bruised too by the world. He was an Iraqi who had been traumatised by a childhood under the rule of Saddam Hussein. He came to CNN as a cameraman during the war, with little English but limitless courage and a determination that his country would see better days. He was a roly-poly figure, bald before his time. He was also an incorrigible gossip, always running stories back and forth, not in a malicious way, but just to put a smile on our faces. His high-pitched voice and wicked humour were always enough to break a sombre mood. Sarmad brought light to the darkness of covering war. We used to love going to a little ice cream parlour in Islamabad called Hot Spot – it was the only alternative to pubs or bars, which are a little harder to find in Pakistan. (To get a licence to drink, I would have to sign a form admitting to being a certified alcoholic, and to be honest I preferred the ice cream parlour to pubs and bars anyway.) Whenever we came back from a hard day, Sarmad would say, in a mock American accent, 'Wanna go to Haaart Spaaart?' I was already thinking about how we would need Hot Spot after this day.

When you spend a lot of time with someone in hard places, you rub off on each other. There are many colleagues I have worked with who are such a part of me that they are family. We learn to read each other's moods, know when to give each other space or make a joke, when to sing a song; we know what each other thinks, and we finish each other's sentences. As the helicopter rose into the air, Sarmad looked to me and asked if I didn't think that man's voice was beautiful. 'He sounded like a holy man, didn't he?' Sarmad said.

I was relieved to hear Sarmad say that. It wasn't just me – I hadn't spent too long out here and become delusional. We agreed that even Imran's face, so serene and noble, was captivating. This is what evil does: it lures us, and it is never what we think it is. Evil is a shapeshifter, a mirror that reflects what we want to see. In Imran, the Taliban had chosen a voice of God to do the devil's work. He was ugly inside, with a tortured, brutal, hate-filled mind, and he preyed on faith and took the goodness of young boys and used it against them.

9

WAR OF THE GREAT FAITHS

'We love death like you love life.'

When Osama bin Laden spoke those words, he believed he was speaking the words of God. His war would be a holy war, and death its highest reward. This was the war he would fight, a war of the soul against a heathen enemy. It was a war of the ages, a continuation of a battle of a thousand years that pitted two great faiths against each other: Islam and Christianity. The Crusades had never ended for Bin Laden: the world would submit or die.

Bin Laden believed the infidels were weak and would run from the smell of their own blood. He would strike the far enemy – the United States – and lure it onto his battleground, where he would light a fire that would engulf the near enemy – those Muslim leaders he saw as apostates, termed kafirs – who had betrayed Islam and become too close to the West. Bin Laden announced his declaration of war with the most spectacular and audacious terror attack we'd see in our time. He would strike at the heart of Western capitalism and bring the Twin Towers of New York down on the American people.

It happened as Americans were heading to work, and I was about to go to bed far away in Australia. None of us would ever be the same, for that moment set off a chain reaction of war, economic collapse, revolution and, in time, a rise of political populism in the West that has shaken democracy to its core. Just ten years before the 9/11 attacks, the Soviet flag was lowered over Red Square in Moscow to signal the end of the Cold War. The world was meant to enter a glorious new era of liberal democracy, but the attacks on the United States brought that to a spectacular end.

This was an attack on everything the West represented. It was a horrific rejection of modernity: for Bin Laden, there would be no world of perpetual peace. To him, America was a symbol of Western hypocrisy: it spoke of liberty and freedom, but represented oppression and occupation of Arab lands. His attack that day would remake the world order: in the years ahead, despots would fall, borders would be redrawn and walls would go back up. Two decades of bloodshed would weaken the most powerful country the world has known, and America in retreat would look like a country no longer sure of what it believes.

For me, watching the television news that night would begin a journey around the world that would end a decade later when I stood outside the home of Osama bin Laden after crack American special-forces troops had come in the darkness and killed him.

I had just finished watching *The West Wing* on television; in the George W. Bush years this was an alternative universe for political progressives, who could suspend reality and believe that the fictional president, Jed Bartlet, was real. These were gentler times, no doubt about it. Australia was in the midst of what would be an unparalleled period of economic growth; the emergency of climate change was just entering our consciousness; the bloom was just coming off Cool Britannia as Oasis – the band that wrote the soundtrack to the Tony Blair years – descended into ever more self-indulgent Beatles parody. Tracey and I had just had our son. She was asleep with him in our room, and I was staying up putting the final touches to my book *The Tears of Strangers*, which would soon be published. I was about to turn off the television when the news broke that a plane had struck one of the Twin Towers in Manhattan. I immediately switched to CNN, thinking like the rest of us that it was probably a light plane that had veered tragically off course. But this was no small plane and no accident. Then the second plane struck. I woke my wife and told her what had happened, then phoned one of my closest friends to see if he was watching.

Jeff McMullen was a former reporter for the popular current-affairs program *60 Minutes*. He had a long and distinguished journalistic pedigree, having been a foreign correspondent covering many of the world's hotspots. Like me, he was back home in Sydney, and in fact we lived in the same suburb. Jeff was married to Kim Hoggard, who had been a White House official during the presidency of Ronald Reagan. Kim had been one of the deputies to Secretary of State Jim Baker, and on the inside of high-powered political discussions. She answered when I called, and I asked if she had the television on. 'Turn it on now,' I said. I knew this would hit Kim, as an American, especially hard. Her country was under attack.

In the days to come, we would all learn of this mysterious figure named Osama bin Laden, the son of a Saudi billionaire who had turned his back on riches to fight in Afghanistan's war against the Soviet Union. He had embraced a doctrinaire, radical version of Islam. It has several names – Wahhabism, Salafism – and as with any ideology, there are power struggles among its leaders. This ideology had grown out of the mosques of the Middle East, based on a fundamentalist reading of the Koran and a rejection of what its followers saw as a decadent, oppressive West. Wahhabi scholars taught at the madrasahs in Pakistan that spawned the Taliban. All advocated violent struggle, yet some argued against killing other Muslims and opposed suicide bombing. But Bin Laden would stop at nothing. This man could have been partying in the nightclubs of Paris, like some of his siblings, but he had chosen an austere life as what he saw as a warrior for God.

Bin Laden was a striking figure, tall, charismatic, with a regal and, if I'm honest, an apparently spiritual bearing. He wasn't a name on most lips, but he was familiar to intelligence officials. He had formed a terrorist network known as al-Qaeda – which translates as 'The Base' – and had carried out attacks on US embassies in Kenya and Tanzania in 1998. In 2000 – a year before the 9/11 attacks – his suicide bombers had struck the USS *Cole* at a port in Yemen. Before we even knew about him, Bin Laden had officially declared war on us. In 1996, from a cave in Afghanistan, he had issued a fatwa; we still live under his order of death.

In some ways we can see Bin Laden as the enemy we created. It was American CIA money flushed through Pakistan's intelligence service – the ISI – that helped Bin Laden establish himself in Afghanistan. Does this make America complicit in the rise of al-Qaeda? Was Bin Laden a de facto agent of the United States? No, that would be wrong. But he was perhaps an agent of convenience. American intelligence established contact with Bin Laden's Arab jihadists via the back door: through Pakistan into

Afghanistan. But everything Bin Laden stood for and the subsequent war on terror are unintended consequences of the Cold War.

After the Red Army's invasion, Afghanistan became another front in the ideological battle between the West and the Soviet Union. Bin Laden was never 'on our side'; he despised the United States and what he saw as decadent Western liberalism. But if my enemy's enemy is my friend, then America and Bin Laden could conveniently join forces.

Bin Laden led his Mujahideen – jihadists – to join the battle alongside the warriors who would become the Taliban, armed and funded by the United States. It was in Afghanistan that the myth of Bin Laden was born. He slept in the trenches and fought on the front lines with his men. In their book *The Exile*, journalists Catherine Scott-Clark and Adrian Levy describe a battle against Soviet troops where Bin Laden's men were outnumbered and facing a near certain death. Inexplicably, the Red Army pulled back, not just handing Bin Laden a victory but making him a legend. The journalists describe Bin Laden picking up a Kalashnikov rifle from a dead Soviet soldier: it became the al-Qaeda leader's totem. 'Men without weapons are incomplete,' he would say.

Bin Laden left Afghanistan and returned to Saudi Arabia, where he grew more embittered. He left for Sudan and spent five years building roads and dreaming of the great battle he saw ahead. When he returned to Afghanistan, he set himself up in a place called Tora Bora ('Black Cave'). Scott-Clark and Levy describe him spending his nights ranting into a Dictaphone about the war he would wage on the West. He believed God visited him in his dreams. It would be wrong though to depict him as delusional. He was in his way rational, committed and deeply read, and he had built an international militant network. He surrounded himself with others who shared his vision and fed his hatred of the infidels.

Bin Laden and his followers lived under the protection and hospitality of the Taliban. But he had a sometimes-tense relationship with the Taliban Supreme Leader, Mullah Mohammed Omar, who demanded the al-Qaeda leader bow to his authority and keep a low profile. Mullah Omar himself was a legendary figure who stood around two metres tall and was powerfully built. Like Bin Laden, he forged his reputation in the war against the Soviet Red Army. Also like Bin Laden, he lived an austere life of near silence. He spoke very sparingly, rarely left his stronghold of Kandahar, and shunned outsiders. Mullah Omar shared something else with Bin Laden: he too saw his fate in a dream, where a young woman appeared and called him to lead Afghanistan out of chaos. In 1994 he founded the Taliban, recruiting from the madrasahs on the Pakistan–Afghanistan border. A year later he seized power in a civil war with other Afghan warlords.

Bin Laden would not allow Mullah Omar to interfere with his plans for a global war. He said to one of his aides that it was 'not the prerogative of Mullah Omar to prevent me from embarking on Jihad'. This war, Bin Laden said, would be the 'gateway to the future'. The planned 9/11 attacks already had a code name: 'Planes Operation', a scheme to hijack aircraft and strike multiple targets inside the United States. New York's World Trade Centre was already marked out.

It had been bombed in 1993 by a Pakistani, Ramzi Youssef, killing six people and injuring a thousand. Now Youssef's uncle,

Khalid Sheikh Mohammed, a Kuwait-born Pakistani militant nicknamed Mokhtar, had penetrated Bin Laden's inner circle. Some thought Mokhtar crazy, but his plan to finish the job of his nephew intrigued Bin Laden. Sheikh Osama, as his followers called him, had already issued a decree that it was the duty of all Muslims to kill Americans and their allies; in a rare interview with CNN, Bin Laden accused America of 'hideous, criminal acts'. America, he said, was under the control of the Jews and had occupied Muslim holy lands. Now, in Mokhtar he had found someone who would help him fulfil his vision, and he funded the Pakistani to bring his apocalyptic vision to reality. Planes Operation now took on a new code name: Holy Tuesday. The date for the attack was fixed: 11 September 2001.

We can't say we were not warned. In the months leading up to the attack that would change the course of our world, American intelligence was intercepting messages about an impending big operation. President George W. Bush had even received FBI briefings that al-Qaeda was planning to hijack planes and strike buildings in New York. Bin Laden himself made no secret of this coming war – in fact he wanted the world to know. Sheikh Osama summoned a Saudi television crew for an interview where he told of what was to come. Down the barrel of the camera, he proclaimed that 'Islam's victory is coming'. First al-Qaeda would strike the Twin Towers, then lure America into Afghanistan – long called the graveyard of empires. Like Alexander the Great and the Soviet Union before him, America, said Osama, would meet its end in the mountains of the Hindu Kush.

On the day of the attack, Bin Laden had told those close to him that 'it is very important to see the news today'. The al-Qaeda leader himself did not get to see what he had orchestrated.

He was on the road, in a convoy travelling to the Pakistani border, and the satellite signal was too weak; instead, he and his men tuned into news reports on a short-wave radio. Reporter Jason Burke, in his book *The 9/11 Wars*, describes Bin Laden holding up a finger for each strike: first one, then another, then a third for the strike on the Pentagon. He was expecting a fourth, but the hijacked plane had crashed into a field in Pennsylvania after passengers had bravely wrestled back control from the terrorists. With each strike, the men 'wept and prayed'. Mullah Omar, far from Bin Laden, knew the Americans would come: soon they would rain down missiles on his land and sweep the Taliban from power. But despite strains with Bin Laden and warnings from the United States, Mullah Omar would not give up Sheikh Osama. The war of civilisations had begun, just as Bin Laden had dreamed it would: this was a forever war passed down through the generations. A war of the great faiths.

*

The nineteenth-century French author Victor Hugo wrote, 'For six thousand years war has pleased the quarrelling peoples and God has wasted his time making the stars and the flowers.' Was he right? Are we condemned to war? Is this our natural state, and the stars and the flowers and the dream of peace are just the folly of God?

I have asked myself this question over and over; it is a question that has haunted me for as long as I can remember. I have given my life over to this question. Not only have I spent much of my career reporting on the horrible things we do to one another, I myself was born into the shadow of war and suffering.

From the time I was a child I was told the stories of my own history: how my family had endured invasion and colonisation. I saw the toll that took on the lives of those I loved. No land has been spared the killing; Australia is no different. Yet I saw also the bravery and courage of those in my own family for whom the heavy weight of history was lightened by the strength of faith.

I am one of those who can say that they are blessed by the presence of God, call it what you will. I have never felt the absence of a loving spirit guiding my life. That same spirit lives in the struggles of ordinary people staring down adversity and suffering in countries like Syria, Afghanistan, Pakistan, Iraq, China and North Korea. And yet I know too that we are weak, and I know how easily we can bend to tyranny. More than that – we are drawn to it; some part of us craves the certainty that tyranny brings. In the battle for our souls, I can't help but wonder if the darkness will forever devour the light.

This question has troubled the minds of scientists, philosophers and poets through the ages. Love and war are the eternal themes of art and politics and faith. The earliest surviving work of literature, *The Epic of Gilgamesh*, written two thousand years before the birth of Christ, is a meditation on love and war. Gilgamesh embarks on a great journey to discover the secret of eternal life, but he learns that he will never find this life he searches for: 'For when the gods created man, they let death be his share, and life withheld in their own hands.'

Are we all smeared with the blood that the biblical Cain drew from his brother Abel? Surely we know by now how easy it is to kill and to command others to do our killing. The history of humanity tells us that much. History, Hegel wrote, is a 'slaughter-bench at which the happiness of peoples, the wisdom of states, and the virtue of individuals have been victimised'. Where is God in all this carnage? Victor Hugo was wrong – God is not always in the flowers and the stars. For much of the past two thousand years, God has been at the head of his armies. From Constantine's spiritual awakening in battle outside Rome in the year 312 AD to the end of Europe's bloody Thirty Years' War in 1648, war shaped the birth of the modern world. Historian Arnaud Blin writes in *War and Religion* that 'the many wars that rocked and shaped Europe, the Mediterranean, and the greater Middle East were in one way or another driven or influenced by religion'.

Of those warring faiths, two stood above the rest: Christianity and Islam. What can be a source of love or forgiveness can also be a force of destruction. These two monotheistic religions sought control of the world and have sacrificed countless millions of lives to impose their universal truth. From the seventh century, the armies of Muhammad had conquered territories from Europe to North Africa, carving out previously Christian territory. For two centuries from 1096 to 1271, Christians waged their war to recapture the Holy Land from Islam. What began as a small pacifist sect had, by the twelfth century, Blin writes, become a force 'to wage and support holy war'.

Christianity was at war with itself from the Reformation of 1517, Martin Luther's Protestant rebellion against the Catholic Church. The invention of the printing press the century before put Bibles into the hands of ordinary people, sparking what today we might see as a populist movement to overthrow absolutist rule from Rome. By the seventeenth century, the wars of religion – the Thirty Years' War – destroyed half of Europe, leaving eight million people dead and remaking the world. It ended with the Treaties of Westphalia, which would set out the parameters of what has become the modern political state. The West has now prised apart God and Caesar: the separation of church and state is a foundation of liberal democracy. But in fundamentalist Islam, God is inseparable from politics.

The prophet Muhammad believed God spoke to him in a dream. It is no wonder that his twentieth-century followers, Bin Laden and Mullah Omar, would claim the same divine inspiration. From the start Islam was a warrior faith. The word 'Islam' means submission: there is no God but Allah, and no word higher than the word of God. Muhammad spread Islam at the point of a sword. When he was driven from Mecca in 622 AD he counted just dozens of followers, but fewer than ten years later he would return with an army of a thousand men. Arnaud Blin argues that, compared to other faiths, 'Islam has been much more consistent in its attitude to war': it understood the need to keep the peace within but prepare for war from outside, revolving around the Dar al-Islam (house of Islam) and the Dar al-Harb (house of war). According to Blin, 'Islam was committed to violence almost from the very beginning, and violence has remained a part of its makeup, including its message.'

Middle East scholar Raymond Ibrahim says Muhammad spoke to the powerful Arab tribalism. Under Islam, Muslims everywhere would form a 'super tribe' – the Umma – and 'its natural enemy remained everyone outside it'. The Islamic doctrine of *al-wala' wa-l-bara"* ('loyalty and enmity') became a battle cry. The Koran describes non-Muslims as 'vile animals and beasts, the worst of creatures and demons'. It says non-believers 'are to be beheaded; terrorised, annihilated, crucified, punished and expelled'. Those Muslim martyrs who fall in battle 'are to be forgiven from the first drop of blood. He sees his throne in paradise.' Muhammad sent messages to his Christian enemies to 'submit to Islam and have peace'. This doctrine underpinned Islamic imperialism, and it is used to inspire violent jihad today.

Terrorism is a rejection of what the West calls civilisation. The butchers of Pakistan's Swat Valley, including the evil Imran with his voice like honey, rebel against everything that Western modernity stands for. In their eyes the West is weak. Everything it advocates – the values of pluralism, tolerance, cosmopolitanism, the belief in a perpetual peace of shared humanity – is a lie. These Islamist militants have been shaped by colonisation and Western imperialism. They feed on a diet of vengeance, a history of humiliation whispered into their ears from childhood. The world is against them; they hear this week after week in mosques from Mecca to Kabul. Theirs is a selective reading of the Koran: like the other great holy books, it also preaches love and peace and charity.

The war these militants are fighting is a war for the soul of Islam as much as it is a war against the West, and they use their faith to justify the slaughter of their own people. More Muslims have died at the hands of these so-called defenders of the faith than at the hands of American soldiers. I have lived with Muslim people, shared their tables and slept alongside them. I have worked with people of astounding charity, goodness and love, and I know they draw those values from the same Koran that others use to inspire hate.

*

Before dawn in a run-down neighbourhood in the Afghan capital of Kabul, a boy pumps water from an old well. In the background a rooster calls to mark the breaking of the day. Dozens of boys slowly file into a decrepit house, with a bare floor and tattered walls. This is a madrasah, and I have come here with my CNN television crew. It is a rare chance to see up close what these boys are learning. These children have known nothing but war. Their parents were raised in conflict. Afghanistan has been a land at war for centuries; in modern times, the guns have rarely fallen silent since the Soviet invasion in December 1979. These children were not being taught literature, science or mathematics: their lessons were in the ways of holy war.

The Red Army marched into Afghanistan to support the country's communist government, which had seized power just three years before, when left-wing military officers overthrew the centrist government headed by President Mohammed Daoud Khan. The new government had little public support and brutally purged any opposition. It implemented a range of land and social reforms that further enraged a devoutly Muslim populace. Insurgencies rose up against the government, sparking a civil war. These militias were known as Mujahideen – jihadists – and they were ultimately joined by Arab fighters including Osama bin Laden, inspired by dreams of a great battle for God. Moscow ordered the deployment of thirty thousand troops to prop up its client state; it would be bogged down in Afghanistan for the next ten years as some of its own soldiers deserted. The Afghan War helped bring about the end of the Soviet empire.

The power vacuum prompted by the Soviet pull-out led to the Taliban seizing control. Initially, the Islamist insurgents were greeted as saviours by a fractured nation ruled by rival warlords. As a Pashtun movement, the Taliban represented the single biggest ethnic group in the country. It cemented its stronghold by defending the rights of women in particular. But the Taliban would become an oppressor, banning girls from school, stopping some from working, and imposing strict Islamic law. Simple pleasures like music were banned, other than the human voice singing the praises of God. By the time I visited this small madrasah in Kabul in 2011, the Taliban government had been toppled by the United States and its allies, but its message lived on.

Working in countries like Afghanistan depended on building strong relationships of trust with local people. CNN employed Afghan journalists to help organise and set up stories and interpret the Afghan languages. It had taken several weeks to get access to this school, as the imam was suspicious of outsiders. The school had been raided before, with police discovering weapons hidden under the floorboards; the previous imam was arrested.

I worked closely with an Iranian-American cameraman, Farhad Shadravan, who was the most talented camera operator I had ever worked with; he also became one of the closest friends I have in the world. His family is my family, and we are bonded in ways that can never be broken. It helped that Farhad understood the local language – his native Farsi and Pashto are very similar. It also helped that we were not white. Unshaven and dressed in local clothes, Farhad and I could move more easily around the city. We would often skip out from our heavily fortified bureau to eat in local restaurants and get a feel for life on the ground.

On this day, the boys in the madrasah barely pay us any mind. It may have something to do with the type of learning they are being trained in: I watch for hours as they slowly rock themselves into a trance. Back and forth, back and forth, moving in hypnotic repetition. They chant passages from the Koran over and over. The imam beats time with a stick as the boys commit the word of God to memory. It is an unnerving sight, watching children surrender themselves this way. The imam commands unquestioned authority. It is so different to any classroom I grew up in: there is no laughter, no schoolboy pranks. No boy even raises his hand to ask a question – and of course there are only boys, no girls allowed. In this classroom there is just obedience and the same message repeated time and again: that there is no god but Allah, and the non-believers are infidels to be hated.

The imam himself is a smiling, rotund, gentle man. His demeanour could not be more different from the words that come from his lips. When I sit cross-legged with him on the floor, he tells me that 'God says we can never be friends with unbelievers. What do they know of our religion? We can never be friends.' By this stage the United States and allies have been in Afghanistan for nearly a decade, and this is a chilling reminder that, for all of its force and despite toppling the Taliban, the foreign troops have failed to win Afghan hearts and minds. In fact, the resentment has only deepened.

The boys I speak to damn America and praise Osama Bin Laden. 'The Americans are doing suicide attacks and they blame Osama Bin Laden,' one boy tells me. The imam says that his children are 'like fruit' – they need to be ripened. When they come to him, he says, 'I train them the right way'. That way is strict sharia law. The boys tell me that girls must stay indoors: to go outside without a veil 'is filthy'.

These boys were being schooled to fight for Islam. I was left in no doubt that they would sacrifice themselves for their faith. In the raid on the school, police found not only guns and grenades but suicide vests. When I visited, the school was under constant watch. But the boys remained loyal to their old teacher, now in prison. He was linked to a Pakistani militant group. To these boys, though, his arrest was part of an American conspiracy. One boy told me that American troops would drug and kidnap imams and take them far away – 'They would stick needles in their chests and pull them out the other side,' he said.

Like boys anywhere, these children played outside during their school break, but when they did they played with toy guns. They engaged in mock battles and pointed the guns at me and Farhad. They were laughing like boys do anywhere, but behind those smiles there was a much deadlier intent: they were being raised to fight Americans, to continue a holy war of a thousand years – and they believed that God was on their side.

10

MURDER IS THE QUESTION

The things I have seen weigh heavily on my soul. It isn't just the violence and the misery that I reported on, but the stories of these people, which connected deeply with my own. When I looked into the eyes of a child or a parent in a refugee camp, I saw the eyes of my own family. Reporting the world was my way of trying to understand myself. Like the people of Afghanistan, Pakistan, Iraq or China, I had been shaped by history. My family's story, too, was one of invasion, occupation, colonisation and oppression. We had been left on the margins, excluded, impoverished and imprisoned. I knew how easy it was for small peoples everywhere to feel the humiliation of history, to feel angry and grow bitter at some still-open wound, and to hate the people you believe inflicted it. In other circumstances in another country, I too could have been one of those boys rocking backwards and forwards in the madrasah in Kabul, surrendering my mind to hate.

I was an exile, I suppose. I chose to live away from Australia because it weighed down on me too hard. I didn't want to feel as though I had to fight the battles of my ancestors. Where is the freedom in that? And yet wherever I went, I took my history with me. I could never be free from its shackles. So I sought out those stories that would speak to me. In the lives of others I could ask the questions of myself that burned inside me. If history does live in us – and I know that to be true – then aren't we also doomed? Those who don't remember the past are condemned to repeat it: another lie. Those who remember the past too well repeat it over and over and over again. The truth does not always set you free: the truth can handcuff us to a history that we cannot change. The boys in the Kabul madrasah were not being taught about freedom; their minds were not opened to the great thinkers of history, those philosophers who had imagined a world beyond warring tribes. But the West had betrayed its own ideals; Western nations had built empires and invaded nations bringing suffering and misery to subjugated people. To these boys America had become the symbol of Western hypocrisy. They were taught that the Americans were their enemy – that I was an enemy – and that history defined them.

This is the return of history. It is a fever, a rage. Where injustice lives, this anger festers. I have said it before, but it bears repeating: history can be the poison in the blood of our identities, what the Polish Nobel laureate poet Czesław Miłosz called 'the memory of wounds'. History is a festering wound, to be picked at over and over, never allowed to heal. This has been my world: my nightmares.

It is standing in a bombed-out marketplace where the blood boils; it is so hot it gurgles under my feet. It is twisted metal and the stench of burning flesh. I remember a double bus bombing in Beersheba in Israel, a scene of dead bodies, broken glass – and there among it all was a small packet of chocolate teddy bear biscuits, and on the box the bloodied handprint of a child. These are the things that rattle me the most. The thought that here was a child – just like my children – on a bus ride with his parents, eating biscuits and talking excitedly, and then in an instant gone. Why? Standing there, that night, the only answer I had was that the world is insane. We cling to our tribes, waging a historical blood feud without end. Within hours the glass was cleaned up, the blood washed away and the wrecked buses removed; the road was reopened and life proceeded as if this were any other day. I called my wife on the way back to the bureau and we arranged to meet for dinner.

Albert Camus wrote: 'In the age of ideologies, we must make up our minds about murder. If murder has rational foundations, then our period and we ourselves have significance.' It is this violence that can give our lives meaning. We have made up our minds about murder, and we have decided we are okay with it. If we weren't, we would not keep committing it, as we have done from World War to World War, from Korea to Vietnam, to the Balkans, to Afghanistan and Iraq and Syria and Yemen. We are okay with it. Sometimes it comes to us – it is true, sometimes war is necessary. Tyranny cannot stand. The slaughter of innocents cannot stand. Terrorism that can strike in our streets cannot stand. So we choose our sides and we do our killing and we are okay with it. As Camus wrote, '[I]deology ... limits itself to repudiating other people ... this leads to murder. Everyday masked assassins slip into some cell: murder is the question of today.'

*

My dear friend Farhad was an exile too, just like me. His life too was shrouded by history. His family were persecuted for their

Baha'i faith and fled Iran for the United States. He was a child of the 1970s, again just like me. We shared a love of movies, books and music. We both played guitar and would spend hours locked down in our bureaus in Kabul, Islamabad and Iraq swapping songs. It was our way of dealing with the stress.

'Hey, do you know this one?' And I would start strumming David Bowie's 'Starman'.

'What about this?' And Farhad would play something by Fleetwood Mac.

So many songs: I would strum 10cc's 'I'm Not in Love' and Farhad would chime in with a pitch-perfect vocal, knowing all the lyrics. He loved it when we were editing and I'd play a little jazz version of Hank Williams' 'Hey, Good Lookin'' and he would do a little whispered introduction – 'Welcome to the happy hour at the Sunset Motel, my friend and I would like to do this little number for you' – like we were in some smoky bar in the American south.

Music was our great solace over one hot and bloody summer in Pakistan. The Pakistani Taliban had continued its offensive. The Swat Valley, where I had interviewed Imran, was still a battlefield. I had struck up a friendship with the commander of Pakistan's Northern Forces, General Nadeem Ahmed. He had responsibility for the most brutal parts of the country, the Federally Administered Tribal Areas, or FATA, which ran along the border with Afghanistan. This was a hotbed of insurgency and a Taliban stronghold. It was an indication of the crazy freedom of Pakistan – what drew me there – that if we wished, we could go right into the heart of the battlefield. There was no guarantee we would come back, but there was nothing stopping us if the story was worth the risk.

General Ahmed flew his own helicopter, and offered to chopper Farhad and me into the war zone over Swat. We woke early to meet him at the Islamabad military airstrip, and as usual put on our favourite song of that summer, 'She's Been Talking' by the New Zealand rock band The Mutton Birds. I had introduced Farhad to a lot of antipodean music, and he loved The Mutton Birds – there was something in their swooping, jangly guitar and minor chord melodies that touched the sadness in both of us, but they also lifted us out of our gloom with soaring harmonies that reminded us of the great pop bands of the sixties. We needed a lift on this day.

The Swat Valley, as I have said earlier, was ruled by a brutal Taliban commander, Maulana Fazlullah: public executions and beatings were common. The people lived in fear. Each time the Pakistani military would drive the militants out, they would return and Fazlullah – the FM mullah – would again take to the airwaves to broadcast his terror. General Ahmed had arranged for us to be embedded with Pakistani troops: it would offer us an up-close view of this war. Words can barely describe the beauty of the Swat Valley: flying low over its rivers and ravines was breathtaking. In the mountains surrounding the capital, Mingora, General Ahmed pointed out the Taliban positions. Down below, we could see militants moving through the area.

War moves at lightning speed. Riding in the back of a military vehicle isn't at all like you see in the movies; it is more frightening than that. We had to wear Pakistani military bulletproof vests and helmets. The vest may be able to dull a bullet if it hits you in the chest, and the helmet may save you from a ricocheted bullet, but we were facing snipers who, I had no doubt, could shoot me right between the eyes. The military truck moved at top speed; even going around corners, the driver barely applied the brakes and we were tossed from one side to the other. We came to a stop at Mingora's Slaughter Square, where the Taliban dumped headless bodies. Farhad and I wanted to film what we call a stand-up – a piece to camera that puts the reporter in the scene. The soldiers told us we had two minutes; any longer and they would leave without us.

Farhad and I had a telepathic connection. Instinctively I knew where he would be, and vice versa. He knew what I would say before I had even said it, and he'd have a shot framed to illustrate my words. Here we would need to be of one mind. Farhad started filming and I started talking as the military convoy screamed to a stop. We jumped off the truck and Farhad circled me as I pointed out what I could see around me. There was blood on the ground, shattered glass, and bullet-riddled buildings. The people of Mingora squeezed into dark alleys, watching us but afraid to come out. As I talked and pointed, Farhad picked up every shot. In two minutes we had told an entire story and were back on the truck before the militants could ambush us.

That afternoon, General Ahmed was due to fly us back to Islamabad, but he had to take another passenger, one of his senior officers, and that increased the weight in our small chopper. Every kilogram counts – if it was too heavy we might not get airborne. As we took off, the helicopter struggled to get high enough to cross the mountains around Mingora. Farhad and I grew more nervous, knowing the Taliban fighters were thick on the ground. We looked at each other and nervously smiled.

Then I saw General Ahmed tapping at the controls as the chopper just hovered in the air. I don't know a lot about helicopters but this could not be a good sign. Tapping the controls on the dashboard made me worry that the General was out of ideas. I looked across at Farhad and he started to panic, hyperventilating. I was genuinely concerned, but in circumstances like this I have always felt oddly calm. I think I just surrender to whatever fate may bring.

As we hovered for what must have been only a few minutes, it really did feel like we entered a time warp. Everything seemed to stop. Then General Ahmed caught what he was waiting for, a gust of wind lifted the chopper high enough to clear the mountains and we headed for home. The General buzzed over his home as we circled Islamabad to let his wife know he would be home for dinner. When we landed, Farhad and I stepped from the helicopter with our legs like jelly; Farhad crawled off to the side and threw up.

Farhad and I returned to Swat Valley soon after. This time General Ahmed arranged for us to travel with a Pakistani psychologist, Doctor Fariha Peracha, whom the army had brought in to assess a group of boys who had been kidnapped and brutalised by the Taliban. From the moment the boys walked in – there would have been about a dozen of them – I could see they were damaged, likely beyond repair. They shuffled in, each of them eyes downcast, pointedly avoiding contact with me. When I did catch sight of their eyes they appeared empty, soulless. They were dead to the world.

This is a look I have grown sadly used to. It is a vacant stare, as though the eyes are fixed on some far horizon – or maybe they are just unable to see anything ahead and so stare into a hazy distance. But I saw something else too, a spark of something: something deeply human. In their eyes I saw a plea, a yearning to make a connection – anything that might jump-start their soul.

Could I reach them, when all they saw in me was an infidel, something to be reviled?

In situations like this I always try to make some small talk, something that might build a rapport. It is a tool of the trade, the ability to warm to people and encourage them to drop their guard. But how would I start with boys like this? There seemed nothing we had in common. We did not speak the same language, share the same culture or worship the same god. These were Pakistani farm boys, largely uneducated; some could barely read. They were raised to work the fields like their fathers and grandfathers before them.

Each of these boys had been kidnapped by the Taliban. The army had rescued them in a raid on a Taliban stronghold. In hours of interviews, Dr Fariha had pieced together their traumatic experiences. They had been tortured, deprived of sleep, beaten and sexually assaulted. For hours on end they were forced to recite the most violent teachings of the Koran: chanting over and over, rhythmically rocking themselves into a trance just like the boys I had seen in the Kabul madrasah. Their minds had been corrupted by hate for foreigners or non-believers. These were precisely the sorts of boys that Imran would have preyed upon. These boys were being trained to kill. Now they looked at me with disgust.

It was Dr Fariha's job to assess if these Taliban boys could ever be rehabilitated. She was part of a de-radicalisation program that the army hoped might cleanse boys like these of the violence that had been drilled into them. She wasn't hopeful; they were too far gone, she said. There was a wildness now in them that could never be controlled. They could just never be trusted again. She told me that at least two of the boys could kill 'and they would not even feel it'. It was unlikely, she said, that they would ever return to their families or hold down jobs; they would likely need to be institutionalised.

What a tragedy. These boys had not signed up for this – they were the victims of war. Yet, had they not been rescued, I would doubtless have been reporting one day about a suicide bombing that one of them had carried out. They might have killed dozens of people and blown themselves up for the promise of a martyr's paradise. This is how it works: evil preying on weakness to inflict evil on others.

I needed to tell this story to CNN viewers; I needed to try to make sense of this cycle of violence. We need to understand the minds of suicide bombers, how they are so often stripped of their humanity and programmed to murder. They become part of the apparatus; they are the bomb itself. I had to interview the boys.

As I sat in front of them, I had no idea where to start. What do you say to someone who has been so traumatised? In asking questions, I knew, I was risking reinforcing that same trauma. As I cast about for something to say, I introduced myself and told them where I was from. The boys had likely assumed I was American – all Westerners were Americans to them, and especially a CNN television reporter. But when I told them I was Australian I saw something flicker in the eyes of one of the boys. He looked curious, as though there was something he wanted to say.

I had seen this before among Pakistani boys: when they knew I was Australian, it was as if there was some bond between us. It all came down to cricket. Pakistanis are fanatical about cricket – every spare field or path of dirt is filled with boys playing with a bat and a ball. 'Do you like cricket?' I asked. A couple of them said yes, and in halting English reeled off the names of some

Australian players: Ricky Ponting, Shane Warne, Steve Waugh. I asked them if they played cricket. Yes, they replied. Were they bowlers or batsmen? Both, they said. 'All-rounder,' said one boy.

This was what I was looking for – a human connection that could penetrate the suspicion and hatred these boys felt. Maybe there was something here after all? Just a glimmer of the sweet kids they had been before the Taliban abused them and poisoned their minds. Even the psychologist was surprised, as she had thought there was nothing left to work with.

But the moment passed: as quickly as the boys had seemingly sprung to life, they retreated again. They lowered their eyes and stared at the floor, and further questions were met with monosyllabic replies. They told me a little of their old lives, of their families and their villages. A couple told me how they were taken, snatched by the militants who raided their homes, but they told me nothing of what had happened after that. I asked what they thought of me. I was an enemy, they said. Would they kill for God? Yes, they replied. Dr Fariha said one had told her if he had a suicide vest he would use it.

*

Pakistan is the head of the snake. It is where hard-line Islamic militants plotted the most horrendous attacks. There is a map of global terrorism that can be traced to the mosques and madrasahs of Pakistan. Terrorism is built into the nation: there is an alliance between the military, the intelligence service and the militant groups. It is a deadly double game: a nation that has been our ally in the war against terror, and that has received hundreds of millions of dollars to aid in that fight, has also enlisted terrorist groups to further its own ends. Militancy that runs from the India–Pakistan border to the borders of Afghanistan and Iran forms part of Pakistan's strategic depth. It is a bulwark in Pakistan's existential struggle with India: a nuclear-armed stand-off against a mortal enemy. But those same militants can just as easily turn on Pakistan.

Pakistani journalist Zahid Hussain has called Pakistan a 'nursery for jihad'. Its Islamic schools have not only inspired a new generation of home-grown militancy, but have also drawn recruits from far and wide. According to Hussain, 'The development of simple, sparse religious schools into training centres for Kalashnikov-toting religious warriors was directly linked with the rise of militant Islam.' The 1979 Islamic Revolution in Iran sparked a bidding war for Pakistan. Shia Iran began funding new madrasahs, so Sunni Saudi Arabia followed suit, each supplying money and teachers. Students were from poor families or orphans. The schools were crowded and the children regularly beaten. To show how rapidly these schools spread, Hussain notes that at Pakistan's independence in 1947, there were only 147 madrasahs; with the explosion of jihad during the Soviet war in Afghanistan in the 1980s, there were more than 13,000 schools, with nearly two million students enrolled.

This was not about religious education as much as it was about religious identity. It is identity that is the wick in the dynamite. It is when identity shrinks to its essence – when we are defined by one thing and one thing alone, brainwashed to reject all others – that we are primed to kill. This is the story of every country I have covered. As Zahid Hussain says, 'The Islamisation process nurtured many, often mutually hostile, varieties of fundamentalism. In a society where many sects coexisted, the measures representing the beliefs of the dominant sect acted as an identity marker.' The militants were locked in an arms struggle with each other, and from there with the world at large.

In the lead-up to the 9/11 attacks, one particular Islamic school, the Darul Uloom Haqqania madrasah, hosted a conference of militants loyal to Osama bin Laden. At this point, planning for the attack on the Twin Towers was well advanced. American intelligence had intercepted chatter about a big event. Knowing the reach of Pakistani intelligence and its close ties to Islamist militancy, it is unthinkable that they would not have known what was soon to take place. Yet on Pakistani soil, masked gunmen could stand outside this madrasah and guard the doors against those inside who had vowed to wage holy war on the West. What's more, former senior Pakistani officials were inside the room. As Zahid Hussain points out, as well as 300 leaders of radical Islamic groups, the meeting 'was also attended by former army chief General Aslam Beg, and a former ISI [intelligence] chief, General Hamid Gul'. They declared it a religious duty to protect Osama bin Laden, whom they 'described as a great Muslim warrior'.

The terrorism that was born in the Pakistani nurseries of jihad was felt around the world. Thousands of students from countries like China, Malaysia, Chechnya and the Philippines enrolled in these Islamic schools. Thousands would fight in Afghanistan or Kashmir. When we filmed in deserted Taliban camps, it was not unusual to find books in Chinese or Russian. One student at a popular madrasah in the Pakistani city of Karachi had enrolled under a fake identity. He was not in fact Ahmed Hadi, but Gun Gun Rusman Gunawan, a member of Indonesia's Jemaah Islamiah. Gunawan was the brother of

Hambali, the mastermind of the 2002 Bali bombings, which killed more than 200 people. Hambali himself had links to Khalid Sheikh Mohammed, the shadowy Pakistani figure nicknamed 'Mokhtar' who grew close to Bin Laden and orchestrated the greatest single terror attack on the United States. Another foreign student in Pakistan, Shehzad Tanweer, was involved in Britain's 9/11, the coordinated bus and subway attacks of 7 July 2005. As Zahid Hussain says, 'There are strong suspicions that Shehzad might have met the mastermind of the London bombings during his brief stay there.'

While the world had been focused on Afghanistan and Iraq, the real theatre of terror was Pakistan. At one point while I was working there, Pakistan endured more terrorist attacks and casualties than either Iraq or Afghanistan. It was nuclear armed, with an unstable civilian government, a place where leaders like Benazir Bhutto could be assassinated. Her father, a former prime minister, Zulfikar Ali Bhutto, was executed in 1979. Along with a weak government, Pakistan had a strong military that could and would intervene to seize power. Everywhere was the shady hand of the ISI. For me as a reporter, it was a perilous place to work; I had Pakistani colleagues who were kidnapped or killed. Pakistan was unlike Afghanistan or Iraq in that there was no front line – terrorism could strike anywhere. As journalists, we were constantly on guard. I could never get a full night's unbroken sleep; there was always the fear – even in our heavily guarded compound – that someone might break in and kill us.

We were watched continuously. The Pakistani intelligence agencies regularly called our local staff and drivers and interrogated them about the stories we were covering, where we were travelling and whom we were meeting. One morning

Farhad woke to a frantic phone call from his wife. She told him that someone had hacked into his social media profile and personal information – bank accounts, addresses, websites – and accessed the phone numbers and emails of his family. His Facebook page had been altered, and vile allegations made against him. None of them was true; it was wild and crazy stuff, much of it of a sexual nature. He was distressed; his family was worried for him. In his panic, Farhad suspected everyone, even our loyal staff.

We immediately made plans to get him out of the country. If the authorities wanted to charge him, they now had a pretext to do so. They could fabricate allegations, and in this deeply Islamic country it would be impossible for Farhad to defend himself. We could never prove it was Pakistani intelligence, but the operation had their fingerprints on it. They had made threats against us, they had intimidated our staff and warned them that we should leave the country – and now this. They wanted us out, and they were prepared to show us how close they could get to us and how far they were prepared to go.

*

Every journalist who works in Pakistan knows the name Daniel Pearl. The *Wall Street Journal* reporter was kidnapped and beheaded in 2002. Like me, he wasn't based permanently in Pakistan: he worked from his newspaper's Mumbai office in India. He had crossed the border to investigate the background of Richard Reid, the 'shoe bomber'. Reid was a Muslim convert who had attempted to detonate a bomb in his shoe on an American Airlines flight from Paris to Miami. He was believed to have links with al-Qaeda, and like so many terrorists he had trodden the familiar path of mosques and madrasahs from Pakistan to Afghanistan. Pearl was snatched by terrorists on his way to an arranged interview with Sheikh Mubarak Ali Gilani, a scholar who had founded the organisation Muslims of America Inc. to help spread Islam. But Pearl didn't make it; he disappeared. He was next seen in a video, handcuffed and with a gun to his head.

The militants had sent a message to the United States to free all Pakistani terror prisoners and stop a shipment of fighter jets to the Pakistani government. The terrorists warned that in one more day they would kill Daniel Pearl and go on killing, and no American journalist could enter Pakistan. True to their threat, Pearl was beheaded, and his body was cut into pieces and buried in a shallow grave. Years later, after being captured, Khalid Sheikh Mohammad – the man who plotted the 9/11 attacks – told a US tribunal that he had beheaded Pearl. 'I decapitated with my blessed right hand the head of the American Jew Daniel Pearl, in the city of Karachi, Pakistan,' Mohammad said.

I tried not to think too much about Daniel Pearl when I was in Pakistan. I tried to live as normally as possible: taking walks, having coffee; reading. Even in the most volatile or stressful places life finds its regular rhythms. But what happened to him could have happened to any of us, especially American journalists – and nothing screamed 'American journalist' more than the red CNN logo. I may have been Australian, but to Pakistani militant eyes I was an American infidel.

Imagine, then, how we felt when we were contacted by a high-ranking Taliban official who told us that we could interview one of the most wanted men in all of Pakistan: a leading figure in the bloody siege that had opened a brutal new chapter in the war on terror. The siege of Lal Masjid (the Red Mosque) was a shootout between Islamic fundamentalists and Pakistani government forces in the heart of Islamabad, between 3 and 11 July 2007. In the end, nearly a hundred people were killed and a similar number wounded or captured.

The Red Mosque had been taken over by hard-line militants who wanted to impose severe Islamic law and overthrow the government of Pakistan. For eighteen months they carried out violent protests and abducted female workers from a Chinese health care centre. China applied pressure to Pakistan and the government laid siege to the mosque, finally storming the building. The attack broke the fragile but mutually beneficial alliance between Pakistani intelligence, the military and the militants. Taliban rebels on the Afghan border tore up a peace agreement with Pakistan and launched what became known as the Third Waziristan War, an outbreak of violence that killed at least 3000 people. Most of the leaders of the Red Mosque siege were now dead or in prison but some had escaped, including one who now sat at the right hand of the Supreme Leader of the Taliban, Mullah Mohammed Omar. Now, we were told, he had crossed the border back into Pakistan from Afghanistan and wanted to talk – and talk to us.

We were never allowed to reveal this right-hand man's name or show his full image, so we will call him 'Sheikh Hamza'. This man had links to the highest levels of international terrorism. When Pakistani officials sifted through the aftermath of the Red Mosque siege, they found letters from Osama bin Laden's deputy, Ayman al-Zawahiri. Zawahiri had directed the imams of the mosque to carry out their violence, and it was said that foreign fighters from Uzbekistan and Egypt had arrived at the mosque in the weeks leading up to the siege. On 11 July 2007, Zawahiri released a video calling Pakistanis to war to avenge the Pakistan army's bloodshed.

Sheikh Hamza had a direct line to the top. He had been sent to Pakistan on what might appear a strange mission. Mullah Omar had grown frustrated with the Pakistani Taliban, whose brutality even he could not stomach. Mullah Omar feared the Pakistani arm of his organisation had gone rogue: he was appalled at how the Taliban there were targeting ordinary Pakistanis. The slaughter was indiscriminate. He was also disgusted at the widespread sexual abuse of children. Now the Supreme Leader issued a code of conduct: no more civilian deaths. Kill as many foreigners as possible, but no more Pakistanis. Once a man grew facial hair he was not to share a room with a child: there must be no more rape of kidnapped children. On and on the code went, a strict edict to enforce more discipline and focus the fight against what Mullah Omar saw as the real enemy: the West and its sympathisers. Sheikh Hamza was dispatched to read the riot act to his fellow Pakistani militants. But more than that, he wanted the world to know that Mullah Omar had spoken.

In Pakistan we always had back channels open to the Taliban; we spoke on the phone, and the militants would send us press statements and videos – sometimes horrendous videos of the worst torture and killing. We always used intermediaries: people we trusted and the Taliban trusted, at least as much as any side could. Now our guy had told us that Sheikh Hamza – a man the Pakistani government wanted dead – would meet us for an interview. At times like this, I felt a surge of excitement – I can't deny it – as in journalistic terms this was a coup. But then came the dread: what the hell were we doing? How could we possibly be safe? Remember Daniel Pearl.

An enormous amount of planning goes into an operation like this: what time we would leave, what equipment and supplies we would take, what our lines of communication would be, how long it would take, what our estimated times of arrival and departure would be, who would act as our point person back at the bureau, and from there at our news headquarters in Atlanta. Even getting permission for this was difficult. CNN had lost staff in war before. My crew and I at times had come under fire, and been surrounded by angry people wielding guns, threatening us; we knew there were enormous risks. Was this worth it? That's the first question, but from my point of view the easiest one to answer: it was always worth it. Even death was worth the risk. If it wasn't, what on earth was I even doing here? Luckily, our bosses were news people: they looked for ways to say yes, not no, but they were responsible for us too. With the correct safeguards in place, we got the go-ahead. Now the morning had come for a job that, we had to accept, came with no guarantee we would return safely.

Farhad and I were as relaxed as on any day. We got up, had breakfast; messed around with guitars just as we always did. We teased our Pakistani driver, Dildar, who always loved our good-natured ribbing, and he made fun of us in return. It was how we bonded; the banter always lightened the mood. We got our things together, packed our car and got ready to leave. Not all of us could go on this trip. There would be Dildar; our security man, Al, a former SAS soldier who came with us on every mission – he carried a gun and was prepared to use it; our local Pakistani producer, Nasser; and Farhad and me. We went in two cars and used phones to make regular contact. We had promised Atlanta that we would call in every half an hour: there would be a checklist we would have to tick off, and if at any time we sensed it was getting too dangerous, we were to abort the job. Every minute was accounted for, and every contingency considered.

We had to leave Islamabad and drive for about an hour into a small village that really was in the middle of nowhere. We were told by the Taliban that we were to enter the village and come to a T-junction; we were not to stop but should slow down and flash our lights. Two cars would be waiting for us, and one would go in front of us and one at the back. I know it's a corny thing to say, but this really did feel like something out of a movie. Normally on a trip like this we would playing music and having a laugh, but on this day everyone was quiet.

We did as instructed, the cars joined the convoy and we were led down several winding lanes until we came to a sudden stop outside a small house in an otherwise empty field. The militants from the cars in front and behind leapt out with guns pointed at our vehicles and motioned us out. We were taken into the house and told to set up our camera. We were reminded that we were not to show Sheikh Hamza's image: no face. We could not blur the vision to disguise him as they did not trust that; all we could do was film the back of his head and his hands. As Farhad positioned his camera, one of the armed men looked down his viewfinder and another pointed his gun towards us.

After a few minutes, Sheikh Hamza appeared. If I had been told it was Osama bin Laden himself I would have believed it. The Sheikh bore an amazing resemblance to the al-Qaeda leader. Like Bin Laden, he was very tall; I am 187 centimetres and he towered over me. He had a long beard and the same mystical expression.

He wore all white: long, flowing robes and a turban. He would not meet our eyes or shake our hands: to him we were unclean. He spoke softly and looked at the floor. Our interview lasted about thirty minutes, then the Sheikh rose to leave. Now came the task of getting out.

I was confident nothing would happen to us on the way in, but I grew more nervous about leaving. One of the risks with missions like this is the potential for someone to get spooked, some gunman to panic. Now that the interview was over, I think it really hit me that we were in Taliban-controlled country. Our lives were in the hands of the people who sent us videos of beheadings and torture. We were given strict instructions about leaving: how much time we were allowed, each checkpoint we had to pass. If we were late or took a wrong turn, the Taliban would suspect that we had set a trap and tipped off the Pakistani military. We left and did exactly as we were told.

When we cleared the town, we were like giddy children. We had shot an amazing interview; our rivals would be envious. We had gone into enemy territory and come out alive. And we were hungry. None of us had eaten since breakfast. On the journey back, I wrote my story and Farhad edited it in the back of the car, and we had it ready to file by the time we reached Islamabad. That night we ate at Pizza Party, a makeshift pizza shop at the back of a house that made the best pizzas anywhere.

A story like this raises many ethical questions – and, frankly, I don't have terribly ethical answers. Sheikh Hamza was a wanted man who had been involved in a shootout that tipped Pakistan into a new war with the Taliban. He had the blood of people on his hands. He was a direct line to Mullah Omar – a man the United States was seeking – and probably beyond that to the highest echelons of al-Qaeda. But this is the journalist's dilemma: are we an arm of the law? If we go down that path, where does it end? Do we become spies? I had certainly been approached in the past to 'share information', as it was put, with foreign embassy officials. But I knew that would be asking for death. Should we carry weapons? Again, that would be an invitation to be shot. We were not in America or Australia; how could we trust the Pakistanis? Knowing what I knew about the double game Pakistan employed – playing militants off against each other, using militants for its own ends, taking American money and placing it into the hands of Islamist groups – how could I be sure that this would not backfire on us?

No, I decided. Pakistani intelligence did its job and we did ours. If we did not talk to the Taliban, then how would the world know what went on in the minds of those on whom we were waging war? That's my job – to tell stories, to inform people and to allow them to make their own judgements. I am still not sure if that is right. But that's the way it was: these were the decisions we made. And of course, if I am being honest, we loved the thrill of the chase.

*

How do you defeat an enemy that can't be killed? And more than that – an enemy that welcomes death? The type of Islamist holy war launched by the likes of Osama bin Laden is based on an idea more than an organisation, and ideas don't easily die. Killing its leaders does not end the fighting as others soon take their place. The names of these terror groups change – Taliban, al-Qaeda, ISIS, Abu Sayyaf, al-Shabaab, Ansar al-Islam. The theatres of war shift from the deserts to the cities, from the United States to

Europe, the United Kingdom, Africa, Asia, Australia. People have died on buses, trains, in hotels, theatres, cinemas, cafes. None of us can say we are safe anymore; the tentacles of terrorism can touch us wherever we are. Violent extremism takes hold wherever resentment festers: it feeds on fear, anxiety and hate. The germ of extremism crawls out of the dark pit of history; it attaches itself to the vulnerable, weak and oppressed, and weakens them, eating into their souls and poisoning their minds. When a historical narrative of oppression and humiliation attaches itself to religion, race, politics or class, then people can become hard-wired for hate.

Scholar Shadi Hamid has spent his career trying to understand what drives Islamic militancy, and he says that, despite his best efforts, 'the one element I continue to struggle with is what might be called the willingness to die'. The militants are willing to die because it brings glory to God. They believe they will be rewarded in the afterlife. But they also have earthly political motives: a deep enmity for the West and a desire to avenge history. They blame the post–World War One carve-up of the Middle East as the cause of so much contemporary suffering. The Sykes–Picot Agreement, made between England and France in 1916, redrew the borders and created new countries ruled by strongmen installed and funded by Western countries. Islamist movements, Hamid says, seek to recapture the faded glories of the faith. They want to recreate the caliphate, an Islamic state where religion and politics are indivisible. Where people are governed by God's law. As Hamid writes, 'The gap between where Muslims once were and where they now find themselves is at the centre of the anger and humiliation driving political violence across the Middle East.'

The resurgence of Islamist political movements has been baffling to the West. They simply do not fit into the Western arc of historical progress. We are meant to move beyond feudalism or theocracy to a more enlightened liberalism of individual rights, where religion retreats from the public to the private realm. The West is built on *freedom from* as much as *freedom to*. I am free to belong where I choose, to worship as I wish, and free from the imposition of your faith or beliefs. Our society cannot hold unless we all surrender, to some degree, to a shared public square. Liberalism presents itself as a civilising idea of compromise, responsibility and respect. So many Western thinkers have believed that, given time, Islam would undergo a change similar to the Reformation of Christianity: that the lure of Western freedoms would be irresistible, and if necessary we could hasten it with intervention and be rewarded with flowers and kisses from a grateful public. We couldn't be more wrong. As Shadi Hamid says, 'The vast majority of Christians in the West – including committed conservatives – cannot conceive of a comprehensive legal order anchored in religion.'

Hamid calls this 'Islamic exceptionalism': it is not like the West and will not be like the West. Islam, he says, 'is distinctive in how it relates to politics, Islam is different'. This exceptionalism, he says, is neither good nor bad, it just is – and it needs to be understood and respected.

Is this correct? It is difficult and can be very misleading to discuss any one group of people as though they are homogenous, all thinking with one mind. I remember sharing a public discussion with the Muslim journalist and writer Mehdi Hasan, who, when asked what Islam thought about a particular issue, replied: 'Who is this Islam? I've never met him.' There are many majority Islamic countries that are to varying degrees functional democracies: Indonesia, Pakistan, Malaysia, Turkey, Tunisia. There are 1.7 billion Muslims in the world, and at least half of them live in democratic countries. In countries like India there is a large Muslim minority, and they participate in and accept the democratic process. Many millions of Muslims live in majority Christian countries in the West, and like all other faiths and ethnicities embrace a multicultural pluralism. It is wrong to think that all Muslims hanker after public executions and stoning for adultery.

But scratch a little deeper and things are much more complex. What is Islamism, and how does it differ from Islam? Islam is the faith, while Islamism is a modern political movement. Not all Muslims are Islamists: over time many if not most have embraced secularism or socialism or nationalism. But for those who would call themselves 'true believers', those who are angry with foreign intervention or who feel betrayed by the world, Islamism has an emotional and spiritual hold. It is not archaic or backward, as popular media portrayals would suggest. Images of people with long beards and black robes and turbans, and horrific vision of beheadings and beatings, may suggest something medieval but that is wrong: Islamism exists now and is a reaction to Western modernity as much as a rejection of it. As Shadi Hamid says, 'Muslims were never compelled to choose between their own tradition and another.'

Democracy is not antithetical to Islamism; instead Islamists, not unlike fascists, work inside democracies. Hamid points out that 'the most democratic countries ... are the ones where Islamism, or Islamists, have fared better'. He also makes clear that countries hailed as models of democratic pluralism –

Indonesia and Malaysia, for example – 'feature significantly more shariah ordinances than Egypt, Tunisia, Turkey, Algeria, Morocco or Lebanon'.

Islamists claim a strict reading of Islam, founded on the teachings of Muhammad. Indeed, Islamists believe that the Koran is the word of God, celestial teachings beyond any interpretation or nuance. Islamism puts no law above God's law – the faith cannot be separated from politics. The Christian teaching to 'render unto Caesar what is Caesar's and unto God what is God's' has no place in the Islamist worldview. It is a point of difference between the two great faiths that Jesus – who is revered as a prophet within Islam – preached that someone could come to God through him, not through observance of the law, while Muhammad brought the law of God to the world. Islamism centres faith at the heart of society, and emerged as a reaction to what some Muslims saw as the failure of Islam to defy the march of Western modernity. It is not unlike the existential crisis that gripped China during the fall of the Qing Dynasty. Then too the rise of modernity sparked violence and revolution. For the Islamic world the collapse of the last caliphate, the Ottoman Empire, in 1924 came to be seen as the great humiliation. In its wake, majority Muslim nations flirted with nationalism, socialism and secularism, but something was missing. A politics without Islam was a politics that did not speak to the soul.

Egypt's Muslim Brotherhood emerged as the first of the great Islamist movements. It existed to oppose secularism. It bridged the divide between the old and the new, between the teachings of the prophet Muhammad and the modern cosmopolitan world. The Brotherhood is a political party of theology and resistance, and its message spread quickly from Egypt to other parts of the

Muslim world. The Muslim Brotherhood's founder, Hassan al-Banna, saw a complicated world and simplified his message: Islam was the answer. He spoke not only to faith but to history: if Muslims wanted to recapture their former glory, then they must turn away from the world and back to God. As Shadi Hamid says, 'Banna looked around and saw passivity and fatalism. This infuriated him. Muslims had fallen. Muslims were weak, divided, bickering and in the thrall of foreign ideologies.'

Now we are getting to the heart of the matter. This was not simply about faith; it was not just about history or politics: this was about identity. Faith and history and politics all serve identity. It is the law of the tribe, who belongs and who doesn't. It is the law of opposites: I am what you are not. This toxic identity breeds in the dark corners, and preys on weakness and vulnerability: it turns victimhood into a virtue. Writing about al-Qaeda, philosopher John Gray identified its appeal to 'deracinated Muslims in Westernised societies; it provides meaning, and purpose in lives that lack them and recreates an identity where one has been lost.' Of course the lure of al-Qaeda is not confined to 'Westernised' Muslims; to impressionable Muslims everywhere it offers a voice to speak back to a world of hurt. It is not that the tragedies of history are not real. It is not that people should not be angry; anger is often righteous. Faith is real and faith lifts our spirits. The fight for justice is real. But identity can turn us away from the world; it can turn us inward where a seething anger at the world festers and at its worst explodes in violence.

In this, Islamism is not exceptional at all: wherever history and politics and race or faith meet, you find demagogues who seek to exploit fear and turn it into hate. It is the white supremacist, the Stalinist and the Maoist; it is in Rwanda and the Balkans and Northern Ireland and China and Korea and India and Pakistan and America and France and Hungary. It is everywhere we are. We are all potential recruits in this war of our time: the war of identity. It is identity forged out of resentment and a thirst for vengeance. It is identity that draws its narrative from the open wounds of history.

Cemil Aydin, in his book *The Idea of the Muslim World*, rejects much of the Islamic exceptionalism argument, but he also traces the rise of Islamism to the spread of modernity. The collapse of the caliphate was the spark for the rise of a new militant political faith that would restore Muslim pride. Aydin says Islamists are born out of Western racism. It was the West that sought to racialise Islam, to see all Muslims as a homogenous people, not capable of modernity. This justified the intervention and meddling in Muslim nations that produced what has become a violent backlash. Judged as one people, Muslims, he says, responded as one people. He says amid the Arab–Israeli conflicts and the Iranian revolution of the 1970s and '80s, those decades 'witnessed a resurgence of pan-Islamic patterns of thinking born in the imperial age'. Islam, of course, has its own deep divisions between Shia and Sunni – its own wars of identity – and it is not therefore a singular religious or political entity. But whether Shia or Sunni, the various regimes all sprang from the same source and saw faith and politics as inseparable. As Aydin writes, '[With] its true spirit recovered, Muslim modernists claimed, Islam would be an instrument in the revival of the victimized, declining Muslim world.'

Identity. It is everywhere. Identity, identity, identity. It is inescapable, and at its worst – at its most toxic – it is the scourge of our age.

11

NO ONE GETS OUT ALIVE

For a reporter, the world can turn when you least expect it. Even when I was out walking my dog on a frozen winter morning in Beijing, somewhere history would be being made. So it was one morning when my phone rang. It was one of CNN's senior producers, Licia Yee, calling from Hong Kong to alert me that something was up. President Barack Obama was expected to make what we were being told would be a big announcement. Through back channels we heard it was about Osama bin Laden. 'I think they might have got him,' Licia said.

At times like these I immediately switch into reporter mode. I called my cameraman, Brad Olson, and told him to get ready. We needed to pack our bags and book our flights to either Islamabad or Kabul. CNN would throw all its resources at big stories – we needed to cover every angle. I was one of a group of senior international correspondents who would be deployed from different parts of the globe to cover breaking events. I was based in Beijing but regularly travelled elsewhere. It helped that China and Pakistan were close, and that we could fly direct on Pakistan International Airlines from Beijing to Islamabad, rather than the long way round, via Dubai. We could be on the ground in a few hours. I always kept my visas up to date so I could leave immediately.

I soon learned that CNN wanted me in Afghanistan – this was where the war was. We would fly directly to Islamabad and then straight on to Kabul. We would be back in the country Bin Laden had come to for the first time during the Soviet War to forge his jihadi reputation and plot the attacks on the United States. If Bin Laden was dead, we needed to be on the ground to get the reaction.

Everyone braced themselves for violence. Before leaving, I watched President Obama tell the world, 'We got him.' Like everyone, I was stunned. Ten years before, I had sat in my living room in Sydney watching the Twin Towers in New York fall. How my life had changed; how many miles I had travelled. The things I had seen ... so many lost lives. I was scarcely the same person.

This decade had changed me. I read voraciously, I asked questions insatiably, I watched news endlessly; night after night I slept only a few hours at a time. It was not enough to just cover the world, I needed to understand it. I needed to make sense of this, to try to make sense of myself, of those things I had seen as a boy and the family I was from. For all I had learned, there was still wisdom to be gained. Journalism had not answered all my questions, so I read more and more philosophy. I had to know about the people who had shaped the modern world; philosophy obsessed me. On this day I packed more books into my bag and boarded a plane for what was really the last big story of this phase of my career.

On a job like this, we never rest. As I disembarked from the plane in Kabul I was on the phone to CNN headquarters. CNN is a voracious beast; it always needs more and more. The producers in Atlanta wanted me up immediately. I hadn't even seen anything yet, but they wanted to know what it was like to be in Kabul after Bin Laden was killed. I told them to give me ten minutes.

As I walked through the airport to customs and immigration, I spoke to people: baggage handlers, immigration officials, fellow passengers. Had they heard the news? What did they think? Would there be a backlash? Was this the end of the war? When the news producers phoned back, I was ready to go with something: little more than immediate first-hand responses and my deep knowledge of Bin Laden, al-Qaeda, the Taliban, the war. I had enough to stay on air for as long as they needed, and CNN had what in journalism we called a locator: by-line: Afghanistan.

My old friend Farhad had flown into Kabul from Dubai, and it was good to see him and work with him again; it put my mind to rest, and I was pleased that in our quiet time we could play guitar and sing together.

I was up all night that first night and then again the next day, before Atlanta phoned again and said they wanted me in Pakistan: leave now! I arrived that evening in Islamabad; the next morning I would travel to Abbottabad, the military garrison town where Bin Laden, incredibly, had been hiding in plain view. This tells us something about Pakistan and Islamist militancy: how easily they can exist side by side. Here was the most wanted man on the planet, a tall, unmistakable Arab man living at the heart of Pakistan's military establishment, and we were expected to believe no one knew?

On 1 May 2011 Barack Obama joined his senior staff in the White House to watch a US Navy Seal team, under cover of darkness, fly into Pakistani airspace and kill the man who had tipped the world into an endless war on terror. In the house in Abbottabad where Bin Laden and his family were hidden, the sound of the choppers grew nearer. Bin Laden's wife looked at him: she knew this was not normal. This was not a drone strike – it was much more than that. At 1 am on 2 May, Bin Laden's son ran into his father's bedroom. The Americans are coming, he said. When the Navy Seals entered the room, one of them was surprised, he later revealed, by how tall Bin Laden was. Bin Laden had his hands on a woman's shoulders – his wife Amal – and was thrusting her forward. There are conflicting reports about what happened, and about who fired the fatal shot, but within minutes Osama bin Laden was dead.

Abbottabad was on edge when we arrived. We managed to get right up outside the Bin Laden compound. It was an easily identifiable house, by far the largest in what was a very ordinary neighbourhood. It was remarkable that a man as infamous as Bin Laden, surrounded by security and with his family living with him, could have been living there with no one knowing. Our job was to speak to as many people as we could to piece together the last months of Bin Laden's life.

By now the world had seen the final images of the al-Qaeda leader, and he was far from the revolutionary figure he had cut just a few years earlier. We had become so used to seeing Bin Laden in military greens, with his Kalashnikov resting beside him,

that this figure, grey and stooped, wrapped in a blanket, was shocking. In his last minutes Bin Laden looked pathetic. He was the leader in exile, but it looked like his movement had progressed without him. New militant leaders like Abu Musab al-Zarqawi, a Jordanian who had studied and fought under Bin Laden, had established new al-Qaeda offshoots, breaking away from the old guard. Zarqawi's al-Qaeda in Iraq was in fact a much more brutal organisation – so much so that Bin Laden and his lieutenant, Ayman al-Zawahiri, had asked him to pull back.

The invasion of Iraq that toppled the tyrant Saddam Hussein had also lifted the lid on simmering sectarian tensions in that country, and these were now tearing Iraq apart. I had travelled in and out of Iraq several times over a decade. I first went there in 1996, just a few years after the Gulf War. It was a country that shivered in fear of the dictator Saddam. Everywhere there were reminders of his presence and his power. Statues of Saddam stared down at his people, and monuments celebrated weapons and guns. The Iraqi leader – himself for a while propped up by Western nations, especially during the brutal Iran–Iraq War – operated a secret police network that monitored Iraqi citizens and could make people vanish in the middle of the night.

Yet Iraq was a paradox. Saddam's Ba'ath Party had socialist roots, and he kept a tight hold on Islamist militant groups. The capital, Baghdad, was a long way from a fundamentalist Muslim state: women and girls were educated, and worked. They could appear in public without having to be covered. I visited the university and saw young men and women openly socialising like they would on any Western campus. One of my enduring memories of my early visits to Iraq was eating at a fish restaurant on a balmy night by the river. As the *masgouf* (a grilled fish dish) cooked over an open fire, my colleagues and I relaxed with other Iraqi people as though we were in any other great city of the world. But appearances were deceiving: Saddam, a Sunni Muslim, kept his boot on the necks of the Shia majority.

Iraq, long considered the cradle of civilisation – the ancient home of science and maths and literature – was also the ancient home of terrorism. The Assyrians who ruled Mesopotamia also ruled with totalitarian fear. In his book *The Caliphate at War*, Ahmed Hashim says that the Assyrians' 'army, system of totalitarian rule, and infliction of terror as state policy was the scourge of the Middle East between 2500 and 605 BC' (to use the Gregorian calendar). Assyria was an expansionist power that used its army as an instrument of terror with the power to depopulate and repopulate. Iraq was also the home of the great schism of Islam: Sunni versus Shia. When the prophet Muhammad died, he left no male heir, so competing alliances formed to determine who would lead the faith. One group supported Muhammad's father-in-law Abu Bakr; another said the prophet had designated his son-in-law Ali Ibn Abu Talib as his successor. Supporters of Abu Bakr formed the Sunni, and Ali's followers the Shia. Over time the two groups formed different theologies. Ali became caliph in 656 AD but was assassinated in southern Iraq in 661. Ali's son Hussein was murdered in Karbala, Iraq, in 680. Shiism is a minority belief in Islam, but its strongholds are Iraq and Iran.

It is no surprise or coincidence that Abu Musab al-Zarqawi built his power base in Iraq. The fall of Saddam had unleashed bloodshed between rival Sunni and Shia militias. Zarqawi had no problem killing his fellow Muslims – in fact, he made it a duty. Zarqawi wanted to start a civil war, to pit Shia against Sunni and drive the minority Sunni population to his side. In a letter to Osama bin Laden, Zarqawi wrote: 'Shia are the lurking snake, the crafty and malicious scorpion, the spying enemy and the penetrating venom ...' Zarqawi would slaughter Shia to provoke reprisals, to 'show their rabies', as he colourfully put it in his letter. He told Bin Laden: 'If we succeed in dragging them into the arena of sectarian war it will be possible to awaken the inattentive Sunnis as they feel imminent danger and annihilating death.'

As Zarqawi encouraged others to kill, he was also prepared himself to kill. The world saw the depths of his brutality in a video posted in 2004. Zarqawi appeared wearing a black mask standing behind a man in an orange jumpsuit. This was an American, Nick Berg, who had been captured in Iraq. Now Zarqawi produced a large kitchen knife and decapitated Berg for all the world to see. Zarqawi wanted to send a message not just to the West but to other Muslims: he wanted to strike fear into non-believers and issue a bloody call to arms to other Muslims to join him in his holy war. It is tempting to see this as wanton violence, as an orgy of bloodshed carried out by butchers from a dark age; that is often what we get from the media as it searches for simple answers and someone to blame. But Zarqawi, like Bin Laden, was steeped in theology and political ideology. He studied the ways of war and knew precisely what he wanted to achieve, and what he was prepared to do to achieve it. He had a playbook, and its title tells us everything: *Management of Savagery*.

Zarqawi was fulfilling a master plan, a program that began with the 9/11 attacks, and incorporated the US and allies' invasion of Iraq, the following sectarian war and ultimately the establishment of a new caliphate – an Islamic state – between 2013 and 2016, leading to the final victory that would unite Muslims worldwide and overthrow the state of Israel. But the plan was nothing without a strategy, and that strategy was savagery. *Management of Savagery* was a document released online in 2004 by an Islamist strategist who called himself Abu Bakr Naji. It was an outline for endless war, to weaken the enemy, drain the United States of blood and treasure, and bring about the collapse of local regimes. It was based on an age-old formula of divide and conquer, pitting against each other people who, in desperation, will seek shelter in a truly Islamic state. In his book *The Master Plan: ISIS, al-Qaeda and the Jihadi Strategy for Final Victory*, Brian Fishman says *Management of Savagery* 'offered strategic and operational plans for Zarqawi's war in Iraq and beyond'. This was a plan for global domination, but what is often overlooked is that it came not from within Islam, but from a revolutionary of another time and another country: *Management of Savagery* was torn from the pages of China's Communist Party leader, Mao Zedong.

Chairman Mao wrote the book on asymmetrical warfare: how to use a smaller force to defeat a larger and more powerful one. It was how he triumphed over Chiang Kai-shek's American-backed Nationalists. Mao pursued what he called the 'Three Stages of Revolutionary Warfare', a protracted war built around (1) strategic defence – the long game to wear down your enemy; (2) strategic stalemate – digging in and building political and military strength; and (3) strategic offence – the transition from guerrilla warfare to political power. Mao's plan required mobilising people behind a clear ideology – in Mao's case, a peasants' Marxist revolution (as opposed to a workers' revolution), and for Zarqawi binding Sunnis to a fundamentalist Islamic doctrine that shows no mercy.

Guillaume Beaurpere is a US Army lieutenant colonel who served in Iraq and studied al-Qaeda ideology. He joined the dots between Islamist strategy and Maoist doctrine, and says that while the 'circumstances and motives' of the Chinese Communist Revolution were different to those of Islamist terrorism, it is 'most evident' that the strategy is Mao's. As someone who has spent so much time covering the rise of China and the terror wars, I see revelations like this as like light bulbs that illuminate the deep connections between identity movements the world over, and the common pattern: manipulate a people; discover their weakness and fear; bind them to an ideology; give them a story of oppression and historical humiliation; arm them and send them to war.

As I stood outside Osama bin Laden's house in the days after he was killed, I had little sense that this moment was already being overtaken by the spread of an even more virulent ideology, an al-Qaeda mark II that would, in the years to come, plant the flag of a new state, a caliphate reborn. To many in the world, Islamic State, or ISIS, seemed to come from nowhere, but it had many fathers: the growth and spread of the Muslim Brotherhood, the rise of the Taliban and al-Qaeda during the Soviet–Afghan war, the birth of Abu Musab al-Zarqawi's al-Qaeda in Iraq after the fall of Saddam; each iteration was more brutal than the last. The failure of the West was to think it was fighting the same enemy.

Western leaders did not heed the lessons of their mistakes: they failed to win the hearts and minds of the people they were supposedly liberating from terror. In this they were repeating the pattern of their own history. Through Muslim eyes the West had betrayed or exploited them too many times. They had meddled in Muslim countries propping up despots who tortured and brutalised their own people. Now Western military might had toppled the Taliban in Afghanistan but unleashed a brutal blowback that took more civilian lives. Saddam Hussein had been captured and killed but the United States then stripped Iraq of its military and political leaders, people who had served under

Saddam but were not necessarily loyal to him. The de-Ba'athification strategy meant many senior politicians and generals were locked up. It hardened animosity towards America and removed many who could have been essential to restoring good government to Iraq. Inside prison, Saddam's military leaders – many of whom would have had little time for the likes of al-Qaeda – were enlisted in a new war: they took a fundamentalist turn and ended wearing the uniforms of Islamic State.

Killing Bin Laden did not kill his movement. The celebrations were premature, and those in power were blind to what was already right in front of them. When ISIS placed its flag in the ground and drove back the Iraqi military, Barack Obama blithely dismissed these new jihadists as a 'JV [junior varsity] terrorism group' – how stupid it was to see this as the equivalent of a second-tier college basketball team. But Obama never was a great foreign policy president. His record reveals a leader unsure of American power and how and when to use it. To his critics and enemies, Obama was weak and indecisive. He underestimated ISIS, and later failed to enforce his own 'red lines' in Syria when Bashar al-Assad – the Syrian president – gassed his own people. Obama left open the space for Russia to reassert itself as a global power. Vladimir Putin would never waste a good war: he inserted himself into the Syrian conflict, propping up the besieged Assad and building an arc of influence across the region.

It is tempting to say that Putin played Obama off a break. Many Muslims I spoke to thought the American president weak; the Chinese leadership was quietly dismissive of him. When Obama left office, ISIS had established its caliphate, Putin had changed the borders of Europe by reclaiming Crimea, North Korea was a nuclear-armed state, and China, richer and more powerful than ever, had claimed and militarised the disputed islands of the South China Sea. What's more, the war on terror continued, with military tactics drawn from China's own revolutionary leader, Mao Zedong.

*

Covering world-shaping events can be surreal: there is danger and excitement – a sense of being in the front row of history – but it is sometimes mundane. There are long hours of travel; the boredom of being locked down inside heavily armed compounds; decisions about what to have for dinner; and hours spent binge-watching mindless television drama. Even on the ground, it is the little things I remember, and sometimes the small stories that tell us so much.

Outside Bin Laden's house, I saw a young boy bouncing a cricket ball on his bat. I walked over and asked if he wanted to play – I would bowl a few balls down at him. I have never met a Pakistani kid who would say no to a game of cricket. As I got talking to him, the boy told me the most unlikely, fantastic story. He said he had befriended the children inside the Bin Laden compound and regularly played with them. This small boy, no more than nine or ten years old, had been so close to the most wanted man in the world – Osama bin Laden's children were his playmates.

'What was that like?' I asked.

'Good,' he said. He told me the children were nice, and he especially liked their mother, one of Osama's wives. She was kind, he told me; she used to sit with the children when they ate a meal. Then this boy dashed inside his house and returned holding a black and white rabbit – Osama's wife had given it to him as a gift, he said.

Here was something so utterly normal: a little boy playing with his neighbours, and a kindly mother giving him a gift. It was so at odds with how we might imagine the secretive life of the al-Qaeda leader. I couldn't help but think of what the philosopher Hannah Arendt said, when writing of the Nazis, about the banality of evil. Those we would rather imagine as monsters can also be so human: so pathetic or kind or sad or afraid, or indeed so evil.

The West cannot shake itself of its belief in destiny. It perceives that the world is just waiting to be discovered and will greet Western democracy and universalism with open arms. As I have written, the fall of the Berlin Wall only reinforced this view of the glorious march of liberal progress. Why wouldn't the Muslim world be the same? Surely all Muslims craved McDonald's and Nike; surely they wanted to watch Hollywood films and shop in mega-malls. The great conceit of Western leaders is that they fail to imagine that Muslims themselves may want those things and yet remain who they are. In the corridors of power in Washington it was not thought that what was cast as a seventh-century-style holy war was sustainable. Yet the fall of Saddam was not met with flowers and cheering crowds. Democracy did come to Iraq but it did not immediately bring stability. Far from it. Indeed the wider Middle East instead descended into ever more brutal conflict. The killing of Osama bin Laden did not mean that jihadists downed their weapons. Some Muslims may have been relieved, some may even have rejoiced, but so many still saw the West as evil and decadent. Some still blamed America for bringing war to their countries.

During a break in filming in Abbottabad I went to a local food stall to buy a drink; to the man who served me, I was just another American working for CNN. As he handed me my Pepsi he spat at my face.

In the days after Bin Laden's death, I went to a run-down neighbourhood in Islamabad, where one of the leaders of the Red Mosque siege had started his own madrasah to keep alive the soul of Islam. I sat on a bed across from Mullah Azam Aziz as he sat cross-legged, singing with his eyes closed. He rocked gently back and forth, repeating words from the Koran. Aziz had been imprisoned for his role in the Red Mosque violence, but as is the way of things in Pakistan, he was later acquitted and was now under the protection of the state.

When I arrived to meet him, my crew and I were greeted by heavily armed security. As is the custom, they gave me a hug and I could feel the ammunition belts strapped across their chests. We were led down a dirt path into a series of old white buildings. This was where Mullah Aziz ran his school. We were taken to meet him in a sparsely finished room, and a meal was laid out to welcome us. Islam is a religion of hospitality; I have never gone hungry in Muslim countries. During the holy month of Ramadan, when the devout fast between sunrise and sundown, I was always offered the first taste of food at the end of the day. No one else would eat until I had broken the fast, usually with fresh dates. Now I sat across from a man I know believed I was dirty – an unbeliever destined for hell – yet he greeted me as a brother.

Mullah Aziz's time in prison had done nothing to soften his militancy. He still pledged allegiance to the Taliban – the same force that America and its allies had vowed to defeat. It was the same Taliban that killed their fellow Pakistanis and Afghans. The same Taliban that locked women and girls out of work and school. That flogged men for not wearing beards or for listening to music. Mullah Aziz told me the United States was his enemy, and Osama bin Laden was a heroic leader. To be martyred, he told me, was the dream of all Muslims. His own son had been killed in the Red Mosque siege, and as he sat beside his five-year-old adopted son, he told me it was his greatest wish that his youngest boy too would die for his faith. His mother and sister were also killed in the siege. At his school he kept reminders of that battle, bullet-riddled cabinets and furniture. Mullah Aziz did offer me a solution to end the violence: President Obama, he said, needed to convert to Islam.

I followed the trail of terror from Pakistan to Afghanistan to Iraq, Egypt, Jordan, Palestine and Israel, and across South East Asia, including southern Thailand and Bali. These things never leave me. I know it took an enormous toll on the people I worked with. Two of my closest friends, cameramen Brad Olson and Sarmad Qaseera, have passed away, both gone years before their time. I was so lucky that I got to spend precious time with them before they died.

I was back in Australia working in Sydney when my phone rang and I recognised Sarmad's unmistakable high-pitched voice. He was in Australia following the royal tour of the Duke and Duchess of Cambridge. Sarmad was laughing about being part of the William and Kate circus – it was a long way from Pakistan and the Taliban. He was happy: he was now living in America and caring for his mother. He had seen enough war and misery and wanted an easier life now. We caught up for a coffee and laughed just like old times. After he returned home to the United States, I got another phone call telling me Sarmad had died.

I saw Brad for one last time in Singapore. We were covering the meeting between Donald Trump and Kim Jong-un, he still with CNN and me for the ABC. We went for dinner and spent hours talking about the world and our families and our adventures. We hugged each other before we parted, and I felt that bond that only those who have seen the worst of the world together could have. We spoke again in the coming years on the phone, although not as often as we should have. One morning my wife came downstairs and asked me if I had heard the news – Brad had died. I could not comprehend what she was saying. 'Who's Brad?' I asked. 'Brad Olson,' she said. He had been feeling unwell and had called an ambulance to his home in Hong Kong, but died of a stroke before help could reach him.

My friends, my brothers – I will never meet people like them again. I can't help but think that those hard years in hard countries played a part in their deaths. But we relished it and I know they would not have had it any other way. In many ways parts of me have died too. It's an old cliché I know, but it stands: none of us truly gets out alive.

*

To survive, we need to look for little moments of joy, those moments when if you like, the light of God shines. We take those moments where we find them and hold them close; sometimes this is all that gets us through. This is what the fundamentalists of any faith, any political ideology – the identity warriors – hate the most: they hate love. They hate joy. And most of all they hate the freedom that only love and joy can bring.

When the Taliban took control of Afghanistan, all music stopped. Nothing but the human voice could be heard. Under the Taliban's version of Islamic law, music was sacrilege. The militants shut down the thriving music stores of Kabul; some musicians were even murdered. When the Taliban was toppled, the streets came to life again.

There is a strip of music stores in Kabul that is called Music Street, just like there is Chicken Street for the chicken restaurants. I'm not sure if those are official names but it is what we knew them as. No matter where I am in the world, I can never pass by a guitar shop without walking in. I just love the look of instruments, the feel of them in my hands and how the sound of strings on wood can lift my spirits. One day I walked in and saw hanging on the wall an old beat-up guitar with rusted strings. I pointed to it and motioned the shop owner to get it down for me. I managed to get it roughly in tune and started playing. Farhad was with me, and he was able to interpret when I asked the shop owner where this guitar came from. It had been left behind by a Soviet soldier after the Red Army pulled out of Afghanistan, he told me.

Here in my hands was all the recent history of this troubled land. What had started with the Soviet invasion had led to the rise of the Taliban, to al-Qaeda, and now to me sitting in a store tuning these rusted old strings in a land where music had been silenced. I started playing Led Zeppelin's 'Stairway to Heaven' – yes, what else – and as I played, something truly magical happened. The shop owner picked up a traditional Afghan instrument – a *rubab*, which is a little like a lute – and slowly started picking out the tune. Soon we two men, from different lands, each bound to his country's history, but who could not speak each other's language, were speaking through music, connecting across time and defying the brutality of the world.

I am given to dark visions of the soul. I have seen too much anger and violence, and I often fear that may be close to our true nature. But every now and then I am redeemed by the pure glory of being human.

12

WHITE PANIC

W e are bound to each other, this man and me. I have known him barely an hour, and I will soon leave and never see him again, but I know him as I know myself. I have come to his house in a time of war, in a city where to venture outside is to risk not coming back. I will never forget him.

That may sound melodramatic, but I lost CNN colleagues who were killed doing their jobs. This is the deal: we get to be up close to history, to see and write about the things we humans do to one another, and for that we put our lives on the line. This day, as on all days, I left the bureau in Baghdad wearing a bulletproof vest hidden under an oversized shirt. (You sometimes see reporters wearing visible vests, but that's usually for dress-ups – theatre. It is also a guarantee you will be a target: one of the first lessons I learned was that vests are not for show.) I was flanked by security personnel carrying guns inside their jackets; and we travelled in a heavily armoured car with an outer shell strong enough to repel gunfire. Of course, there was always the chance of a roadside bomb or an ambush, but we had to accept that. I was on my way to interview a man whose entire life had been framed by war: he had fled war in his homeland to come to Iraq, where war had found him again.

Muhamad lived with his family in a typical Baghdad neighbourhood. In another time it would have been teeming with life: kids playing, women out walking, men sipping coffee amid the bustle of local shops. But it was now a shelled-out ruin. The locals had endured the worst of the war; Saddam Hussein was gone and elections were looming: Iraqis would soon get to elect their own government. This was the 'flowering of democracy' that George W. Bush had promised when he concocted his lies about Saddam's weapons of mass destruction as a pretext for invading the country. As the people would find, democracy was no answer to their problems. But there was hope at this moment back then.

Muhamad was not a local, but he had lived in Baghdad for most of his life. He had endured the fear of Saddam's rule and was excited about a new future. Muhamad had come here as a young man after the 1967 Six-Day War between Israel and the Arab states. Like many other Palestinians, he had fled his hometown, leaving behind his house and all his possessions as the Israelis occupied more Palestinian territory. He had never seen his home again – but his home was never more than a touch away.

'Wait, I want to show you something,' Muhamad said.

Our interview had finished and we were talking about our lives. I told him my story, of my heritage and the history of Aboriginal people, invaded, dispossessed and occupied by foreigners. He saw something of his own struggle in mine. I told him what home meant to me; how even though I had spent so many years away, I carried my country – my ancestral country, not the nation Australia – deep in my heart.

Muhamad disappeared into his bedroom and returned a few minutes later carrying a small bottle filled with dirt. He asked me to open my hand and he put the bottle into my palm. This is my country, he said. It was all he had from his garden in Jenin, a town in the West Bank area of Palestine. Muhamad told me how he had scooped up the dirt before he fled. He kept it now in this bottle by his bed. It was the first thing he saw each morning and the last thing at night.

We were each exiles, Muhamad and me, occupying an uncertain place in the world. We were cast adrift, searching for a somewhere to call home with our trues homes always just out of reach. Muhamad and I were prisoners of freedom, captives of the West's dream of the future.

Muhamad was a victim of the *Nakba* – the catastrophe – that befell Palestinians evicted from their lands ahead of the establishment of the state of Israel. I was a product of the great theft – what Australians call 'dispossession' – of Aboriginal land. Two centuries after, my people had still not recovered. And Muhamad and I shared something with the Jews, those people scattered around the world, persecuted and brutalised. The Palestinians and the Jewish people shared so much – they were cousins – and yet they were locked in endless conflict with each other.

The *Nakba*, the Holocaust, the Invasion: what is left after everything has been taken? The philosopher Theodor W. Adorno once wrote that 'to write poetry after Auschwitz is barbaric'. Certainly any poetry that is written will be haunted by loss. Jean Améry, the Auschwitz survivor who carried his resentment to his grave, knew the pain of being homeless, of knowing what the world can do to us. 'There is no new home,' he wrote. 'Home is the land of one's childhood and youth. Whoever has lost it remains lost to himself, even if he has learned not to stumble about in the foreign country.'

And what is left to console we who are lost? It is the promise that in time we might forget, and in forgetting the past we will lose that grip on who we are. And we will welcome that as liberty, as salvation. For this, we are told, is our destiny. It is progress. Then we will belong to this imagined West. In place of our ancestors and our histories, we are offered liberalism and democracy.

The dominant political philosopher of the twentieth century, John Rawls, offered us a new vision for ordering this world in his phrase the 'veil of ignorance'. Imagine, he said, that you are born without knowledge of privilege or wealth or race or gender; you have no idea of the cards life has dealt you, and you now devise a system of government. It is the ultimate appeal to neutrality – a belief that we will set aside our differences and devise a society for all. Yet it would never be that easy. Would some benefit over others? Yes. And Rawls had a model for that, too. The 'difference principle' allowed for inequality, so long as the most benefit flowed to those most in need. So one person could attain untold wealth as long as it trickled down to those poorest. After three centuries of so-called enlightened thought, this is what we have: a veil of ignorance that pretends at equality.

Liberalism is revealed as a timid faith, a tepid, bloodless idea but one with which white people have ruled the world. It has covered for a multitude of sins. Liberalism is a convenient alibi for murder: we were only doing what was right. Or: we meant well, we had the best intentions. Liberalism is what made the likes of me and Muhammad strangers to our homelands. The anthropologist Stanley Diamond called us 'conscripts of civilisation', civilisation being white. We were the 'primitives' to be 'discovered', and we were swept along on history's tide, towards the end of history itself. Liberalism's great reward is that we should vanish into a 'veil of ignorance', a place of 'equality' beyond faith or race or class. Only white people already assured of their place in the firmament could imagine a world where nothing matters and call that virtuous.

Don't get me wrong, I have been a champion of liberalism myself, twisting and turning to try to get it or me to fit. But the price of belonging is often the loss of our souls, and that is too high a price to pay. I am not alone. Now liberalism is in tatters, and the white people whom liberalism has best served are gripped with panic.

*

On 6 January 2021, an American mob stormed the Capitol building in Washington DC. Members of Congress fled and hid as the protesters, some of them armed, overturned offices and stalked the hallways.

I was on air with ABC TV as the scene unfolded. Here were America's worst fears made real. The news anchors and commentators on the US networks competed with one another to describe this moment. Was it a coup? An insurrection? Was this terrorism or treason? All fingers were pointed at Donald Trump, the clown prince of American politics – once called a 'cartoon fascist' by British political scientist David Runciman – who had taken his reality TV show all the way to the White House. I interviewed guests who bemoaned the 'theft' of American democracy. How could this happen in the land of the free and the home of the brave? Where was the glorious city on the hill? This is not who we are, they told me. But of course it was. What we saw in the American capital was America laid bare.

Like everyone, I suspect, I was stunned by what I saw. It was a moment that fixed in my mind as surely as the attacks on the United States on 11 September 2001. Yet I was not surprised. In its own way this was a moment of honesty: a reckoning. The angry mob storming the Capitol building reflected a broken country where tens of millions of people have traded the American dream for American carnage, and no longer know what truth is. American politics, business and media have been complicit in delivering the United States to this moment.

The sad scene of a country that has long billed itself as a beacon of democracy – always contestable anyway – tearing itself apart also revealed the hypocrisy of those condemning it. Former president George W. Bush called it a 'sickening and heartbreaking' attack on democracy; America, he said, resembles a 'banana republic'. This from a man who concocted 'evidence' of Saddam Hussein possessing weapons of mass destruction as a pretext for an invasion of Iraq. His lies led to hundreds of thousands of Iraqi deaths and upturned the Middle East, setting off unending conflict – and cost his own nation US$2 trillion dollars.

Another former president, Bill Clinton, said the attack on the US Capitol building was fuelled by four years of 'poisonous politics' by Donald Trump. This is the same Clinton who, as president, disgraced the White House, perjured himself and became only the second president to be impeached; Donald Trump became the third. While Trump peddled his conspiracies of election fraud, I could only remember that Hillary Clinton had told Democrats there was 'a vast right-wing conspiracy' trying to destroy her husband's presidency. American political leaders have been playing fast and loose with the truth for decades, deepening partisan divisions and whipping up anger among their supporters.

Trump exploited a sick politics: from Richard Nixon's Watergate lies and corruption to Bush and Clinton, all roads led to Donald Trump. His dangerous delusions and his crazed followers should only remind us that America has always teetered on the edge of collapse. It is a nation born in crisis and awash with bloodshed: the genocide of Native Americans and the enslavement of Africans stolen from their lands, on whose scarred backs America built its wealth. Let's not forget this is a nation created by revolution, and torn apart by civil war, and that has seen presidents assassinated. The 1960s was marked by violence, revolt and political killings, and lit the fuse for division and tribalism. America is locked in a perpetual culture war, lacerated by class, race and faith.

Political writer Michael A. Cohen traces today's malaise to the election of Richard Nixon in 1968: a time he calls a 'maelstrom', a violent whirlpool of disorder. Americans then formed battle lines, shouting each other down over Black civil rights, gay equality, family values, gun laws, abortion or feminism. That year revealed a deep cleavage among the American people, and it profoundly reshaped politics. The Democrats lost the white working class, who were captured by an increasingly conservative and religious Republican right.

In their book *Cultural Backlash*, social scientists Pippa Norris and Ronald Inglehart write that Trump's victory 'was rooted in cultural changes that began decades earlier'. They harken back to the mid-twentieth century to track the turn of the Democrats, who became increasingly socially progressive. From the 1970s, they write, Republicans 'shifted toward more consistent social conservatism on key issues including, abortion, affirmative action, or LGBTQ rights'. Republicans also became the home of evangelical Christians, and Norris and Inglehart highlight several key moments. In 1992, right-wing political commentator and broadcaster Patrick Buchanan sought the Republican nomination, campaigning against a Democratic agenda of abortion on demand, gay rights and discrimination against religion. This, said Buchanan, 'is not the kind of change we can abide in a nation we still call God's country'. In 2008 the little-known governor of Alaska, Sarah Palin, became a phenomenon when she was selected as John McCain's vice presidential running mate. Palin traded in simple slogans and 'down home' homilies while railing against the Washington establishment. The Tea Party followed soon after, a conservative movement that was against big government; in the words of Norris and Inglehart, it stoked 'racial resentment ... with a strong authoritarian streak'.

Sociologist Gerardo Marti points out that the Tea Party accused Barack Obama of trying to take America away from 'real Americans'. He says: 'They saw Obama as degrading the status and prestige of America.' Geopolitical forecaster George Friedman, in his recent book *The Storm Before the Calm*, says the white working class looked at the Democratic elite and saw an attack on everything they held holy. 'Members of this class find themselves now in a world where their churches' views, the most authoritative imaginable, are considered not only wrong but a form of phobia,' he writes. They are often derided as racists, sexists, homophobes – but they in turn feel cheated and deserted by their country and its leaders.

Trump was right when he said that America was seriously divided before he got there. Previous presidents had at least paid lip service to unity; Trump never pretended that he governed for all. The country was ripe for his brand of political opportunism, us-versus-them populism feeding on fear and anxiety and exploiting racism. He was a Barnum and Bailey political circus act made for the 24/7 media age, where 'truth' is a matter of opinion. Journalist Matt Taibbi, in his book *Hate Inc.*, says the news media is addictive and anxiety-inducing, pitting people against each other while often failing to hold power accountable. The big cable news broadcasters, he argues, are politically partisan, each speaking into its own echo chamber.

Growing inequality has fractured America, with the working poor left behind while power and wealth is concentrated in the hands of what has been dubbed an 'American meritocracy'. The financial crash of 2008 left the country poorer and deeply scarred: ordinary Americans lost their homes and their jobs, while rich bankers got bailed out. Large parts of white America are poorer and sicker. Even before the coronavirus, the country was in the grip of a deadly health crisis.

Economists Anne Case and Angus Deaton chronicle this downward spiral in their book *Deaths of Despair and the Future of Capitalism*. It is devastating portrait of a lost generation. They reveal an America of 'haves and have nots', where a four-year college degree is the difference not just between better and worse career prospects, but between life and death. This is an America of meaningless or no work, of declining wages and shattered families. Most striking of all, for the first time in a century – not since the 1918 flu – American life expectancy is falling: this generation is dying younger than their parents. And where people live determines their fate. The largest increases in mortality rates for whites aged forty-five to fifty-four are in West

Virginia, Kentucky, Arkansas and Mississippi, which, as Case and Deaton point out, are 'all states with education levels lower than the national average'.

And how are these Americans dying? They are killing themselves. In the words of Case and Deaton: 'They are drinking themselves to death, or poisoning themselves with drugs, or shooting themselves or hanging themselves.' There is no faith in American capitalism, which, Case and Deaton write, 'looks more like a racket' to make the rich richer. I defy anyone to read *Deaths of Despair and the Future of Capitalism* and still cling to the myths of America.

*

I have missed America. I have missed that surge of anticipation and excitement I feel when getting off a long plane ride and walking through the terminal at LAX or JFK. I have missed waiting in the immigration queue and hearing foreign languages all around me, people of the world drawn to this place of dreams. I have missed the immigration officer telling me to have a nice day – that familiar, comforting sound of the American accent, the backdrop to my childhood in front of a TV screen. It has been a couple of years since I last visited, and with the COVID-19 restrictions it may be a couple more until I return. For now, America lives in my memory: hours spent wandering the Strand Book Store in New York, sampling guitars in the best guitar shops anywhere in the world, having a coffee and croissant and settling into one of the leather armchairs at Figaro Bistrot in Los Feliz, or eating dinner at Stamatis Greek restaurant in Queens.

That's what America is right now: a memory. Perhaps that's what it will remain. The mythical America is fading ... if it existed at all. There has always been another America: a counter to Reagan's 'shining city on the hill'. It is the America of slavery, genocide, poverty, segregation and lynching: it is an America that has never atoned for its original sin. America has always been a country caught in a battle between its demons and the better angels of its nature. Mythical America has never wanted for prophets: from George Washington to Abraham Lincoln or John F. Kennedy. Woodrow Wilson built the 'American century' after World War One with a belief that America was the nation chosen to lead others to liberty and democracy.

The American Eden was built on a belief in progress – 'go west, young man' – and in manifest destiny. As historian Greg Grandin has written, 'No myth in American history has been more powerful, more invoked by more presidents, than that of pioneers advancing across an endless meridian.' Barack Obama bought into the same idea, marvelling that 'a skinny kid with a funny name' could become the first Black president of the United States. There was no black America or white America, he said, as if casting a vote could absolve the nation of centuries of brutality and oppression. Joe Biden apparently still believes this, endlessly repeating that there are no 'red states or blue states, just the United States'. It is the price of office: never challenge the myth. But Americans themselves gave up on this a long time ago.

Grandin's book *The End of the Myth: From the Frontier to the Border Wall in the Mind of America* reveals how, after World War Two, 'the "frontier" became a central metaphor to capture a vision of a new kind of world order'. Yet America has also had its true prophets: those who see the country for what it is, and challenge it to live up to its creed. W.E.B. Du Bois, an African-American scholar, revealed that America's true faith was its 'whiteness', and that belief in whiteness assumed 'ownership of the earth'. Martin Luther King Jr gave his life to hold America to account: his civil rights campaign was set against the backdrop of America's war in Vietnam. 'The bombs in Vietnam explode at home,' he said. And James Baldwin wrote that Americans are 'unable to look into their own mirror'. White America, he said, was 'in the grip of a weird nostalgia, dreaming of a vanished state of security and order'.

These American prophets told us the truth of the country – a truth lurking just beneath the surface, and now so devastatingly revealed. Yet old myths die hard. Even now, with Trump impeached for a second time, political pundits are rushing to revive the nation's faded glory, as if the end of Trump will renew the promise of democracy. They cannot see what is before their eyes: it is America that is broken. These pundits are still blinded by their 'weird nostalgia' for a country that, to so many Americans, did not and does not exist. As Grandin writes, this was what Dr King warned America against: a 'constant fleeing forward' that allowed America to avoid 'a true reckoning with its social problems, such as economic inequality, racism, crime and punishment and violence'.

Grandin asks if Trumpism is a 'rupture, a wholly un-American movement' or 'the realisation of a deep-rooted American form of extremism'. The answer is that Donald Trump is an American president, a wholly American creation. He is absolutely a product of America's myth of progress and endless expansion, a twenty-first-century version of the robber barons of America's nineteenth-century Gilded Age. The difference now is that America is no longer on the rise. The nation's horizons have narrowed, and its global power and prestige is damaged. As Grandin says, expansion can 'no longer reconcile the contradictions' or 'redirect the anger'. America's anger has turned inward, and it is 'all-consuming and self-devouring'.

All nations are an invention: they are sustained by their own mythology. It has been so easy to believe in the mythical America, which oversaw the post-war economic boom, gave us the computer age and put people on the moon. Mythical America has drawn to it the world's poor, huddled masses yearning to breathe free. If I close my eyes, that is the America I can still just about believe in. It is the America I miss – the America that lives in my memory, or my fantasy. I can visit that America on holiday, while too many Americans exist in the nation off the tourist map: the urban wastelands, the small towns, the overgrown weeds, the shuttered factories, the rusted-out cars. According to Grandin, Americans could believe they was exceptional, that they had escaped history. Now they find themselves 'trapped by history … prisoners of the past'.

With Donald Trump, he says, 'America finds itself at the end of its myth'.

*

Joe Biden has an opportunity to deliver change to America, he says the right things, yet he is part of the problem. He is a product of the same meritocracy that has sold out so many of its people. The meritocrats are the elite, the richest, most privileged Americans who have a stranglehold on power and wealth. Like the aristocrats of old, they are distant from the rest of the population, often looking down on them, mocking them or exploiting them. Like the aristocrats, they party together, live alongside each other in the same wealthy suburbs; attend the same weddings. Party allegiances come and go – Donald Trump was once a Democrat and Bill and Hilary Clinton were guests at his wedding to Melania.

The meritocracy has rigged the game to suit themselves. Their children dominate entry to the best universities, a pathway to the richest careers, ensuring this new royalty shores up its status for another generation. So entrenched and immovable is this elite that a Brookings Institution study showed that, on current trends, 'it would take six generations for family economic advantage to disappear'. Harvard University philosopher Michael Sandel calls this the 'tyranny of merit'. And he says it is tearing America apart. Consider this: in his latest book, Sandel points out that at Ivy League colleges (the most prestigious in the country), 'there are more students from families in the top one percent (income of more than $630,000 per year) than there are students from all families in the bottom half of the income distribution combined'.

As it is for education, so it is for wealth. Sandel cites figures showing that 'the median income for working age men, $36,000, is less than it was four decades ago'. The richest 1 per cent, he points out, earn more than the bottom half combined. If you're born poor, you likely stay poor. Of those in the bottom fifth of the income scale, Sandel says, 'only about one in twenty will make it to the top fifth'. That's okay, though, as Barack Obama told them, because 'you can make it if you try'. By Sandel's count, he used that line in speeches more than 140 times during his presidency.

Sandel says the members of the meritocracy 'inhale too deeply of their success'. They overlook luck and good fortune, and think success is earned. The idea that 'you can make it if you try', Sandel says, 'congratulates the winners but denigrates the losers'. Obama came from a middle-class family in Hawaii, and went on to Ivy League college, the law and politics. He certainly made it, as did his wife, Michelle, who came from a more humble background. Obama ran a good line in hope, and for a while Americans bought it, enough to make him the first Black president. But when he inherited the global financial crisis in 2008, Sandel reminds us, Obama appointed Clinton-era economic advisers who championed the same financial deregulation that had created the crisis. He then bailed out the banks, because they were 'too big to fail'. Bankers went unpunished, while ordinary Americans lost their homes when they could not pay their mortgages.

Seventy years ago, the British sociologist Michael Young coined the term 'meritocracy', and he warned then that it would lead to social calamity. Yale University law professor Daniel Markovits opens his book *The Meritocracy Trap* with these four words: 'Merit is a sham.' Meritocracy, he says, 'banishes the majority of citizens to the margins of their own society'. Markovits writes that the tyranny of merit serves no one in the end, not even the rich, who are alienated, overworked and stressed, trapped on a treadmill of achievement and success. 'Meritocratic inequality divides society into the useless and the used up,' he concludes.

But it is the 'useless' who have borne the greatest impact, and it has turned them against the elite. The great divide has deformed American politics. Forty years of globalisation that hollowed out working-class jobs and stripped people of their dignity and communities has fuelled a populist blowback. Journalist Michael Lind's book *The New Class War* defines America as a battleground between 'the hub and the heartland'. The hubs are the high-density swanky suburbs of the rich and what Lind calls the 'managerial overclass'. The heartlands are the low-density, low-rise residential wastelands of the outer suburbs, poor and mostly white. Lind says the hub–heartland divide is reshaping politics. It is not just America, he says; the same phenomenon exists in Europe. It is a populism exploited by demagogues who fan ethnic and racial divisions among poor people, who should have more in common with each other than with the elite opportunists who seek to lead by fear.

America deserves better. Michael Sandel says hard work and hope aren't enough. A college degree should not be the measure of a person's worth. The meritocracy holds that unless you are moving up, you are left behind. But what about the strength of community, the dignity of labour, the importance of faith and family? Leaving should not be the only option for a good life. As Sandel says, 'A good society cannot be premised only on escape.' Power must be shared and made more accountable. Michael Lind says: 'A country run by an aristocracy or an oligarchy is a democracy in name only.' Lind's new class war offers us a bleak vision: 'a future of gated communities and mobs led by demagogues at the gates'.

*

Barack Obama was fond of quoting Martin Luther King Jr that the arc of the moral universe is long but it bends towards justice.

King himself was paraphrasing a nineteenth-century American abolitionist minister, Theodore Parker. Parker's idea was more nuanced, but King turned it into a bumper sticker. It is a magical idea, and I admit I have fallen under its spell. I want to believe it. But it is not true – in fact, it is a dangerous idea. It can soothe us that everything will be okay: evil will not prevail, and all we need do is wait and hope. Hope is an opium of the downtrodden and desperate. The moral arc of the universe does not bend to justice; at best, it bends to the appearance of justice, and the rulers of the universe are the powerful.

Obama himself was revealed as a false prophet: he promised hope but bequeathed a legacy of despair. He left behind a country that did not believe in itself. He left behind a country even more divided than when he took office. Black people did not believe in his hope. Too many died under his presidency, killed under the boots of the cops. Black Lives Matter took shape as a movement on Obama's watch. When it came to the question of race, Barack Obama was a bound man: white Americans made him president, but he rarely dared to question American racism. On the few occasions that he did, Obama was quickly put in his place. Even during his candidacy in 2008, he had to denounce his own pastor, Jeremiah Wright, who in a sermon damned America for its treatment of Blacks and its genocide of Native Americans. Obama knew the deal: you don't get elected by telling the truth. By the end of his presidency, he was more often lecturing Black Americans about what he saw as their failings, telling Black men how to be better fathers and reminding Black university graduates of their responsibilities.

Obama begat Donald Trump. Trump built his political base by attaching himself to the 'birther movement', those who questioned whether Obama, born in Hawaii with a Kenyan father, was in fact eligible to be President. Obama had mocked Trump, but he misread Trump's appeal. The poor white American underclass only heard Obama mocking them. Trump is gone but the divisions remain, and now Obama's deputy, Joe Biden, is president and reheating the same unconvincing Obama lines of hope and healing and unity that defy the nation's history.

On air for the ABC, I broadcast the Biden inauguration. CNN had called it a solemn occasion, and it was certainly a different inauguration. Gone were the crowds, and everyone wore a mask, essential in a nation ravaged by coronavirus. But on stage I saw the same American delusion: the same platitudes of hope. Washington cosied up to Hollywood in a choreographed spectacle that served only to remind those disenchanted, angry, poor white or Black Americans of how distant they remained from the American elite. Jennifer Lopez sang Woody Guthrie's 'This Land is Your Land' as if it were a hymn to America, completely misinterpreting the words of a radical folk singer who proudly called himself a socialist. Woody sang for the left behind, but Lopez left out those verses. Woody saw the people lining up for food relief in the American Dust Bowl and wondered if this country truly was their land, yet on that stage on that day Lopez stripped his words of their power and meaning.

It is a measure of how bent out of shape American politics has become that the people Woody sang for were now more than likely Trump voters, and the Democrats, once the party of the workers, was now the party of privilege. And all Joe Biden had to offer was a paean to unity. America, which has proclaimed itself a beacon of democracy, now stands as a symbol of democracy's decline. America is more an idea than a nation: a product of the

Enlightenment. Its creed is liberty, freedom and happiness, and its success depends on enough people believing in it, however elusive those virtues remain.

It has worked: America is an empire perhaps greater than any the world has seen. Certainly it is the richest and most powerful nation in human history. Yet by America we can measure the unravelling of the West. In four hundred years, Western civilisation has gone from Immanuel Kant, Beethoven and Shakespeare to self-help gurus like Tony Robbins, entertainers like Lady Gaga and the famous-for-being-famous Kardashians. The arc of America's moral universe can be measured in the years between Abraham Lincoln and Donald Trump. If this is where American democracy has brought us, there is little wonder it appears to so many of its citizens as utterly bankrupt. Broadcasting the Biden inauguration put me in mind of the words of James Baldwin referring to the myth of whiteness that really is the myth of America: it 'intellectually, morally and spiritually has the meaningless ring of a hollow drum and the odour of slow death'.

In *The Fire Next Time*, Baldwin laid bare America's challenge to stare itself in the face and see the truth of the country beyond the comforting myths. Its failure to do so ensured an inevitable confrontation – the fire to come. White Americans, said Baldwin, do not 'believe that time is real', and so those same white Americans 'do not believe in death'. The same could be said of Western civilisation as a whole. The West has always believed that it has conquered time: it has tamed nature and mapped the human soul as surely as it has mapped the human genome. The West has claimed Christianity as its defining faith, taking the teachings of a wandering, rebellious Jewish rabbi and turning them into a celebration of Western individualism. It is no accident that the story of Jesus is one of sacrifice and resurrection: the defying of death and the promise of eternal life.

In 2020, COVID-19 made death very real. This was the virus of the end times. Hour after hour, television news updated the numbers of infected and dead. America itself became, in sheer numbers, the hardest-hit country. COVID-19 spreads fear even quicker than infection. Everywhere there is fear: fear of the virus, of economic collapse, of terrorism, of rebellion and revolt, of guns, of refugees and immigrants, of climate change – and the great fear of China. China, from where the virus first spread, has more than anything accelerated white panic. China is growing more powerful and rejecting the West, rejecting whiteness. It mocks the belief that freedom is inevitable or even envied. The Chinese Communist Party does not envy Western freedom, and despite its brutality and iron grip on the country, most Chinese people are healthier, wealthier and more secure living without the West's idea of freedom.

Three decades after Francis Fukuyama declared the 'end of history', there is a serious discussion about the end of the West. Our times don't resemble Fukuyama's liberal triumphalism so much as Samuel Huntington's *Clash of Civilizations*. Huntington's book was published several years after Fukuyama's, but it is a riposte to the idea that history ends. More than Fukuyama, Huntington identified the pull of identity. In the post–Cold War world, he wrote, 'flags count and so do the symbols of cultural identity ... because culture counts, and cultural identity is what is most meaningful to most people'. Huntington warned against the belief in Western universalism, instead stressing the uniqueness of the West. Yet he said the West, perhaps more than any other culture, sees its civilisation as the 'central drama of human history'. Now, with the world on tilt, the new so-called leader of the free world, Joe Biden, offers hope for a return to normal – a return to a liberal order that is tattered and torn, led by an America that struggles to lead its own people.

*

Why do we hear so much about the 'liberal global order' when the truth is it has never existed? It was never a global order, and it was not liberal. The phrase itself is a modern invention that came into vogue in recent decades, yet it is presented as holy writ. This mythical order has been invoked as a means of dealing with a disruptive, authoritarian China. Policy-makers like Australia's top diplomat, Frances Adamson, have said we need to reinforce a resilient, flexible and open system that can sustain peace in a more complex and competitive geopolitical era. Adamson, the head of the Department of Foreign Affairs and Trade, has acknowledged that the world has entered a more uncomfortable period for liberal-democratic nations like Australia, but says the solutions are still to be found in a global order.

The promotion of this order accelerated after the end of the Cold War in the 1990s, a period of Western triumphalism when President George H.W. Bush talked about a new world order and, later, President Bill Clinton lectured the Chinese Communist Party that it was on the wrong side of history. This was an example of the type of end-of-history hubris that assumed the supremacy and universality of liberal-democratic values: simply, it meant get with the system or get left behind. Singaporean former diplomat and political commentator

Kishore Mahbubani said this thinking did 'serious brain damage to Western minds'. According to Mahbubani, the 1990s marked the end of Western domination and a turn to the rise of Asia, particularly China.

Harvard University professor Joseph Nye has reminded us that 'American dominance was never as great as some myths make it out to be'. The world is not the West, and liberal values are not universally embraced. Fewer than 20 per cent of the world's population lives in the West, yet Western nations have dominated global power. The post-1945 order was not global, it was American. It did not include the Soviet Union or China. The post-war institutions were controlled by the most powerful countries – what political scientist Michael Barnett has described as a club of liberal states with their own exclusive associations. These Western liberal democracies preached the virtues of liberty and freedom at home, yet would, when it suited their interests, support despots abroad. As Barnett put it, this was not a liberal world order, but 'a world order created for liberal states'.

The seeds of this were sown after World War One and the foundation of the League of Nations. In his magnificent book *The Twenty Years' Crisis, 1919–1939*, historian E.H. Carr reveals a utopian vision of a world built on faith in liberal reason. Reason, it was believed, could banish war and govern politics. As Carr says, 'the wish is father to the thought'. Leaders of the time believed that they could rewire human behaviour, putting the collective good above individual or national interests. It was always flawed, but as American president Woodrow Wilson said when asked about the League of Nations, 'If it won't work, it must be made to work.' Of course, we know now that the world lurched again to catastrophic war in 1939.

John Gray calls this politics as religion – an apocalyptic faith. These visions of ordering society can inspire freedom or darker dreams of total control. It can inspire liberalism, but just as readily Nazism or communism. All draw from the same source – the Enlightenment, and its belief in progress and the forward march of history that ranks human beings, often racially, on a scale of civilisation – and all can be put in service of murder. As Gray writes in *Black Mass: Apocalyptic Religion and the Death of Utopia*, 'The peculiar achievement of Enlightenment racism was to give genocide the blessing of science and civilisation ... the destruction of entire peoples could be welcomed as part of the advance of the species.'

We can hear the echo of Woodrow Wilson's words today from those who insist that if the liberal order doesn't work, it must be made to work. How to do that, when the biggest engine of economic growth and rival to American power is a repressive, authoritarian regime that rejects liberalism and harbours resentment at what it sees as a century of foreign domination and humiliation? Joseph Nye says the so-called global order does not need to be revised, it needs to be replaced. 'It is not enough to think of exercising power over others,' he says. 'We must think of exercising power with others.'

This requires building stronger alliances with nations that share liberal values, while recognising that old-style big-power intervention is limited in a world where Russia and China are stronger. As Michael Barnett writes, 'Wanting a liberal international order and having an international order governed by liberal principles are two different things.' A politically realist view suggests that if we are to have anything akin to a global order in the twenty-first century, it cannot be an American-dominated order. If the old order is having problems, Barnett says, it is less to do with the weakening of liberalism, and more to do with a need to overhaul the rules as power shifts from the West to the East.

Brookings Institution scholar Thomas Wright says global leadership has come at a great cost to America, not just abroad but at home. Americans, he says, 'have never been particularly enamoured with the liberal international order'. As he points out, Americans have wanted to pull back and expect other nations to share the burden. He rejects the idea that China or Russia can simply be 'accommodated' in a global system; it is a 'fantasy' or, at worst, a 'devil's bargain'. China and Russia want more than just accommodation. The return to rivalry was inevitable, Wright argues, a clash of the 'free world and a neo-authoritarian world'. Maintaining a liberal order 'completely misses the point'. He prefers a 'free world' strategy that preserves liberty 'at home and abroad'. It means pushing back against 'neo-authoritarians', and that requires all 'measures short of general war'.

We are in a world with no easy choices, and a utopian belief in universal liberalism is not the answer. Despite wishing it so, China has not become like the West. It has grown richer, stronger and more authoritarian. It has not been on the wrong side of history. It is one of the liberal fantasies that we can vanquish history. No civilisation lasts forever, and we do not live forever. The late historian Eric Hobsbawm wrote of the twentieth century that 'the historical memory was no longer alive'. Young people, he said, grow up in a 'permanent present'. But in the late 1980s and early 1990s, 'an era in world history ended, and a new one began.' China and Russia have long, hard memories. History has never died there.

Hobsbawm concluded his study of the twentieth century, *The Age of Extremes*, with a warning: we may not know where we are going, but history has brought us to this point. We cannot prolong the past; if we do, we will fail. We must change, he said, and 'the alternative to a changed society is darkness'.

13

THE DEVIL'S CENTURY

In the 1997 film *The Devil's Advocate*, Al Pacino plays the Devil in the guise of the head of a successful law firm who employs an ambitious young lawyer performed by Keanu Reeves. Slowly the Devil breaks down the scruples of his young disciple, tempting him with wealth and power. It is a film that shows how weak we all can be: how, given enough incentive, we abandon our principles. There is one unforgettable scene where Pacino tells Reeves about God. God, he says, is a prankster who sets up the world for his own amusement. God writes the rules and then sets them in opposition – his own private gag reel. The Devil, Pacino's character, says has been here from the beginning: he cared about what man wanted and never judged him for his desires. It has been said that the Devil's greatest trick was making us believe he didn't exist. The world is the Devil's playground. We may want to tell ourselves that evil does not exist, or that there is no divine spirit in the world. Yet we fail to see the Devil even when he is right in front us.

We turned the Devil into a monster, something with horns and cloven feet. At church Sunday school, fear of the Devil is leveraged to scare children into obedience. He belongs to superstition, witchcraft and sorcery: three hundred years ago we banished this medieval Satan. The Enlightenment thinkers of the seventeenth century gave us a new way of seeing the world, what we call the Age of Reason. This was the birth of the modern world, a scientific and philosophical revolution that separated human beings from nature, and that told us we were not bound to our base urges or instincts but by our rational thought we could rule our fate. The Enlightenment gave shape to democracy, individual rights, private property. It inspired revolutions in America and France that told us we are free and equal. One of the greatest Enlightenment thinkers, Immanuel Kant, left us a dream of perpetual peace, in a world beyond our tribes and borders: a dream now within our grasp.

But the Devil made the Enlightenment a philosophy of evil too. The Devil became the master of history. If Enlightenment was progress, then the Devil himself would set the destination. In the name of progress and history, tyrants dreamed of a utopia where human beings were tools of the state. This was a grand historical mission, says Vladimir Tismăneanu, where 'nature, science, language, all had to be subordinated to the sacrosanct goal'. Polish philosopher Leszek Kołakowski warns that the Devil dwells in history: 'the Devil ... invented ideological states ... states whose legitimacy is grounded in the fact that their owners are owners of truth. If you oppose such a state or its systems, you are an enemy of truth.'

Philosopher Zygmunt Bauman said, 'How safe and comfortable and cosy it would be if it were monsters and only monsters who perpetrated monstrous deeds.' So we see evil as something inhuman. It is what we call the Nazis: monsters. What we fail to see is that evil can live right next door, in the most seemingly normal people. It is precisely how normal they are that makes such evil possible. When we – ordinary, good, loving, honest people – stop asking questions, when we blindly follow the leaders, when we refuse to say no, we are capable of the worst atrocities. As Hannah Arendt pointed out, evil is banal. Heinrich Himmler orchestrated the holocaust by enlisting everyday Germans – parents, husbands, wives, sons and daughters – to do the Nazi's duty. The gas chamber, the guillotine and the gulag all were made possible by people just like you and me following orders.

We are not immune. Don't think we are somehow above the brutes. Don't think that our civilising democracy makes savagery impossible. I have seen too much of the worst of the world to believe in the better angels of our nature. The Devil carries the virus of tyranny, just waiting to infect us. That's what happened in Weimar Germany in the 1930s. In his book *The Death of Democracy: Hitler's Rise to Power and the Downfall of the Weimar Republic*, historian and lawyer Benjamin Carter Hett describes Germany then as 'some kind of apex of human civilisation'. Its constitution protected individual rights and freedoms; there was an active social justice movement and widespread gender and sexual equality. Germany was home to high culture and science. It gave the world Albert Einstein. But it also gave the world Hitler.

The Nazis are a Rorschach test: we can see in their rise whatever we wish to see. So what is it we see today? To some, 1930s Germany is a mirror of our times: we are living through some Weimar redux. Benjamin Carter Hett argues that after basking in the post–Cold War liberal triumph of the 1990s, we are seeing the cracks appear again. We see this everywhere: a blowback against globalisation is fuelling right-wing populism;

an international refugee crisis threatens our sense of belonging and nationhood and hardens anti-immigration attitudes; and we continue to fight terrorism. All of this, Hett writes, 'means that in many ways, our time more closely resembles the 1930s than it does the 1990s'.

What happened then, and how can we learn from that today? I can break it down to four things: hubris, history, resentment and identity. Each feeds the other: the hubris of victory and a faith in moral or political universalism inflicts humiliation that breeds anger and resentment – a victim looking for someone to blame – and this hardens into an identity of 'us versus them'.

The Nazi Party grew out of the German defeat in World War One. Some of its leaders – Hitler included – were soldiers in the Kaiser's army. Hitler gave the Germans a story: how a proud nation had been insulted and mocked after suffering defeat in World War One. The Treaty of Versailles, he said, robbed them of land and wealth: it stole German sovereignty. According to Hett, 'It is not an exaggeration to say that the answer to all questions about Weimar lies somewhere in the First World War.' To that we can add the depression of 1929. Humiliated in war and now impoverished, the German people grew bitter, and Adolf Hitler emerged with a story that seemed to give meaning to German suffering. Historian Lewis Mumford said fascism 'is found in the human soul'.

Nazi propaganda chief Joseph Goebbels wrote that what set modern Germans apart was a willingness to sacrifice for the people. Goebbels drew a nation into his dark vision and enlisted ordinary German people into acts of evil. Psychoanalyst Erich Fromm explored the psychology of Nazism in his book *The Fear of Freedom*. He says that by the 1930s the German people were tired and ready to submit. Having fought a war and then suffered through economic collapse, many had little fight left with which to counter a Hitler. The liberal bourgeoisie and the Catholic Church, especially, Fromm says, 'did not show the kind of resistance one might have expected'. The poor flocked to Hitler because they saw in him a symbol of resurgent German pride, as the Nazi Party 'became identical with Germany'. Someone may even oppose what the Nazis represent but not oppose the Nazi Party itself, Fromm writes: 'if he has to choose between being alone and feeling that he belongs to Germany, most people will choose the latter'. It was the middle class – those who had lost money and prestige, and felt the humiliation of the past – who sealed Hitler's rise. As Fromm saw it, they projected 'social inferiority onto national inferiority'. The younger generation especially, writes Fromm, 'was driving for action'.

What of the soul of Hitler himself? In his biography/manifesto *Mein Kampf*, Hitler describes himself as a 'nobody', the 'unknown man'. In remaking Germany he was remaking himself. This World War One corporal, failed artist and beer hall rabble rouser had for a time performed the Devil's greatest trick, convincing people he wasn't real. A smart, cultured, democratic society allowed itself to descend into tyranny. People stopped asking questions; some were silent when they should have spoken; others who felt betrayed and humiliated found in Hitler someone who would give voice to their resentment. We are foolish to think this can't happen today.

Fascism is a shapeshifter: it takes on new names, but it still plays on fear, anger, resentment; it still uses history as a weapon and rallies people to a shared victimised identity. Is this what we see today? We should not expect that fascism today should imitate the Nazis' version; like the Devil himself, it is good at disguise. But new and dangerous fault lines – economic, social, political – are being exploited by a new generation of charismatic leaders and political parties, just as the Nazis did in Weimar Germany.

Across Europe, neo-fascists, some of the more extreme of whom openly praise Hitler, are on the rise. Radical right-wing politics is finding success at the ballot box in France, Italy, Poland, Austria, Denmark. In Germany itself, the Alternative für Deutschland (AFD, or Alternative for Germany) is the third-largest political party in the Bundestag. The AFD is avowedly nationalistic: its leaders have flirted with Nazi-era language and defend Germany's wartime past. In Hungary, the democratically elected and increasingly popular prime minister, Viktor Orbán, flaunts what he calls his 'illiberal democracy'. He has weakened the courts and the media, wound back freedoms, reinforced his country's border with barbed wire to keep out refugees – and increased his political majority.

Is fascism even the right term for this new far right? Scholar Enzo Traverso, who has studied these groups closely, prefers 'post-fascism'. It helps distinguish them from the fascists of the past. Islamic fundamentalist groups like Islamic State, he says, can be described as fascist, even though ISIS itself would be opposed by European right-wing political parties who see Muslims as an enemy. There is no one-size-fits-all fascism; instead, Traverso says, it has mutated. The parties of the extreme right do not follow the same rule book. They adapt to local political conditions; some – like the National Rally in France, previously called the National Front – soften their rhetoric to appear more moderate. We cannot ignore 'the fascist womb from which they emerge', Traverso writes, but they have 'transformed themselves, and they are moving in a direction whose ultimate outcome remains unpredictable'.

Australian political scientist John Keane has devoted his career to the study of democracy and says that rather than see the new right as fascists or autocrats or authoritarians, we should view them as despots. Unlike twentieth-century fascists, the new despots don't seek to repress people, but they 'are masters of deception and seduction'. Like a parasite, he says, they attach themselves to democratic institutions, they are savvy media players, and they 'know how to employ the law to defeat the law'. They 'cultivate submission', he says, and 'produce cowards'. Keane says the world has not seen such dangerous times since the 1930s. He warns us that 'everywhere something sinister is being born of our darkening times; a kind of despotism the world has never seen before'. Keane's preference of the word 'despotism' over 'tyranny' or 'authoritarianism' may be a distinction in search of a difference, but it does illustrate that the resurgence of populist politics is a hydra, a beast with many heads.

Like the Nazis, the operatives of the extreme right operate under the cover of democracy. Look, they say, we are peaceful, democratic politicians – and if the people elect us, how can the people be wrong? Indeed, as I have argued, people have reason to be drawn to these groups. When right-wing politicians talk about reclaiming their country, stopping the flow of refugees, reopening factories, wresting control from political and business elites – when they salute the flag and sing the anthem – they are speaking to the souls of people who need something to believe in. It is not enough to dismiss this as ugly or deluded; democracy means people have a voice. Progressive liberals increasingly risk losing the 'hearts and minds' battle to this resurgent right. These liberal cosmopolitans losing their grip on power often sound as though they would rather blame the voters than look at themselves. They remind me of something the German poet Bertolt Brecht once asked: would it be easier to 'dissolve the people and elect another'?

Fear makes us see things that are not there: in the dark, we may mistake tyranny for freedom. Illiberal, small-t tyrants like Viktor Orbán – a declared enemy of the open society – may appear as saviours. The resurgence of proto-nationalist groups, linked to a hard-right ideology, unsettles core liberal beliefs in human nature: that we aspire to greatness, that we heed our better angels. But history is witness to a much darker humanity, one that turns the idea of freedom on its head. It is what we saw in 1930s Germany, and in the Soviet Union: it is the notion that true freedom can come only from the state. The Nazis and the Soviet Communists fell, but the philosophy endures: it is something Adolf Hitler knew only too well. His chilling warning in *Mein Kampf* remains relevant: people would rather 'submit to the strongman than dominate the weakling ... they are far more satisfied by a doctrine that tolerates no rival than by the grant of liberal freedom'.

These broken people submit to the strong leader: the ultimate defender of their freedom. It is only there, in the embrace of the all-dominating state, that we feel the wounds of our soul heal without scars.

*

So now we must stare it down, this tyranny. Coronavirus has pressed fast-forward on our world. How we thought we had time;

how we still wanted to believe that our vaunted global liberal order could hold. The truth is we were unravelling before COVID-19 hit. We have been drifting for years, unmoored: our society has been eating itself from the inside. We are atomised, disconnected from each other, turning in ever smaller circles; in our echo chambers we cling to our tribes, four legs good, two legs bad. We have been witnessing the slow death of that which should be most precious to us: democracy. It is in retreat around the world.

As I write this, Freedom House – a think tank that measures the health of our political institutions – now counts thirteen consecutive years of negative freedom. The rule of law, a free media, political accountability, human rights and universal suffrage – all have been declining. To that you can add rising inequality, a loss of trust and a cynicism about the dominance of politics by a small educated, privileged elite. People are turning away from 'politics as usual'; as a community, we are more polarised and hostile as we engage in identity-based culture wars. All of this is contributing to a wave of populism that is shaking up the global order.

We are already inscribing democracy's headstone. Political scientist Peter Mair opened his 2013 book *Ruling the Void: The Hollowing of Western Democracy* with this sentence: 'The age of party democracy has passed.' Political parties, he argues, have become disconnected from wider society. This has implications for their legitimacy and effectiveness, and the political landscape is fractured. Democracy's path, since it emerged out of ancient Athens, has been troubled. Philosopher A.C. Grayling says in his book *Democracy and Its Crisis*, 'For most of recorded history political power has been held by the few over the many.'

Not long ago, we were talking about a golden age. The second half of the twentieth century was good for democracy: by 2000, Freedom House counted 120 democracies, or 63 per cent of the world's nations. It had accelerated after the Cold War, with the proclaimed triumph of Western liberal democracy, Fukuyama's 'end of history'. Now that sounds more like a myth. What happened to us? History, that's what. Out of a morning sky a plane crashes into a building; a New York banker logs onto a computer and sends the world's financial system into a tailspin; in an ancient country, for a century on its knees, a dictator orders the army to shoot down protesters.

Three events stand out. First, the 11 September 2001 terrorist attacks in the United States, which triggered the war on terror, the invasions of Afghanistan and Iraq, wars we are still fighting. Second, the 2008 global financial crisis – something more akin to a depression in much of the world – which not only revealed the weakness of the world's financial system, but shook confidence in our politics and way of life. And third, the biggest political earthquake of all: the return of a powerful China, an authoritarian regime that is on track to become the biggest economy in the world. It is a nation to which we have hitched our futures, and yet it rejects so much of what the West stands for.

While the liberal-democratic West has struggled, China has continued to grow. Despite warnings of imminent collapse, the Chinese Communist Party has proven itself remarkably resilient. In two decades from the 1990s, it has lifted more than half a billion people out of poverty. China is walking a high wire: getting rich while refusing to become free. The world has never seen anything like this. Western leaders have refused to believe it, predicting that China will go the way of the Soviet

Union. The Communist Party's leaders were lectured that they were on the wrong side of history. But it is the West that history may count out.

China does not want to become like the West; it regards the West as weak. President Xi Jinping is considered the most powerful person on the planet, and he believes China has a better model. Its authoritarian-capitalist system is spreading its influence, and other countries are taking their own autocratic turn, shedding their freedoms. Turkey under Recep Tayyip Erdoğan is cracking down on opponents and locking up journalists; Vladimir Putin jails his rivals in Russia; and Hungary's Victor Orbán has transformed from one-time student democracy campaigner to political demagogue.

In the past five years, two further events have shaken global politics: Brexit and the Trump presidency. In the words of British political writer David Goodhart, these marked 'not so much the arrival of the populist era but its coming of age'. They were about a 'core values divide', Goodhart argues. Britain's vote to leave the European Union highlighted a flaw in the EU project and in globalisation more broadly: it weakens national sovereignty. Europe political watcher Ivan Krastev, in his book *After Europe*, says the EU 'has always been an idea in search of a reality'. When countries lose control of their borders and their economies, blowback is inevitable. According to Krastev, Europeans have lived with a 'paralysing uncertainty', and 'what was until now unthinkable – the disintegration of the union – begins to be perceived as inevitable'.

Across the Atlantic, Donald Trump exploited similar anti-globalisation, anti-deindustrialisation tensions to win the White House, campaigning for secure borders and a tougher trade position: America first. He rode the wave of populism that has seen disrupters win office or strengthen their foothold in elections around the world. Liberal cosmopolitans – those rich, educated, live-anywhere elites – fear they are losing the battle and say democracy is being weakened. Those left behind see it entirely differently: this is democracy's revenge.

Yet Harvard University professors in government Steven Levitsky and Daniel Ziblatt have told us how democracies die in their book of that title. Democracies die in war, they write in *How Democracies Die*, but they also die at the hands of elected leaders, 'presidents or prime ministers who subvert the very process that brought them to power'. Writing in 2018, they worry about Trump's attack on some of the institutions of democracy – judges and the media – and fear that the United States will abandon its role as democracy promoter. But, as they argue, this democratic drift preceded Trump: 'The soft guard-rails of American democracy have been weakening for decades.'

The West is in a turf war. Arrogant globalists have dominated power, playing Monopoly with other people's money and roulette with the jobs of blue-collar workers. They have shut down industries and relocated factories, leaving people stranded in fly-over ghost towns. They want people's votes but give every impression off not liking the people themselves. Barack Obama accused the white poor of America of 'clinging to their God and their guns'. Hillary Clinton called them 'deplorables' and wondered why they didn't elect her president. Elites mock the food people eat, the sports they play and the TV shows they watch. It is a broad-brush caricature, I know, but all too real to many people. They have been lied to, asked to send their children to endless wars, lost their houses in big bank Ponzi schemes and then watched politicians bail out the banks, and seen their jobs shipped offshore, only to be told they can retrain for the tech sector. No wonder they are fed up. And then those same ridiculed masses turn to arch-nationalists, racists, snake-oil salesmen who pledge to 'drain the swamp', leaders who are just as rich and elite as any other politician but claim to be driven by the voices of the left-behind.

This is where the virus of tyranny thrives in the West: in the West's loss of confidence, its political divisions, the steady erosion of its values. We are meant to be at the end of history; we thought we had banished politics, elevated morality and the market, cast off ideology. Instead we entered a post-historical slumber, marked first by hubris and then by lethargy and cynicism. While the West goes through an identity crisis, caught between the tyranny of the elites who want to rule the world and the tyranny of the Trumps who want to retreat from the world, the tyranny of a powerful China grows. That is where people are jailed for their words, their thoughts or their faith. Where a Communist Party that ordered the army to shoot its own people protesting for democracy remains in power. China did not become like the West – it is threatening the West. The Communist Party knows what it is; the West is unsure what it believes, let alone whether it should fight for those beliefs. The words of the philosopher Leo Strauss, from last century, bear repeating: '[W]hen we were brought face to face with tyranny – with a kind of tyranny that surpassed the boldest imagination of the most powerful thinkers of the past – our political science failed to recognize it.'

In *The Devil's Advocate*, Al Pacino finishes his speech by telling us that the Devil has won: he has nurtured every sensation that humanity has aspired to have. I am the Devil, he says, and

I have never rejected man. The Devil lives in history; he lurks in the dark corners, waiting for us. He is a shapeshifter: he has had many faces, and each time he appears we are fooled again. We don't even want to believe he is real. The Devil speaks to that part of us we don't want to see. He has the upper hand because he knows our terrible secret: we so easily bend to fear; we so readily surrender our freedom for security. That's the Devil's grand bargain: give me your souls and the world will be yours. Hitler knew this; Stalin knew it when he spoke of producing a new human; and Mao knew it when he said the Chinese people were a blank sheet of paper. As Al Pacino's Devil asks, 'who in their right mind could possibly deny that the twentieth century was entirely mine.'

*

For three centuries the West has believed that it can bend the rules of time and space – that it has conquered nature itself. I wonder whether, a hundred years from now, someone will write of our folly. I can imagine what 2020 will look like all those years hence, how politicians in some of the world's most powerful countries will be seen to have failed their people in the face of a new threat, how this virus will be seen to have undermined our freedom and our faith in progress. This future writer will tell how we cringed in fear, locking ourselves away, trying to forestall death. *What were they thinking? Did they believe they were immortal, that death would not find them anyway?* But that's what happens when people rule the planet: they believe in their own immortality. How different the world of our writer will look to our own, as foreign as our great-grandparents' time is to us. They may write of how the West fell, just as the Mongols, the Abyssinians and the Persians fell, the Romans too. Those empires did not see their end either; they believed they had harnessed the power of the gods and answered the questions of eternity.

The virus will be a chapter in our writer's book, but it will not be the most important part of the story – that is us. That's what our writer will say: these people lost sight of themselves. These people, who carried a world of knowledge in their phones, no longer heeded history. They were immersed in a world of things, of possessions and vanity. They fouled themselves on mindless entertainment and forged themselves on processed food while nature stored up its vengeance. Even when the storms grew more intense and the fires more frequent, they fiddled and danced while the planet burned. Coronavirus stalked them and shut them down, but the virus revealed a deeper malaise: the West had been unravelling for decades. In fact, the West had known nothing but turmoil: war and disaster. In 2020, the defenders of the West were increasingly panicked, flailing at culture wars and forming warring tribes, only to destroy the thing they wished to save. All the while the great threat to the unchallenged supremacy of the West loomed, a nation set on an inexorable rise to power – the most populous nation on the planet. For the first time in three centuries, the world's greatest power would not come from the West. Our future writer will see what we did not ourselves so clearly see: the coronavirus pandemic revealed the depth of the West's existential crisis. It was China the West feared – but the virus merely came from there.

If I were that writer, who would I turn to as my guide? There is none better or more prescient than Dietrich Bonhoeffer. The Lutheran pastor and philosopher, who sacrificed his life to stand against the Nazis, warned us of the slow death of the West. He told us that our pride, vanity, and lust for power and treasure would be our undoing. Power, he told us, sacrifices justice and destroys peace. Democracy, supposedly rule with the consent of the governed, is hijacked by special interests who weaken the authority of the state. This is man's sorry fate, he wrote. '[I]t may be that there will be no salvation for the human spirit from the more and more painful burdens of social injustice until the ominous tendency in human history has resulted in perfect tragedy.'

Bonhoeffer knew what evil was; he knew that it was real, and what we must do to stand against it. Yet he also knew that we were weak, that human nature was brutal and it hunted in packs. Reason, he told us, would never be enough; our faith in human reason may even be the source of our misery.

As a young reporter, I was tossed into a changing world. I was told this world was new. The old order was gone, and we would not be cursed by history like our parents and grandparents were. Three decades later, we know that was not true. There is no end of history. What a Western fantasy that is. Only those who do not come from the other side of history can believe we can tame the past, that each generation can be washed clean of the blood on their hands. I am too drenched in the misery of history, in the unrelenting torture of it all, how it grips one's soul and will not let go, to ever believe that it is in the past. History is, as James Joyce said, a nightmare from which I am trying to awake.

It has been the struggle of my life to free myself from the chains of my own past, but those ghosts are strong. Is there any way of forgetting history without justice? Are vengeance and resentment themselves virtues? But are there crimes so monstrous they cannot be forgiven? Are there sins so heinous that they cannot be moved from history to mere memory? The great evil of the twentieth century, the Nazi holocaust that raised the courage of Dietrich Bonhoeffer, was a crime beyond forgiveness.

The Austrian philosopher Jean Améry refused to forget what he had seen. He railed against what he called 'the hollow, thoughtless, utterly false conciliatoriness or the pathos of forgiveness and reconciliation'. His words are chilling: 'What happened; what happened. But that it happened cannot be so easily accepted. I rebel against my past, against history, and against a present that places the incomprehensible in the cold storage of history.'

Jean Améry was born in Vienna as Hans Mayer in 1912; his father was Jewish and his mother Catholic. Under new laws passed in 1935, he became legally recognised as Jewish, and that would in time become a death sentence. In 1938 he fled to Belgium but by 1943 he was caught and tortured by the Gestapo, and eventually sent to Auschwitz. He arrived with 655 others – 417 were immediately killed. He saw the totality of the brutality of the Nazis, and wrote that 'the world always dies where the claim of some reality is total'. Améry never relinquished his resentment; in his eyes it would have been a betrayal. For him there would be no place for war monuments acknowledging the Nazi shame or the Jewish suffering: 'To be a victim alone is not an honour,' he said.

Jean Améry's words speak to the divide of history that separates our world. Everywhere I have been, I have felt that unbearable weight of suffering. It is a wound beyond healing. From Afghanistan and Pakistan to Iraq and Northern Ireland,

North Korea and China, everywhere identity is inseparable from resentment. Is there more fertile ground for the Devil to do his work? The suffering that he has inflicted is now his to own and to whisper into the ears of despots and tyrants who will take the righteous anger of the victims and turn it into a force for vengeance. And then, in the darkest hours, there are those who endure and will turn their hearts not to hate but to love. I found that in a place where people who looked like me had been brutalised and oppressed.

The first story I covered as a foreign correspondent was the fall of apartheid in South Africa. There, an evil, repulsive regime saw black people as less than human: they elevated whiteness and ruled mercilessly over black. I had looked to South Africa as a young boy, learning of the heroes who struggled for freedom: Mandela, Biko and Tutu. In 1991, I travelled to South Africa to see this nation transformed. Nelson Mandela had been released after twenty-seven years in prison. This revolutionary leader was on the precipice of history; within three years he would become the country's first black president.

I arrived in a nation that was tearing itself apart. Black turned on black in a struggle for power. More than once we came under fire in the sprawling black township of Soweto. It was indeed a war zone. I can vividly recall one night in the massive Baragwanath hospital – then the largest in the world – watching body after body being brought into emergency. Some had been shot, others stabbed or beaten. There was no room left, and the wounded and injured were treated in corridors, where the floors were smeared in blood.

With my producer and dear friend Peter Charley and a South African film crew, I travelled the length of the country. Apartheid was crumbling but old hatreds and bigotry died hard. We reported in one town, Oranje, in Orange Free State, where the white residents had kicked out every black person. Here they pledged to rebuild a new white homeland. One man, seeing my dark skin, asked me what I was. When I told him I was Aboriginal from Australia, he sniffed that he was sorry for me. I was like an animal, he said.

As black turned on black, so white neo-Nazi groups gathered their numbers for what they expected was a coming race war. One group, the Afrikaner Resistance Movement, was led by a former South African policeman, Eugène Terre'Blanche – his surname translated as 'white earth' – who swore violence against black rule. His group was linked to assassinations and bombings in the 1990s.

I had arranged to meet Terre'Blanche at his stronghold in the Transvaal. Our sound recordist, Milton Nkosi, was black and we were told that he would not be allowed to accompany us. I wondered what Terre'Blanche would make of me. I wouldn't have to wait long. I turn very dark in the sun, and after several weeks in South Africa I was a deep brown colour. Terre'Blanche walked into the room for our interview, looked at me and turned to our South African cameraman, Glen, and spoke in Afrikaans. It needed no translation; I heard Terre'Blanche refer to me as a 'kaffir', an insulting term for a black person. I looked at Glen, who just waved at me dismissively as if to say don't worry about it. I did the interview, and the entire time Terre'Blanche sat his pistol on the table, playing with it to unnerve me.

Like all white supremacists – and terrorists in general – Terre'Blanche peddled a noxious victimhood. Theirs are poisoned minds. Michael Mazarr describes them best in his book

Unmodern Men in the Modern World: they are 'besieged, thwarted; filled with real and invented grievances'. They are overwhelmed by modernity, and 'thrilled with the prospect of revalidating a humiliated nation or ethnic group'. This is, he says, the 'vulnerability of the alienated'. Mazarr could be talking about Eugene Terre'Blanche or Osama bin Laden: Islamist or white supremacist, they drink from the same toxic well. There is one critical difference: it requires a particular indifference to history for white people to imagine they are the most persecuted or aggrieved. Like Bin Laden, Terre'Blanche met a violent end, beaten to death by two black men on his family farm in 2010.

South Africa was a potential powder keg. What pulled it back from the brink? How did black people, for so long beaten down, not rise up and exact revenge? For sure there was violence, but the nation held together. It is a testament to the power of love and forgiveness. As apartheid ended, black South Africa faced a choice: pursue the crimes of apartheid and prosecute the perpetrators or let the truth set them free. Black church leader Archbishop Desmond Tutu chose forgiveness and reconciliation; they were, he said, the 'only truly viable alternatives to revenge, retribution and reprisal'. 'Without forgiveness,' he said, 'there is no future.'

Archbishop Tutu headed a Truth and Reconciliation Commission – critically, it was not a truth and *justice* commission. Justice perhaps would have been easier, and it would have electrified the blood of a people with every cause to want vengeance. By choosing peace, Tutu set the South African people a more profound task. 'Forgiveness is not facile or cheap. It is a costly business that makes those who are willing to forgive even more extraordinary,' he said.

Jean Améry would not – could not – forgive. Jean Améry, who as Hans Mayer survived the Nazi death camps, and who refused to relent in his burning resentment, took his own life at the age of sixty-five in a hotel room in Salzburg. He would never relinquish his vengeance, and perhaps that speaks more to the human condition. We are hard-wired for hate: we commit murder and then we seek retribution, often in the name of justice, even if it kills us. As Albert Camus once said, every cry for justice is an invitation for hate. Of all the stories I have covered, South Africa is the remarkable exception: the shining example of how hatred need not win.

If I could end there, perhaps I could leave you with hope, but the story doesn't end there. History hisses at us like the devil, and to think it can be silenced is as foolish as believing that evil is not real. We lurch from catastrophe to catastrophe, and the ceremony of innocence is drowned. Yeats warned us of a second coming, the 'rough beast' that 'slouches towards Bethlehem to be born'.

BETWEEN TIME AND HOPE

'Where are we going, Dad?'
'We'll know when we get there.'

I had that conversation over and over with my father from the back seat of the car as we moved from town to town. My family was always searching, but we never did seem to find what we were looking for. The world that the West had created could never truly feel like home to us. All we had was movement, the journey itself.

I have never stopped moving, and I have never wanted to get there. Destination is a Western idea: that we must reach the end, even the end of history itself. And what a dangerous idea it has been, inspiring mad dreams of utopia – the perfect, ordered society – that have sent untold millions to their deaths. It defies the laws of nature to believe that time unfolds in a straight line, yet the West has never seen nature as an obstacle. Not everyone views the world this way. Maori people from Aotearoa (New Zealand) say that the future is behind us; my own people believe that all is now – that time is all around us, always. There are alternatives to the West's linear idea of progress, other ways of measuring time and space. Yet we live in a world designed by and dominated by the West.

I am not of the West; I am among those for whom the West is both tyrant and temptress. It is evil and yet seductive. It promises freedom and offers to liberate us from the bonds of ancestry, faith or culture, even if that promised freedom is itself a mirage. I am part of the great sweep of humanity over whom the West has rolled. We have been cast aside, slaughtered, our lands stolen and carved up, our cultures destroyed. People of the West do not know what it is to face your own extinction, to hold on by your fingertips to existence itself. The West has known catastrophic war, it is true; wars of power to determine which ideology would prevail. My people – colonised or oppressed peoples everywhere – know a violence so compete we may well have vanished from the face of the earth.

Yet we have survived. These are the stories I have been drawn to tell: the stories of survivors. From China and North Korea to Central Asia, Pakistan and Afghanistan, to the Middle East, to Africa, to the Pacific Islands. I have witnessed a stirring, a rise of new powers and a return of old, a resurgence of faith and a resilience of ideologies the West had thought it had vanquished. It is a restless stirring, often a violent convulsion. The rules are being rewritten; economic, political and military power is shifting. Our age is more dangerous and disordered than any period perhaps since the years before World War One: there are more pieces in play and the stakes are as high. Just as for our forebears, the world we will live in will not be the world we grew up in.

For the people of the West, the ground is shifting beneath their feet. For at least three centuries, the laws and beliefs of the West have constituted what we have been told is the natural order of things, as if these are as immutable as the law of gravity. The West has defined and written history. It was never simply the accumulation of events or the influence of great people, but history as a destination. Immanuel Kant believed history straightens the crooked timber of humanity, until we converge in a cosmopolitan dream of perpetual peace: a world beyond our tribes. If this perpetual peace could come into existence, it would be peace on the terms set by the West. In any case, it is a dream never realised. Humans need their tribes: they will go to war for the tribe. The quest for Kant's Valhalla has itself set fire to the world. This is the legacy of the Enlightenment, that supposed 'Age of Reason'; as the historian Priya Satia has said, 'the conviction that history is necessarily a story of progress has conveyed us to the brink of disaster'.

In a world ravaged by a coronavirus – where despite wealth unseen in human history, too many still go to bed hungry or are left behind, while the one per cent accrue obscene wealth; where demagogues and political populists exploit fear and anxiety to divide and rule; where the oceans warm and rise and bushfires rage; where old hatreds fester and wars never end – too many Western political leaders offer only the tired shibboleths of liberalism and democracy. Noble ideas perhaps, but whose time may be passing, as they fail to speak to the heart and the soul. Their promise seems, to too many, like a lie. Hitting pause or winding back the clock is no answer.

As much as the accelerated decline of the West may have caught us by surprise, it shouldn't have. The famed philosopher Isaiah Berlin many years ago foresaw this moment. He questioned the assumptions of the West, saying that if the doctrine of Western civilisation – 'that all true values are immutable and timeless and universal – needs revising so drastically, then there is something radically wrong with the idea of a perfect society'.

Hegel, the philosopher to whom I have turned as a guide to our times, believed he had glimpsed the perfect society: a state of freedom at the end of history. Stalin, Hitler, Mao – they too believed that they would be the final word on humanity. Perhaps Xi Jinping believes the same today. Those who cling to the American myth might still believe it is humanity's last great chance. Francis Fukuyama believed he had glimpsed history's end with the fall of the Berlin Wall. The rush to crown the glory of the West has always been premature. Hegel warned that the end of history may also lead to what he called a 'highway of despair'. It is in 'utter dismemberment that Spirit finds itself', he said. What is our despair? It is alienation, the loss of community, the betrayal of leaders, the corruption of capitalism, the rape of the environment, dehumanising racism, the brutality of authoritarianism.

American leadership of the world has helped bring us to this point, and America alone will not deliver us from it. We are now entering what has been called a 'post-American world' – not that America will no longer be powerful, but that it will not be all-powerful. This is a moment fraught with peril, but inevitable. Pope Francis has spoken to this crisis, questioning Western values and 'the American way of life'. A professor of theology, Massimo Faggioli, has explored the pontiff's role in this world of swirling change in his book *Joe Biden and Catholicism in the United States*; he says Pope Francis invites 'a radical critique of the inclination to embrace Western triumphalism as a creed or religious faith that looks forward to the eventual acceptance, willingly or not, of Western-style American-led democracy by the rest of the world'. Democracy is not the natural order of things; it may not even be the natural order of the United States.

Hegel warned that we courted danger when we turned away from despair. In despair we find new ideas: an opportunity to grasp 'truth'. Philosophy, he wrote, reveals 'the progressive unfolding of truth'. It has been described as an engine of change: thesis–antithesis–synthesis. As Hegel poetically put it, 'The bud disappears in the bursting forth of the blossom.' One refutes the other until the fruit of the blossom reveals a new truth. This, he said, was 'their fluid nature'. What begins ends, and begins and ends and begins and ends again, again and again ... Ultimately, for Hegel, the contradictions that drive change are resolved in a universal ethical state. This is what Fukuyama believed he had seen at the end of history. Yet even Fukuyama, in his fervour of Western triumphalism, conceded that it could trigger an 'immense war of the spirit', as he wrote, 'engaged in bloody and pointless prestige battles, only this time with modern weapons'. Presciently, he warned that this 'war' could start within democracy itself: 'that the chief threat to democracy would be our own confusion about what is really at stake'.

Fukuyama recognised that the end of history may just get history started again. This is the world I have reported: the return of history, and the rejection of the idea that liberalism or democracy speaks equally to us all. We are all on the highway of despair. As for the idea of truth, there is debate now about what that even means. Democracy itself has broken with liberalism, hijacked by demagogues who use it as a cover for tyranny. The champions of liberal democracy, like Fukuyama, now confront the prospect that their great faith itself will not outlast history.

As we emerge from the worst of COVID-19, the virus itself has accelerated the change in our world. Writing more than two centuries ago, Hegel could be speaking to our age, and even uses the metaphor of infection. We cannot deny our despair; we must embrace a new consciousness to 'struggle against it', he wrote, 'betrays the fact that infection has occurred. The struggle is too late, and every remedy adopted only aggravates the disease ...'

*

I think often of that train ride to China and the man I saw in a distant field all those years ago. What has become of him? There is no way he could have remained untouched by the momentous change in his country. Back then, he still worked his land, as his ancestors had done. It was still possible for parts of China to remain sheltered from the world. No longer.

When the sun set on the Cold War that pitted the West against the Soviet Union, it rose again in China. We may like to think we can bend time – the universe itself – to our will, that we can capture the human soul and construct a society to fit, but the world is not flat and time is not straight and history goes where it will.

I woke that morning on a train to China in a world of possibility – in a new home and with a new story to tell – but wisdom is not gained in the dawn, as Hegel well knew. 'The owl of Minerva,' he wrote, 'spreads its wings with the falling of the dusk.'

ACKNOWLEDGEMENTS

This book would not exist without the support of Catherine Milne and the team at HarperCollins. Special thanks to Lachlan McLaine and Julian Welch. My agent Tara Wynne thanks for your unstinting belief and loyalty. I have bounced a lot of the ideas in this book off my good friend Andrew West over the years – I owe you lunch. Mum and Dad, you have given me a place to belong in the world. To all my Wiradjuri, Kamilaroi and Dharrawal family – you are my home. Tracey, I love you. My beautiful children, I am so proud of you. Thanks to all the writers and thinkers whose books have lit a fire in my mind. Richard Flanagan and Nam Le, thanks for the inspiration. To all the people I have worked with on the road, it's been a privilege to share the journey with you.

SELECTED SOURCES

Graham Allison, *Destined for War: Can America and China Escape Thucydides' Trap?*, Houghton Mifflin, Boston, 2018.

Cemil Aydin, *The Idea of the Muslim World: A Global Intellectual History*, Harvard University Press, Cambridge Massachusetts, 2019.

Robert Bickers, *Out of China: How the Chinese Ended the Era of Western Domination*, Penguin Random House, London, 2017.

Arnaud Blin, *War and Religion: Europe and the Mediterranean from the First Through the Twenty-first Centuries*, University of California Press, Berkeley, 2019.

Archie Brown, *The Human Factor: Gorbachev, Reagan, and Thatcher, and the End of the Cold War*, Oxford University Press, Oxford, 2020.

Jason Burke, *The 9/11 Wars*, Penguin, London, 2012.

Christian Caryl, *Strange Rebels: 1979 and the Birth of the 21st Century*, Little Brown, Boston, 2014.

Edward H. Carr, *The Twenty Years Crisis: 1919–1939*, Palgrave MacMillan, London, 2016.

Anne Case and Angus Deaton, *Deaths of Despair and the Future of Capitalism*, Princeton University Press, Princeton NJ, 2020.

Gordon Chang, *The Coming Collapse of China*, Random House, London, 2003.

Victor Cha, *The Impossible State: North Korea, Past and Future*, Random House, London, 2013.

Christopher Clark, *Sleepwalkers: How Europe Went to War in 1914*, Penguin, London, 2013.

John K Fairbank, Denis C Twitchett (eds), *Cambridge History of China, Vol 1–18*, Cambridge University Press, Cambridge, 1978–2020.

Brian Fishman, *The Master Plan: ISIS, al-Qaeda and the Jihadi Strategy for Final Victory*, Yale University Press, New Haven, 2016.

George Friedman, *The Storm before the Calm: America's Discord, the Coming Crisis of the 2020s, and the Triumph Beyond*, Black Inc, Melbourne, 2020.

Erich Fromm, *The Fear of Freedom*, Taylor & Francis, Abingdon, 2001.

Francis Fukuyama, *The End of History and the Last Man*, Free Press, New York, 1992.

John Garnaut, *The Rise and Fall of the House of Bo*, Penguin Random House, Melbourne, 2012.

David C. Gompert, Astrid Stuth Cevallos, Cristina L. Garafola, *War with China: Thinking Through the Unthinkable*, RAND Corporation, Santa Monica, 2016.

Greg Grandin, *The End of the Myth*, Henry Holt and Co, New York, 2019.

A.C. Grayling, *Democracy and Its Crisis*, Bloomsbury, London, 2018.

John Gray, *Black Mass: Apocalyptic Religion and the Death of Utopia*, Penguin, 2008, London.

David Halberstam, *The Coldest Winter: America and the Korean War*, Hachette, New York, 2008.

SELECTED SOURCES

Ahmed Hashim, *The Caliphate at War: Operational Realities and Innovations of the Islamic State*, C Hurst & Co, London, 2018.

Georg Hegel, *Phenomenology of Spirit*, Oxford University Press, Oxford, 1977.

Benjamin Carter Hett, *The Death of Democracy: Hitler's Rise to Power and the Downfall of the Weimar Republic*, Henry Holt and Co, New York, 2018.

Samuel Huntington, *Clash of Civilisations and the Remaking of World Order*, Simon & Schuster, New York, 2002.

Zahid Hussein, *Frontline Pakistan*, Columbia University Press, New York, 2020.

Martin Jacques, *When China Rules the World: The End of the Western World and the Birth of a New Global Order*, Penguin, London, 2012.

Yang Jisheng, *Tombstone: The Great Chinese Famine, 1958–1962*, Farrar, Straus and Giroux, New York, 2013.

Stathis Kouvelakis, *Philosophy and Revolution from Kant to Marx*, Verso, London, 2018.

Ivan Krastev, *After Europe*, University of Pennsylvania Press, Philadelphia, 2017.

Gerard Lemos, *The End of the Chinese Dream: Why Chinese People Fear the Future*, Yale University Press, New Haven, 2012.

Steven Levitsky and Daniel Ziblatt, *How Democracies Die*, Penguin, London, 2019.

Michael Lind, *The New Class War: Saving Democracy from the Managerial Elite*, Atlantic, London, 2020.

Julia Lovell, *Maoism: A Global History*, Vintage, London 2019.

Julia Lovell, *The Opium War: Drugs, Dreams and the Making of China*, Pan Macmillan, London, 2012.

Peter Mair, *Ruling the Void: The Hollowing of Western Democracy*, Verso Books, London, 2013.

Daniel Markovitz, *The Meritocracy Trap*, Penguin, London, 2019.

Michael Mazarr, *Unmodern Men in the Modern World: Radical Islam, Terrorism, and the War on Modernity*, Cambridge University Press, Cambridge, 2007.

Richard McGregor, *The Party: The Secret World of China's Communist Rulers*, Penguin, London, 2013.

Pippa Norris and Ronald Inglehart, *Cultural Backlash*, Cambridge University Press, Cambridge, 2018.

Alexander Pantsov and Steven Levine, *Mao: The Real Story*, Simon & Schuster, New York, 2013.

Carl Schmitt, *Political Theology*, University of Chicago Press, Chicago, 2006.

Catherine Scott-Clark and Adrian Levy, *The Exile: The Stunning Inside Story of Osama bin Laden and Al Qaeda in Flight*, Bloomsbury, New York, 2020.

Steven B Smith, *Modernity and its Discontents: Making and Unmaking the Bourgeois from Machiavelli to Bellow*, Yale University Press, New Haven, 2016.

Robert C Solomon, *In the Spirit of Hegel*, Oxford University Press, Oxford, 1983.

Kristina Spohr, *Post Wall, Post Square: Rebuilding the World After 1989*, HarperCollins, London, 2019.

Matt Taibbi, *Hate Inc: Why Today's Media Makes Us Despise One Another*, OR Books, New York, 2019.

Ezra Vogel, *Deng Xiaoping and the Transformation of China*, Harvard University Press, Cambridge Massachusetts, 2011.

Odd Arne Westad, *The Cold War: A World History*, Penguin, London, 2018.

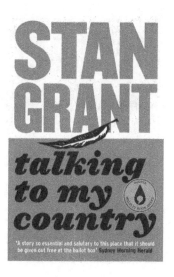

TALKING TO MY COUNTRY

Talking to My Country is Stan Grant's very personal meditation on race, identity and history. It is that rare and special book that talks to every Australian about their country – what it is, and what it could be. It is not just about race, or about Indigenous people but all of us, our shared identity. Direct, honest and forthright, Stan is talking to us all. He might not have all the answers but he wants us to keep on asking the question: how can we be better?

'an urgent and flowing narrative in a book that should be on the required reading list in every school' – *The Australian*

'Grant will be an important voice in shaping this nation' – *The Saturday Paper*

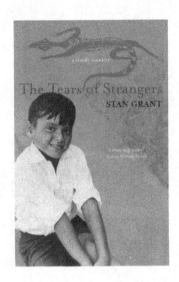

THE TEARS OF STRANGERS

Stan Grant was born in 1963 into the Wiradjuri people, warriors who occupied the vast territory of central and south-western New South Wales. For 100 years the Wiradjuri waged a war against European invasion and settlement. When Stan was born the war had been lost, the remnants of the Wiradjuri were scattered onto mission camps and the fringes of rural towns, and ravaged by alcoholism, poverty, abuse and neglect. Against this backdrop the Grant family waged its own struggle to survive.

From first contact with white settlers to today, *The Tears of Strangers* is an unforgettable Aboriginal memoir of survival, healing and hope. It is the story of the Wiradjuri people, the Grant family and Stan's own journey to come to terms with his Aboriginality and identity.

'a serious, considered and, above all, honest portrait of
both his own life and Australians' attitudes to race.'
– *The Age*

AUSTRALIA DAY

As uncomfortable as it is, we need to reckon with our history. On January 26, no Australian can really look away. There are the hard questions we ask of ourselves on Australia Day.

Since publishing his critically acclaimed, Walkley Award-winning, bestselling memoir *Talking to My Country* in early 2016, Stan Grant has been crossing the country, talking to huge crowds everywhere about how racism is at the heart of our history and the Australian dream. But Stan knows this is not where the story ends.

In this book, *Australia Day*, his long-awaited follow up to *Talking to My Country*, Stan talks about our country, about who we are as a nation, about the indigenous struggle for belonging and identity in Australia, and what it means to be Australian. A sad, wise, beautiful, reflective and troubled book, *Australia Day* asks the questions that have to be asked, that no else seems to be asking. Who are we? What is our country? How do we move forward from here?

'a soulful meditation on who we are by an Australian whose emotional and intellectual range is as vast as the ochreous land itself' – *The Australian*